Free Rein

FRENCH

MODERNIST

LIBRARY

Series Editors

Mary Ann Caws

Richard Howard

Patricia Terry

FREE

REIN

(La Clé des champs)

André Breton

Translated by

Michel Parmentier and

Jacqueline d'Amboise

University of Nebraska Press

Lincoln and London

Publication of this translation
was assisted by a grant from the
French Ministry of Culture.
André Breton, *La Clé des champs*
© 1953, Éditions du Sagittaire
© 1979, Société Nouvelle
des Éditions Pauvert
Translation © 1995 by the University
of Nebraska Press
Manufactured in the
United States of America
∞ The paper in this book meets
the minimum requirements of
American National Standard
for Information Sciences—
Permanence of Paper for
Printed Library Materials
ANSI Z39.48-1984.
Library of Congress
Cataloging-in-Publica-
tion Data Breton,
André, 1896–1966.
[Clé des champs.
English]
Free rein = La clé des
champs / André Breton ; trans-
lated by Michel Parmentier and
Jacqueline d'Amboise.
p.   cm. — (French modernist library)
Includes bibliographical references.
ISBN 0-8032-1241-0 (cl : alk. paper)
I. Parmentier, Michel, 1950– . II. Amboise,
Jacqueline d', 1948– . III. Title. IV. Series.
PQ2603.R35C513   1996
844´.912—dc20
95-22793
CIP

Contents

Introduction

First published in 1953 under the title *La Clé des champs*, *Free Rein* comprises a series of texts written by André Breton between 1936 and 1952. Similar collections were published in 1924 (*Les Pas perdus*) and in 1934 (*Point du jour*), and in 1970 Marguerite Bonnet edited a volume (*Perspective cavalière*) of texts written between 1952 and Breton's death in 1966. As in those other collections, the texts included in *Free Rein* vary in nature and purpose: addresses, manifestos, prefaces, exhibition pamphlets, and theoretical, polemical, and lyrical essays, they display the range of Breton's preoccupations and his enduring faith in the early principles of surrealism, as well as the changing orientations, in the face of that period's crucial events, of a movement of which he remained the leading force and prime embodiment.

The publication of his (first) *Manifesto of Surrealism* in 1924 proclaimed the birth of the surrealist movement and led Breton to assume a leadership role that would remain uniquely his for the duration of the movement. Many of the generation's most gifted poets and artists joined the movement or came under its sway as its momentum progressively increased and its influence spread outside French and European borders. Crises, estrangements, bitter disputes punctuated the evolution of surrealism as it searched for a way to reconcile its own revolutionary intent with political issues. Meanwhile, Breton evolved his most influential theoretical positions in *Nadja* (1928), the *Second Surrealist Manifesto* (1930), *Communicating Vessels* (1932), and *Mad Love* (1937).

In 1936, as Breton rightly observed in "Nonnational Boundaries of

Surrealism," the International Surrealist Exhibition in London marked the highest point of surrealism's influence. Indeed, it would never regain such ascendancy, eclipsed as it was after the war by new intellectual movements and coming under the attacks of such new luminaries as Sartre and Camus. Moreover, ever since he had denounced the Moscow trials of 1936, Breton had made an enemy of the Communist party, a party pledged to Stalinism and whose sway over the French intellectual scene was to increase for many years after the war. Overshadowed by new intellectual and artistic fashions and discredited by a powerful political organization that gave pride of place to former surrealists such as Aragon and Eluard who had faithfully espoused the cause of Stalinism, surrealism was unable effectively to reenter the struggle for intellectual dominance.

It comes as no surprise, therefore, that one of Breton's main concerns throughout these essays is to reaffirm time and again the necessity for revolutionary artistic and literary pursuits to stay clear of political "commitment" and to prevent at all costs their enslavement by a party or a state. While maintaining his support for the social Revolution, Breton had never ceased to emphasize the need for a concurrent revolution of the mind: this was the goal and central focus of the surrealist adventure. His refusal to comply with the subservience expected by the self-proclaimed official revolutionary party was to bring him into direct conflict with that party's minions—at times some of his former closest friends. By chance, his trip to Mexico in 1938 gave him the opportunity to broach this issue with Trotsky and to find in the theoretician of the "permanent Revolution" a supporter of his views. Their discussions resulted in the formation of an International Federation of Independent Revolutionary Art, for which they jointly wrote the manifesto. It proclaims the need to establish, as far as artistic creation is concerned, an *anarchist* regime of individual freedom, against all attempts at harnessing creativity by totalitarian regimes. Indeed, throughout this volume, Breton attacks and derides the socialist realism enforced by Stalinism as the very negation of freedom: that it should have been extolled by someone like Aragon was evidence enough of "true decadence" resulting from a blind allegiance to the articles of faith of a repressive ideology.

Why should surrealism have expended so much energy in trying to situate itself in relationship to communism when it seems that anarchism was its natural ally? That is precisely the question Breton was still asking himself "twenty-five years later," as he confessed in "The Tower of Light," published in *Le Libertaire* in 1952. No doubt, he answers, because of the lure of "effectiveness." It is apparent, however, in this volume that Breton detached himself even further from the theoretical basis of dialectical materialism and turned increasingly toward utopian thinkers. The idea that the Revolution should aim not only at "transforming the world" but also at "remaking the human mind" became all the more crucial as the major events of that period—World War II and the ensuing cold war—evidenced the suicidal course followed by modern civilization. To pit one cause against another with the illusion that the impending conflict can ensure the triumph of Good over Evil remains entirely nearsighted. Such nearsightedness leads to the repetition of new conflicts in a different guise. This was the error against which Breton warned young people in his address to the French students at Yale in 1942 entitled "Situation of Surrealism between the two Wars." Breton observed that nothing had been learned from World War I. He did not know then that the hopes he was expressing for a different tomorrow after World War II would be shattered and that he would have to reiterate the same observations and issue an even more urgent warning when the cold war added a radically new element: the potential annihilation of the entire human species. This new element, as he pointed out in his major essay "The Lamp in the Clock" (1948), compelled a complete rethinking of the human situation: at stake now was the very survival of humanity.

More insistently than ever, Breton undertook to discredit a rationalist approach based on dualistic thinking. Imprisoned within the framework of the "old antinomies," humanity can only find salvation by transcending them and relying on the life-affirming forces within the human unconscious. Hence the central preoccupation with the emergence of a new myth, which surrealism and artistic activity in general must help bring into existence. The primary function of the writer and of the artist is to register the subterranean movements within the id, common to all individuals, to bring to the surface the latent content of the period, to give shape and expression to *human desire*. To this end, the primary tool remains automatism, which Breton here explicitly defines as an ascetic process, thereby implying a withdrawal from all ego-related pursuits. In this regard, the art of the insane, on which he lavished praise in one of these essays, is exemplary in terms of authenticity, in that the admittedly tragic conditions of its production ensure both its freedom from all consideration of personal gain and a total indifference to social constraints. Much of Breton's search for "great isolated messages" focuses on individuals who stand resolutely apart, detached from any form of social recognition (among whom Germain Nouveau, Rimbaud, and Lautréamont stand supreme) and in whose works can be found novel propositions and harbingers of a new myth destined to reunite humanity.

Nowhere is this concern for the therapeutic value of artistic and literary explorations more evident than in the major theoretical statement "Ascendant Sign" (1947), in which Breton asserts that the analogical method is governed by a vector directed toward well-being, thereby making it clear that the aesthetics of surrealism are indissociable from its ethics. This primacy of the ethical sense is central to Breton's attitude in political and artistic matters and drives most of the enthusiasms as well as the vituperations that are omnipresent in this volume. A case in point is the brilliant polemical essay "Caught in the Act" about the fake *Chasse spirituelle* attributed to Rimbaud and published under the patronage of some leading critics but immediately recognized and denounced by Breton as a forgery. Beyond the indictment of those who stood to benefit, in one form or another, from the publication of such a prize "find" and of the ineptitude of the so-called literary experts, this essay emphasizes the proper attitude of receptiveness toward great artistic works: love comes first, understanding and interpretation later. For all its merits, exegesis amounts to naught if it is not inspired by a communion with the work, provided of course that the work in question is one that has the intrinsic power to meet the as yet unrevealed deeper aspirations of those who encounter it.

A recurrent theme in all the prefaces to books and exhibitions in this volume is that of *revelation*: whether they be contemporary or the products of an age-old tradition (Mayan, Oceanian), artistic works worthy of our reverence are those that at the onset claim our passionate adherence, giving the sense that they contain a secret vital to human destiny. Breton's increasing fascination with various esoteric traditions, particularly with alchemy, during this period stems from his hope of recapturing the keys to our inner unity and to unity with nature. The works that exert the greatest attraction for him are those in which he discerns elements of an initiatory process, such as Roussel's *La Poussière de soleils*, which he reinterprets in this light in his preface to Jean Ferry's exegesis ("Fronton-Virage").

Of greatest value are those works that enable us to experience the "marvelous," a concept Breton opposes to that of mystery in the initial essay on symbolist poetry. While the marvelous is the result of dazzling coincidences in life, in art it can only emerge from those combinations of words or visual images which are spontaneously created by the human mind through the automatic process. In them is realized the conjunction of perception and representation, the synthesis of inner and outer realities, whereby we find ourselves simultaneously at one with ourselves and with the world, thus recovering the sense of the sacred. All art forms, including music, to which the essay "Golden Silence" is devoted, and the cinema ("As in a Wood"), have the potential to open up such paths of illumination.

The above are only some of the issues, concerns, and trends that appear in the following texts, whose variety and richness provide numerous insights into Breton's mature thought. While this volume includes some of the major statements on surrealism to be found in Breton's writings, it serves as an indispensable complement to works that appeared during that prolific period of his life such as *Arcane 17* and his epic poems (*Fata Morgana, Les Etats généraux, Ode à Charles Fourier*).

Some of these texts have previously been translated into English by various individuals. The versions presented in this volume, however, are our own and have been entirely rewritten in keeping with our stylistic choices and interpretations. Breton's prose is often discursive and convoluted, sometimes obscure, always replete with literary and philosophical allusions. Because it introduces numerous novel ideas and ascribes special meanings to words that can only be properly understood by referring to his other writings, it requires constant interpretation. Our primary concern has been to render as faithfully as possible this unique process of thought in all its subtlety and complexity.

We have supplied the bibliographic data missing from Breton's references whenever we were able to retrace the title to which he referred. When no date was given and several editions existed, we have provided data for the first edition. We have also added references to published translations of the works cited.

We wish to thank Brian Jenkins for reading and commenting on the entire manuscript and Mary Ann Caws for her warm support of this project.

Free Rein

Marvelous

versus

Mystery

Splendid nineteenth century, before which you have to leap back to
the fourteenth in order to soar into the same formidable sky of tiger-cat
skin! Rejecting life as it is given, either socially or morally, man was steered
toward a series of new solutions to the problems of his nature and destiny.
An extraordinary fermentation that we no longer experience . . . Today, all
eyes are focused on the hopes raised by the *economic* transformation of the
world, and there is no doubt this transformation is urgently needed even
if it is highly unlikely that most of the hopes in question will thereby be
realized. When we are free of that burning question, and only then, I think
it will be time again to start studying the singular and certainly enlightening
curve described by ideas in the nineteenth century, a curve that could not
be better plotted than by the history of poetry.

I have always loved best that orangy-green glow with which, in the
distance, the same fine brush surrounds the conventional romantic scenery
and that almost-buried area of Paris, known as La Boucherie, which is
haunted by the unappeasable ghost of Nicolas Flamel. That perverse glow,
circling round the towers, makes me feel more receptive, in my innermost
self, to that toward which I would consciously consider myself to be most
hostile: Germany as it is in 1936, the country where those towers are being
rebuilt, the country whence came—and will return again—all that we can
regard as being most representative of *what we are*. You know what glow I
am talking about: it starts by hitting broadside on Hugo's gigantic facades,
even filters through Musset's wonderful *Chanson* [Song] of 3 February 1834,
behind the unbearable *Rolla* (despised above all else by *both* Ducasse and

Rimbaud), slips over Aloysius Bertrand's works, cloaks Xavier Forneret, the great mental defective, in imaginary bees, and bursts like a cocoon in Nerval's *Les Chimères* [*The Chimeras*]. It is indispensable to revert to these works, without waiting for symbolism as a professed movement, in order to uncover the original impetus to emancipate man *totally*, one that would draw its strength from language but would sooner or later transform life itself.

Inverted worlds, sheer or not so sheer utopias, dreams of Eden have carved out a place for themselves in language, and blind realism will not be able to take it back from them. The underlying reason, to my mind, is that language, when it is not strictly limited to everyday use, not strictly adapted to practical needs, requires a painstaking effort and involves a certain amount of suffering. The words we need are not always available, they have to be coaxed, or even beseeched. What I am most anxious to say is not what I say best, far from it. I am always greatly disappointed by the absence, which I have noted a thousand times, of any *external* aid when this happens. On the other hand, that assistance has always been provided whenever I have ventured onto more unpredictable paths. Only on those occasions have I felt that I was sometimes awakening musical instruments, that my words might produce some echo. There is in this a stern admonition, most crushing for our pride, particularly the pride that drives us to write. The vexation we experience when trying to convey a clear idea in words that have no resonance and penetrate no farther than the vestibule of the ear, as well as our bitter joy when we see that for which we feel least responsible forming into a pattern of reverberations—these emotions lead inescapably, for the benefit of imaginary worlds, to a rejection of the real world that cannot come to an end before this world does. It is impossible to imagine a Revolution that might abolish this state of affairs, which endlessly recreates the very idea of Revolution. Never will a change of social system achieve a congruence of the mind with the new established order so perfect that this discrepancy, inherent in the human conditions of expression, will vanish once and for all.

On the pretext that current events compel us to take a more prosaic stand, nothing could be more unfair than to deride the efforts of those nineteenth-century poets who were on the horns of that dilemma. Yet that is precisely what a recent intellectual *fashion*, purportedly based on revolutionary ideas, tries to induce us to do. Thus, all the commentaries to which the commemoration of symbolism gave rise make reference, more or less explicitly, to the culpable indifference of its representatives toward the specific problems of their times, to their desertion in the face of everyday life. In my opinion, the issue they are quite needlessly raising is an old one that was set at rest by the discovery of the mechanism of *sublimation*, at work in some individuals but not in others, which consists of channeling "excessive excitations stemming from the various sources of sexuality" toward long-range collective goals. Such a distinctive predisposition implies a profound mistrust of surrounding reality that can, in extreme cases, lead to the total negation of that reality. The unquestionable spiritual enrichment that, throughout the ages, can be attributed to the sublimation process should earn it more understanding and shelter it socially from any new threat of intolerance.

Baudelaire has such a hold over us because he is the last of the French poets to express the all-powerful emotions that possess him in a fairly direct language, a language that fits closely round them and is not broken by them. With him, what is expressed is still almost indistinguishable from the person expressing it: it is preexistent, and this is the crucial point, to the form of its expression. Discounting any possibility of a serious accident, man still has his team of horses well in rein; he knows where he is going. Baudelaire's specification of the road to follow is nevertheless an unsettling one: "through forests of symbols," "deep in the unknown to find the new." Farther down that road, the only relay horses to be had will be ones that are ready to bolt.

The cracks in the foundation of meaning that nonetheless appear in some of Baudelaire's poems, such as "Le Beau Navire" [The Fine Ship], will later on multiply and spread to such an extent that the wall of echoes will totter. This will result from the pressure of the verbal flow that romanticism was only able to direct toward makeshift locks: any one of a number of "subjects" that the poet intends in theory to deal with and that become progressively incrusted with parasitic expatiations. This verbal flow, which had been poorly channeled off for so long, suddenly becomes a torrent.

Once the reins of common sense are dropped, another kind of sense, a compelling and divinatory one, guides man to where he wants to go without knowing it. Always farther! As he goes into the unknown, he has to be willing to let himself be carried along rather than to make his own way. One has to give up that aptitude, long considered the most precious of all: the critical awareness of one's actions. Lucidity is the major enemy of revelation. Only when the latter has happened can the former be permitted to reassert itself. At this juncture, the poetic adventure takes an ominous turn: man's lines of communication with his fellow beings are, at least temporarily, cut off. In everything he does, he seems to be rushing to his downfall. One is struck by how often the contribution of a great poet is regarded by his contemporaries as little more than a collection of visions, auditory hallucinations, and other pitfalls. Even more striking is the fact that, later on, general optical and acoustic phenomena end up vindicating him, often in a resounding fashion. In order to understand Rimbaud, one needs to be farther away from him than Mallarmé was when he wrote that appalling letter to Harrisson Rhodes in April 1896. On the other hand, Verlaine and Mallarmé collected a following right away—and promptly lost it. Lautréamont, the sublime wanderer, the great locksmith of modern life, was only noticed by Bloy and Gourmont, among the whole symbolist generation, and they explicitly referred to him as a madman. Even today Cros is hardly ever mentioned, unless by allusion to the bindweed flower that was to serve as a model for the first phonograph (how is that for the author of *Le Hareng-saur* [The smoked herring] and of those precursory "Illuminations" that *Vanité sous-marine* [Underwater vanity] and *Le Vaisseau piano* [The piano vessel] seem to be?). Someone like Corbière, shivering with contradictions and grudges but endowed with enduring prophetic insights, has less influence than a Laforgue, fortunately on the wane, who can barely whistle. They will soon be vindicated, along with all those who sought or will seek truth, forever elusive but present in new modes of expression, including Germain Nouveau, who pursued it in the mirages of beggary, and Alfred Jarry—the prodigious Alfred Jarry—bicycling to the top of the hill and bursting out laughing.

The ever-brighter flashes of light that after half a century some of these works are beginning to send out and the gradual dimming of some of the others make it possible to separate the jewels from the glass beads. Such a discrimination, however, would still be unsatisfactory if we did not try to elucidate the difference in nature that sets them apart. What is at stake, for the short period in question, is the choice made by human sensibility between two paths, the first one proving, with the benefit of hindsight, to be the one it had to follow while the second one was to be avoided.

At the historical juncture where this problem should be situated—that is to say, at the time of Baudelaire's death—poets are ready to agree on one basic principle: language can and must be protected against the erosion and discoloration that result from its use for basic exchange; it contains possibilities of a much closer contact between men than the laws governing that exchange generally lead us to assume; the systematic exploration of those possibilities would bring about nothing less than the re-creation of the world. Needless to say, the new language we envisage strives to be as different as possible from ordinary language, and the best way to achieve this is to deal exuberantly with the emotional value of words. The emotional life of words, far from being simply contingent on their meanings, predisposes them to be drawn to one another and to make a greater impact than meaning alone, but only if they are brought together according to secret affinities that let them combine in all kinds of new ways. The two paths I was mentioning diverge at the point where the poet *decides to consider himself the master or the slave of such combinations.* Lautréamont, Cros, Rimbaud, Nouveau, Corbière, Jarry—Maeterlinck, the only one after them among all the symbolists proper who accomplishes the miracle of opening the blue plush box of *Serres chaudes* [Hot greenhouses] and *Chansons* [Songs] on a woman's back streaming with golden rain—are among those who, bound hand and foot, gave themselves up to those combinations, who did not try to find out where the sphinx, with all his claws in their flesh, was leading them, and who did not attempt to outwit him. The others, the die-hards of the Mallarmean school, are now sinking in the sand of God only knows what mental Easter Island, their mouths, for the most part, level with oblivion. That is because they thought they could keep at hand the phial of light and the phial of darkness to make us potions—sometimes sweet, sometimes bitter, according to their fancy. I do not know of anything more childish than Mallarmé's concern with postponing, until he had "applied some shading," the publication of one of his texts that he had just read aloud and was afraid might have been too readily understood. Such a deliberate distillation can only lead to self-dissolution. By the light of that artificial midnight sun, only René Ghil, Stuart Merrill, and Francis Vielé-Griffin can still sometimes be seen dominating the taller waves. Not touched, as they were, by the hand of sugar, Saint-Pol-Roux turns toward us sky-blue eyes left ever clearer and brighter by the blowing wind of images.

From the moment when words are perceived in a more or less exclusively emotional light, when their association, in some forms, is felt to establish a profound, unique link between two entities, and even more so when we start dreaming of "grasping the Essence" through them, it is clear that behavior in matters of language will tend more and more to be modeled on amorous behavior. I say that, in both cases, what we have to face squarely is the problem of passion. The poet and the lover must aim, in the presence of the form haunting them, at being infinitely less mystifying than mystified. *Mystery* as an end in itself, intentionally injected—at all costs—into art as into life, looks not only like a cheap trick but also like an admission of weakness, of jadedness. Symbolism has not yet sunk into total oblivion only because, forsaking the mediocrity of such stratagems, it occasionally determined to abandon itself purely and simply to the *marvelous*: in this abandon lies the only source of eternal communication between men.

1936

Nonnational

Boundaries

of Surrealism

The International Surrealist Exhibition that ended a few months ago in London, which served as a prelude to a series of events organized by a surrealist group that has been formed in England and is presently working in close connection with those in other countries, marks the vertex of the *influence* curve of our movement, a curve that has been ascending with ever increasing rapidity over recent years. As Guillaume Apollinaire said,

> *It is difficult to imagine*
> *How stupidly complacent people are made by success*

but surrealism, precisely because it maintains its *invariable* original principles, is immune to that kind of stupor. We use the word "vertex" intentionally to call to mind the generating curves intersecting at that particularly significant point, to help place it in relation to the coordinates of time and place. This concern alone should be enough to refute any allegation that surrealism has come to a standstill and to let it forge ahead unhindered, unfettered by laurels. The International Surrealist Exhibition opened with great success at the very moment when the French workers, using totally unexpected tactics, proceeded by force to occupy the factories and, simply by making that stand collectively, succeeded overwhelmingly in getting their main demands satisfied. The spontaneity and suddenness of that departure (for which none of the existing political parties claims responsibility, and rightly so), the way that action, once initiated, was able to spread like wildfire, the impression it gives that nothing can prevent it from gaining its primary objectives, the resounding refutation it inflicts on those who, ever since the war, have continually denied that the French proletariat had any fighting spirit, and finally the *precedent* it creates—a precedent that cannot but give the bourgeoisie concrete evidence that their rule is drawing to an end—all this is apt to convince the clear-sighted observer that "the French Revolution has begun." Those, I repeat, were the circumstances in which our exhibition opened in London, but when it closed, we found that events had taken another turn, equally disturbing and no less dramatic: beyond the Pyrenees, a counterrevolutionary offensive was putting in jeopardy the well-being, the liberty, and the hope that had just been wrested from an age-old malevolent oppression. Everyone realizes that this conflict is a decisive one, that much more is at stake than just the fate of the young Spanish Republic. What is being decided is whether man is fated to prey on his own kind, whether in striving to escape this condition he only falls from one trap into the next, or whether, on the contrary, it lies within his power, it depends on his degree of energy at first, and of watchfulness later, to loosen the knot of the hydra and ensure that its heads *will never grow back*. If, at the time I am writing, the French Revolution has no doubt begun, it is certain that the Spanish Revolution is reaching its zenith. Thus we are able to observe this revolution, which in its essence must be one and the same, at two different stages and to note in particular that, if it has proved possible to overthrow certain transitory forms of exploitation by collective *inaction*, nothing short of *taking up arms* is necessary to prevent a return of that exploitation in forms infinitely more overt and more sinister. Under this threat, it has been necessary to call upon workers' militias, the formation of which is urged only by a revolutionary minority in France, while the Popular Front government—well aware that the appearance on the scene of those militias marks, in terms used to characterize war, "the continuation of politics by other means"—postpones for as long as possible the time when the social crisis will come to a head in the only conceivable place, namely, *in the streets*. It is my contention that the recent conduct of the French workers and that of the Spanish avant-garde (even more soul stirring!) represent two necessarily successive moments of a single movement, a movement destined to carry the whole world forward. It is of the utmost importance to realize that this movement follows the most constraining course in defiance of political forecasts and beyond the contradiction of party slogans. Surrealism, at this particular stage of its development, cannot disregard those events without losing sight of the *prow of history*. Beyond the obligations undertaken by men in order to serve what they believe to be the truth by fighting to the death, the earth turns on its hinges of sunlight and darkness. Nothing can prevent surrealism from seeing the reflection of the whole future in the dying eyes of the men and women who fell in July 1936 outside Saragossa. The whole future includes the unlimited hope for the liberation of the human spirit that surrealism, perhaps the only existing intellectual effort to be both concerted and sustained on an international scale, can infuse into that word.

In such troubled times, when all of Europe—maybe the entire world—could at any moment be set ablaze, it is quite understandable that, for many people who look at it from the outside, an exhibition such as the one in London may conjure up images of an extravagant Saturnalia and arouse a questionable curiosity. That is why we do not take as evidence of its thorough success the fact that this curiosity spread to twenty thousand visitors, nor the fact that it received a blaze of publicity in England. Rather, that success lies in the fact that it provided ample and conclusive evidence that surrealism now tends to unify under its banner the aspirations of the innovative writers and artists of all countries: indeed, members of fourteen nations were exhibiting, and even so we were unable to include certain particularly important collaborations, for instance, that of the Japanese. This unification, far from being simply a unification of style, corresponds to a new awareness of life that is *common to all*. I can guarantee that no effort has been spared since the inception of surrealism to drive off those who would be hesitant to support a fundamental and indivisible set of propositions that I will now briefly restate:

1. Adherence to all the principles of dialectical materialism endorsed in their entirety by surrealism: the primacy of matter over thought, the adoption of the Hegelian dialectic as the science of the general laws of movement pertaining to the external world as well as to human thought, the materialistic view of history ("all social and political relations, all religious and legal systems, all theoretical views appearing in history can only be explained

by the conditions of material existence during the period in question");
the necessity of social revolution as the end result of the antagonism aris-
ing, at a certain stage of their development, between the forces of material
production in society and the existing relations of production (the class
struggle).

2. As Marx and Engels pointed out, it is absurd to maintain that the
economic factor is the *only* determining one in history, the determining
factor being "in the final analysis, the production and reproduction of
life itself."[1] Since, as they themselves declare, "the various parts of the
superstructure ... also exert their influence on the course of historical
struggles and in many cases determine to a great extent the *shape* they take,"
intellectual effort cannot be put to a better use than the enrichment of that
superstructure, which will only reveal the secret of its development at that
price. It is a matter of pointing out the trail that leads to the center of those
"chance events" (to keep on using the same authors' terminology) through
the multiplicity of which "the reciprocal action and reaction" of the factors
determining the movement of life go on. This is the trail that surrealism
claims to have laid out. Nothing is less arbitrary than the direction this path
takes, considering that it can only be the logical and necessary continuation
of all the *paths of great spiritual adventure* that have been followed or
indicated up to our time. Ever since the publication of the *Manifeste du
surréalisme* [Manifesto of Surrealism] in 1924, I have not ceased to point
out those more or less solitary, more or less hazardous paths and to call
attention to their *convergence*. Quite recently, I tried to show how, to the *open
rationalism* that defines the present position of scientists (as a result of the
development of non-Euclidean and subsequently of a generalized geometry,
of a non-Newtonian mechanics, of non-Maxwellian physics, etc.), there had
to correspond an *open realism* or *surrealism* that brings about the ruin of
the Cartesian-Kantian edifice and a drastic transformation of sensibility.[2]
Without consulting or even knowing each other, Isidore Ducasse and Arthur
Rimbaud set an entirely new course for poetry by systematically challenging
all the habitual ways of reacting to the spectacle of the world and of
themselves by throwing themselves headlong into the marvelous. It is worth
noting that they adopted this attitude right about the time of the Franco-

German War of 1870, that is to say the time of the great preliminary attempt at proletarian revolution that ensued from that war. This fact is all the more striking since it is also right about the time of another war, that of 1914, that Picasso and Chirico produced works which revolutionized the field of painting: as a result, as it had to be acknowledged sooner or later, human modes of visual representation have changed. Freud's magnificent discoveries came just at the right time to illuminate for us the depths of the chasm that was opened by this withdrawal of logical thought, by this suspicion about the reliability of sensory evidence. What they reveal to us about the nature of human relationships threatens to destroy the institutions hitherto considered the most solid, starting with the family, and calls for the establishment of a real science of mores on the ruins of a ludicrous morality. To these various influences that combine in shaping surrealism we must not forget to add two distinct modes of awareness that go back, without a doubt, much farther and have numerous antecedents. One of these modes expresses itself in *objective humor*, in the Hegelian sense of a synthesis of the imitation of nature in its accidental forms on the one hand and of humor on the other. Humor, as a paradoxical triumph of the pleasure principle over real conditions at the moment when they are considered the most unfavorable, is naturally bound to take on a defensive character during the period so fraught with menace in which we live. From Swift to Lewis Carroll, the English reader is in a better position than anyone to appreciate the resources of that humor that in France is represented by Alfred Jarry and that hovers over the origins of surrealism (the influences of Jacques Vaché and Marcel Duchamp). The second mode of awareness in question resides in the need to inquire passionately into certain situations in life that are characterized by the fact that they seem to be part at the same time of the real and an ideal series of events, so that they constitute the only observation post available to us inside that prodigious mental domain of Arnheim that is *objective chance*, defined by Engels as the "form of manifestation of *necessity*." Novalis, Achim von Arnim, Gérard de Nerval, and Knut Hamsun had already taken that viewpoint, but all too often with them, the layout of the place they set out to describe—that layout being, from the standpoint of knowledge, the only thing that ultimately matters to us—would get lost in the heady fumes of their own enchantment. I have tried for my part to present facts of this nature with the same sobriety and accuracy that characterize medical observations.[3] *Objective humor* and *objective chance* are, strictly speaking, the two poles between which surrealism is confident it will produce its longest lasting sparks.

The path pointed out by surrealism would not be sufficiently defined were we only to mention where it leads and what it cuts across. We must also bring to light the underlying driving force: is there a common link between the various intellectual modes of exploration enumerated above, from which surrealism proceeds and of which it claims to be the sum total? Our primary concern has been to establish the existence of this link: this constant, this driving force is *automatism*. Only by resorting to automatism in all its forms can we hope to resolve, outside the economic sphere, *all* the antinomies that, since they already existed before our present social system became established, are not likely to disappear along with it. We must do our utmost to remove those antinomies that are the cause of great mental anguish, because they imply a servitude even more profound and permanent than the temporal one: that suffering should not—any more than the other one— find man resigned. Those are the antinomies of being awake and sleeping (of reality and dream), of objectivity and subjectivity, of perception and representation, of past and future, of collective sense and individual love, even of life and death.

With the greatest examples of the past in mind, we confidently deny that the art of a period might consist of the pure and simple imitation of its surface manifestations. Just as forcefully, we reject and denounce as *erroneous* the dogma of "socialist realism" that would constrain the artist to depict nothing but the plight of the proletariat and the struggle for liberation it is waging. As a matter of fact, this dogma is in glaring contradiction with Marxist teachings: "The more the [political] opinions of the author remain hidden," Engels wrote to Miss Harkness in April 1888, "the better it is for the work of art." We emphatically disagree with the view that it is possible to create a work of art or even, for that matter, to do anything at all worthwhile by striving to express only the *manifest content* of a period. What surrealism sets out to do, by contrast, is to express its *latent content*.

The "fantastic," which the implementation of a program such as that of socialist realism rules out completely and to which surrealism has never ceased to appeal, is in our view the ideal key to this latent content, the way for us to explore the secret depths of history that disappear beneath the web of events. It is only when the fantastic draws near, at a point where human reason loses its control, that the innermost emotion of a human being has every chance to express itself: in its haste to do so, being unable to externalize itself within the confines of the real world, that emotion has no other outlet than to yield to the eternal lure of myths and symbols. In this regard, it has always seemed to me that nothing could be more appropriate than to call attention to the extraordinary proliferation of gothic novels in England at the end of the eighteenth century. When today we consider that literary genre that has fallen into disrepute or sunk into oblivion, we cannot help but wonder not only at its tremendous success but also at the quite remarkable fascination it held at one time for the most critical minds. Schedoni, one of Ann Radcliffe's heroes, does seem to be the character on which Byron modeled his own persona; Thomas Moore was to evoke fervently time and again the lovely diaphanous maidens who wander among the bird songs and the trees in *Romance of the Forest*. Victor Hugo's first novels (*Bug-Jargal, Han d'Islande*), as well as Balzac's (*L'Héritière de Biragne* [The heiress of Biragne], *Le Centenaire ou les deux Béringheld* [*The Centenarian: or, The Two Beringhelds*], etc.) are directly inspired by Lewis's *The Monk* and Mathurin's *Melmoth*, the same *Melmoth* that would make such a lasting impression on Baudelaire and was probably, along with Young's *Night-Thoughts*, the most invigorating of the sources tapped by Lautréamont's all-powerful inspiration. Such popularity and influence, in contrast with the extreme disfavor in which those and similar works have generally been held since, would be inexplicable if it did not lead us to infer that they were perfectly adapted to a particular historical situation. The truth, which the Marquis de Sade was the first to bring to light in his *Idée sur les romans* [Idea on novels], is that we are looking at a genre that, in its heyday, must be regarded as the "indispensable fruit of the revolutionary upheaval whose effects were felt all over Europe." It is easy to understand how invaluable we find this assessment. Human curiosity in its most common, most spontaneous form, as well as in its most individual, most purely intellectual form, was focused in this instance not on the scrupulously exact depiction of the external events that occurred at the time but rather on the expression of confused emotions oscillating between nostalgia and terror. The pleasure principle has never more obviously taken its revenge on the reality principle. Ruins suddenly acquire so much significance only because they express visually the collapse of the feudal age; the inevitable ghost haunting them reflects, with special intensity, the fear that the powers of the past might return; the underground passages represent the slow progress of the individual toward the light in the perils of darkness; the stormy night only transposes the incessant roar of the cannon. Such is the turbulent background against which beings of pure *temptation* choose to appear: they are the supreme embodiment of the struggle between, on the one hand, the death instinct, which, as Freud has shown, is also an instinct of preservation, and, on the other hand, Eros demanding, after each human hecatomb, that life be restored to its fullest exuberance. Let me emphasize that the substitution of one setting for another (of the typical romantic setting for the real setting) was in no way deliberate on the part of the authors of gothic novels nor indeed preconcerted by common accord. Their undoubted lack of awareness in this respect lends all the more significance to the insights their sensibility provided. "*Udolpho,*" writes Mme de Chastenay, who was the first to translate that work into French, "gave my imagination a shock from which my reason was incapable of shielding it. Even now, without my being able to find the cause of this, its muffled sounds, stretching shadows, fantastic effects still inspire the same fears in me that they would in a child." A work of art worthy of the name is one that gives us back the freshness of childhood emotions. This it can only achieve on the express condition that it does not rely on the history of current events, whose deep reverberations through the human heart can only be produced by a systematic return to *fiction*.

No attempt at intimidation will make us give up our self-allotted task, which, as we have already made clear, consists in elaborating a *collective myth* appropriate to our period in the same way that, whether we like it or not, the gothic genre must be regarded as symptomatic of the great social upheaval that shook Europe at the end of the eighteenth century. It is interesting to note that the reading public was first introduced to this genre, in 1764, by Horace Walpole, a man who, owing to his social origin and early experience in public life, was very well informed about the actual political situation of the time and who, moreover, was a year later to capture the whole attention of Mme du Deffand until her death—Mme du Deffand, the close friend of the French encyclopedists, that is to say of those intellectuals who were by definition most hostile to the literary conception revealed in *The Castle of Otranto*. It is fortunate that we are acquainted with the process whereby such a book was written: what it illustrates, and that for which it provides added justification, is nothing less than the *surrealist method*. It seems to me all the more appropriate in this respect to quote from a letter dated 9 March 1765, from Horace Walpole to William Cole, since it reads as though, in the *Manifeste du surréalisme*, I had done nothing but paraphrase and unknowingly generalize the affirmations it contains: "Shall I even confess to you what was the origin of this romance? I waked, one morning in the beginning of last June, from a dream of which all I could recover was that I had thought myself in an ancient castle (a very natural dream for a head, filled as mine was, with Gothic story), and that on the uppermost banister of a great staircase I saw a gigantic hand in armour. In the evening I sat down and began to write, without knowing in the least what I intended to say or relate. In short, I was so engrossed with my tale, which I completed in less than two months, that one evening I wrote from the time I had drunk my tea, about six o'clock, till half an hour after one in the morning, when my hand and fingers were so weary I could not hold the pen to finish the sentence." This account bears witness to the fact that the message in question, which was to beget so many others whose cumulative effect was highly significant, could only be obtained by relying on the *dreaming* process and on *automatic writing*. It might even help us resolve an important question that has hitherto been left unanswered: are there places that conduce by their very nature to this particular kind of psychic activity? Yes, there must be observatories of the inner sky. I mean, naturally, observatories already existing in the external world. This we may describe, from the surrealist standpoint, as the *castle question*: "A considerable part of his youth," a biographer says of Lewis, "was spent in a very old manor house." J. K. Huysmans, incontestably the leader of French naturalism, sets the action of his masterpiece *En rade* [*Becalmed*] in an abandoned castle— an action interspersed with such splendid dreams that it is finally ruined by them. When I myself tried to find what would be the most favorable place to receive the great prophetic waves, I ended up, on paper at least, in a tumbledown castle of sorts.[4] Only a few months ago I was able to satisfy myself, while pondering the singular theme of a remarkable film entitled *Berkeley Square*—the new occupant of an old castle manages, by bringing back to life in his hallucinations those who occupied it in former times, not only to mingle with them but also, as he takes part in their activities, to solve the problem of his present behavior, a most difficult sentimental problem—that the myth of spirits and of their possible intercessions is still very much alive. Yet I do not think that the "gothic" element, even though it is almost constantly present throughout the cycle of productions that concerns us, should be deemed essential. As a style, its historical evolution toward the "flamboyant" and the way it went up in flames seem to me alone responsible for the marked predilection it enjoyed. The human psyche, in its most universal form, found in the gothic castle and its accessories a point of fixation so precise that it would be essential to discover what would be the equivalent of such a place for our own period. (Everything leads us to believe that it is definitely not a factory.) But surrealism is still in the process of registering the transfer, occurring between the period of the gothic novel and our time, of the highest emotional charges from miraculous *apparitions* to wondrous *coincidences*: it only asks that we allow ourselves to be guided toward the unknown by the *glimmer* of those coincidences, which is at present brighter than any other one, isolating it whenever possible from the minor events in life.[5]

.   .   .   .   .

I had occasion to speak last June of the anxiety I felt at the prospect of presenting a comprehensive exhibition of surrealist works in London, since the reception it would get was, in my view, to serve as a criterion. I felt that the objectification and internationalization of surrealist ideas, pursued more or less actively in the last few years, were reaching their critical point at this juncture. The preceding months had focused the attention of the Western world on England. She was the one who had been desperately expected to issue the call to order—unfortunately, when she did, it was in a form that proved ineffective—necessitated by the unspeakable aggression of a powerful country against a weak one and by the shameful policy of support for the aggressor adopted by other countries. She is the one as well, I could not help thinking, who is in the best position continually to arbitrate the latent conflict between the two *wretched* nationalisms of France and Germany that cannot wait for the people of these two countries to start once again tearing one another apart like dogs. Searching as we were—and still are, now more than ever—for a European consciousness, if not a world consciousness, it is, in spite of everything, toward England that we turned. Not that it was possible for us, of course, to pay an unconditional homage to her attitude in such matters. We shall not forget that the multiplication of capitalist contradictions, from which she is not spared, may lead us to call her leadership into question in matters of law. It is nonetheless true that the language she has repeatedly spoken, and spoken loudly, is among those to which we are most receptive and to which we will continue to listen as long as the *disinterested* language of truth and justice will not prevail. It has seemed at times, when the most inadmissible passions were being unleashed, that she needed all of her authority to make herself heard. In view of the situation elsewhere, particularly in France, we cannot underestimate that authority, which she demonstrates both in the economic and the intellectual spheres. To recognize it, I had no need to be in London, where it spreads its wings over every old stone. I perceive it plainly at every turning point in history and, I may say so, at every turning point in legendry, wherever man has recorded for man what has been or could be accomplished toward lofty purposes. Insofar, I repeat, as surrealism aims at creating a collective myth, it must endeavor to bring together the scattered elements of that myth, *beginning* with those that proceed from the oldest and strongest tradition (it is indeed in this sense that we may speak of a "cultural legacy," to use an expression that has caught on in revolutionary circles). This tradition seems at the present time to be more enduring in England than anywhere else. Hence, I was frequently told that this tradition posed an insurmountable obstacle to the penetration in that country of a new current of ideas such as surrealism. To myself, I thought that this current of ideas, unless diverted from the course I had set for it twelve years ago, would only gain strength from such an encounter. Considering the specifically English sources from which, for centuries, sensibility has sought refreshment, I became convinced that surrealism itself had drawn enough from them to have nothing to fear. Sooner or later it would become obvious that it had endeavored to carry along with it all that is truly inspiring in the art and literature of the past, so that it was bound to pay a considerable tribute to the art and literature of England. Thanks to the happy initiative of our English friends, recent events have confirmed this assumption and paved the way for a mutual understanding and a collaboration that, at a distance as well as in their midst, I feel is growing closer and more effective by the hour.

1937

Gradiva

Gradiva? This title, borrowed from Jensen's wonderful book, means primarily

SHE WHO MOVES FORWARD

Who could "she" be, other than tomorrow's beauty, as yet hidden from the multitude, and only glimpsed here and there as one draws near some object, goes past a painting, turns the page of a book? She adorns herself with all the lights of the *never seen* that force most men to lower their eyes. Yet she haunts their dwellings, gliding at dusk through the corridor of poetic premonitions:

> *No more than a vague notion of my life did I retain*
> *And what until then, a larva by glimmers guided,*
> *I had called my soul was no longer a certainty,*
> *But a figment afloat within me.*
> *What was left of me was a thirst for knowledge,*
> *A longing for what could be,*
> *A mouth craving some elusive water*
> *Even from the fateful hand of night.*
> *—Hugo*

She may even become an ever greater source of light as she stands on the landing of this confession:

> *I liked idiotic paintings, over-doors, theater sets, the painted cloths of the traveling circus, shop signs, cheap illuminations . . . —Rimbaud*

And more and more naked as she climbs the stairs of these injunctions:

One must be absolutely modern.—Rimbaud

Well, you should know that poetry can be found wherever the stupidly derisive smile of the duck-faced man cannot be seen.—Lautréamont

> *We do not relish enough the joy*
> *Of seeing beautiful new things*
> *O my beloved hurry*
> *Beware lest one day a train stir your heart*
> > *No more*
> *Quick look at it for your own sake*
> *—Apollinaire*

We conceived the idea of a repository, an ageless place located anywhere outside the world *of reason*. In that space would be stored those manmade objects that have lost their utilitarian purpose, or have not yet found it, or have markedly deviated from it and that therefore conceal some internal secret lock. Those objects could then emerge in an elective way and continuously from the river of ever-thickening sand that blurs adult vision, restoring to it the transparency that children enjoy. They would alternate with highly singular natural objects, primarily those whose structure corresponds to a most unfathomable necessity, those whose very appearance is enough to cast a new light on the problem of that necessity. Both categories of objects could exert a rather mysterious attraction, arouse ideas of possession, and especially help reveal to each individual his own desire, or at least act as an intercessor between that desire and its true and often unknown object. A tentative list of such objects has been drawn up:

Natural objects	Savage objects
Interpreted natural objects	Mathematical objects
Integrated natural objects	Objects made by the insane
Disturbed objects	"Readymade" and assisted-
Found objects	"readymade" objects
Interpreted found objects	Surrealist objects

Just as poetry must be made by all, so those objects must be of use to all.

*

A most amusing tale published in the French magazine *Lu* (16 August 1935) shows that the Hungarian novelist Alexandre Maraï came close to this idea when he imagined a store called "A Bit of Everything," which he described in some detail:

> *We started by placing in the center of the window a piece of basalt, fairly big but not too unwieldy, well brushed and laid delicately on a bed of cotton like some very fragile object. On the right and on the left, imitation crystal goblets held white and yellow sea sand and common calcareous sand. . . . A variety of leaves—beech, locust, oak—were pasted on a sheet of black cardboard at the back of the display. Each leaf was identified by its origin, from the soft green of May to the golden yellow of October. . . . One page, dog-eared, numbered 165, from one of the least engaging novels by M. Pierre Benoit, a member of the French Academy, was displayed in a frame under glass . . .*

The humor of this description stems from the presence of objects that are obviously valueless, but one need only replace those with others of some value and the store imagined by Maraï could serve as a model of disorientation.

As well, however tiny that space might be, it would open onto the largest, the most daring structures presently under construction in the minds of men. There, one could *leap beyond the retrospective view* to which we are accustomed when looking, for instance, at true artistic creativity. From this diminutive yet unlimited space, one could enjoy a panoramic view of all that is being discovered, while at the same time thinking: "Here, one might have read *Delfica* by Nerval, seen Borel make a quick visit . . . or yet: Seurat could have left there one of his *Poseuses* [Women posing], it's here that Henri Rousseau would have enjoyed sitting."

Like a vestibule between two cars of a train, those phantoms you so love await you in the doorway of *Gradiva* to guide you inside.

Finally, this would be a book heaven—so few are chosen—but the shelves would really have to be rays of sunshine. On condition that all the books selected are worth reading, that *they and they alone* make up the phosphoric substance of what we have to know and love, of what can propel us to action—no longer backward but forward.

From the children's picture books to the poets' picture books:

GRADIVA

On the bridge between dream and reality, "hitching up her dress with a small gesture of her left hand":

GRADIVA

On the borders of utopia and truth, which is to say right at the heart of life:

GRADIVA

1937

Memory
of Mexico

Red, virgin land impregnated with the most generous blood, a land where man's life has no price, always ready like the omnipresent agave expressing it to burst into a single final bloom of desire and danger! At least there is still one country in the world where the wind of liberation has not abated. That wind in 1810, in 1910 has irresistibly rumbled with the voice of all the green organs that thrust up over there into the stormy sky: one of the earlier images one has of Mexico consists of just such a giant candelabralike cactus, from behind which a gun-bearing man with fiery eyes suddenly appears. There is no dismissing this romantic vision: centuries of oppression and wretched destitution have twice shown how utterly real it was, and nothing can prevent this reality from enduring in its latent state or from smoldering under the deceptive slumber of the desert. The gunman is still standing there in his magnificent rags: he may, at any time, rise unaided from the depths of unawareness and adversity. He will once again emerge from the nearest bushes along the road; driven by an unknown force he will go to meet the others; for the first time he will recognize himself in them. One should not pay undue attention to the apparent rigidity brought about by the formation of any military hierarchy as a result of such adventuring: in Mexico, the title of general can be assumed by anyone who has been or is still capable of mobilizing, on his own initiative, any number of men individually recruited in rural areas. The "generals" of whom I speak, most of them trained the hard way under Emiliano Zapata and some of them currently in power, are still part, it should be said, of the admirable upthrust that, nearly thirty years ago, led the "peons," those Indian day laborers who made up the most shamefully exploited section of the population, to victory. I do not know of anything more exalting than those photographs that captured the light of that period, such as the shot of those bivouacs of barefooted insurgents whose eyes, despite the wide variety of getups and attitudes, all show the same fierce resolution. Great uprisings may seem to be a thing of the past, the villages may appear to have closed their eyes to the pathetic barter of peppers for pottery pieces, and even if corruption, there as elsewhere, may have gotten the better of the state apparatus, it is nevertheless true that Mexico is bursting with the hopes that have been successively placed on other countries—the USSR, Germany, China, Spain—and that, during the last historical period, have been dramatically thwarted, even though we know that they will eventually subjugate the forces crushing them, that they are inextricably linked to what is most mysterious, most indestructible in the human impulse, that it is their nature repeatedly to come back to life and blossom on the ruins of this very civilization.

Mexico imperiously urges us to join in this meditation on the ultimate aims of human activity, with its pyramids made up of several layers of stones corresponding to very distant cultures that have covered and obscurely penetrated one another. Drillings provide learned archaeologists with opportunities to speculate on the various races that occupied this land, one after the other, and ruled it with their weapons and their gods. But many of those monuments are still disappearing under the short grass and they become indistinguishable from the hills when seen from any distance. The great message of the tombs, which is spread by unfathomable means much better than it is deciphered, charges the air with electricity. Mexico, having barely awakened from its mythological past, keeps evolving under the protection of Xochipilli, the god of flowers and lyrical poetry, and of Coatlícue, the goddess of the earth and of violent death, whose effigies, more impressive, more intense than any of the others, exchange winged words and raucous calls from one end of the national museum to the other, above the heads of the Indian peasants who are the more numerous and more reverent of its visitors. This ability to reconcile life and death is doubtlessly the principal lure of Mexico. In this regard, it offers an inexhaustible range of sensations, from the mildest to the most insidious. There is nothing like Manuel Alvarez Bravo's photographs to reveal to us its extreme poles.[1] That workshop where they make caskets for children (the infant mortality rate in Mexico is 75 percent): the relationship between light and shadow, between the stack of boxes by the ladder and the one by the gate, and the poetically dazzling image created by placing the phonograph horn inside the lower coffin are exceptionally evocative of the emotional atmosphere in which the whole country is steeped. That composition made up of a head and one hand, both mummified: the way the hand is placed and the endless spark produced by the proximity of the teeth and the nail describe a suspended, buzzing world, torn between conflicting poles of attraction. That corner of an Indian cemetery where daisies, sprung up from the gravel-covered soil, maintain mysterious relations with hoops of bleached feathers. Finally, if a girl or a woman appears in the picture, a dramatic element is introduced under the blazing sun by the white hat tilted back, wide enough to block the porthole of darkness, by the chipped surface of the wall, by the sense of time standing still one gets from seeing the effortless, ever so graceful tiptoeing; or yet that element appears when a black veil is suddenly lifted and stands out sharply against a glacier of wash drying in the sun. Chance seems to have been completely excluded from such an art—the black horse against the black house—for the greater benefit of that sense of fate, pierced by divinatory glimpses, that has inspired the greatest works of all time and that is today in the custody of Mexico.

*

The palace of fate: isn't that where I found myself on several occasions in Guadalajara, in the very heart of the city? As Diego Rivera and I went in search of old paintings and objects, the museum curator had referred us to an old broker whose face resembled that of Elisée Reclus. That friendly, shabby-looking man who prided himself on his ability to find what we were looking for told us from the start that he would only accept lottery tickets as a commission. He said that, in the course of his life, he had already bought twenty-six thousand pesos' worth of such tickets and that, since he had never won anything, he could not reasonably be expected to leave it at that. While taking us to his lodgings, he insisted on giving me a small polished stone in the veining of which he had recognized the image of Our Lady of Guadalupe, but he indeed refused any payment in cash. To reach his dilapidated dwelling, we had to cross a bizarre courtyard and climb a genuinely fantastic set of stairs. However accustomed the eye may be in Mexico to the baroque architecture and decoration of colonial times, it is impossible for it not to react in a unique way to the interior layout of this former private mansion that had fallen prey to some sort of parasitic disease of the most corrosive kind. The monumental stairs open out onto landings made to look like grounds-facing perrons with faded green half-balusters.[2] Those landings are lined with tall streetlamps repeated in trompe l'oeil on the walls. Colonnades whose shafts are real at first end up disappearing, as one moves forward, in a fog of illusion. The paneling, lashed by blue strips and deceptive like theater mirrors as one draws near them, has been painted in gradations of color, in imitation of thickening air, of still waters. On the second floor one passes by a wide blocked-up door, condemned to being its own shadow. As I was to be told later, all the exits of the room onto which it used to open were walled up as soon as the former mistress of the house had been embalmed inside it. She was the mother of the current titular occupants and she had expressed the wish to rest in peace in that room forever. Naturally, the presence of that great lady, all the more oppressive for being invisible, seems to account for the dreamlike atmosphere of the house. That morning, an elegant-looking man was singing at the top of his voice on the upper gallery. Looking at him from down below, I had difficulty in taking my eyes off him even though another sight vied for my attention. The corners of the courtyard, half-enclosed and covered with makeshift roofs, were used as shelters by entire families of destitute people who went about their business and played their games, as unconcerned as gypsies around a caravan. Other groups had taken possession of all the nooks on the stairs: in the lacustrine shade, one could see women bustling about a fountain, two or three men around a workbench. The singer who, as we drew near, had not lowered his voice at all did not seem to notice us. He was one of those characters from an El Greco painting whom one encounters every day over there. His importance in that place seemed to me disproportionate to his size and even to the externalization, in exceptionally appropriate circumstances, of his delirium. That importance was indisputably a social one, as I was able to ascertain later, when I was told that he was the eldest son of the former owner and that his mental condition alone had until then prevented, in accordance with the laws of the land, the sale of the house and the distribution of the proceeds of that sale among himself and the other two heirs. I still marvel at his solitude in those surroundings, at everything that his behavior implied in terms of the miraculous survival of feudal times. While the barbarians, myself included, were camping out in front of the very doors of the bedrooms, while their sacrilegious and magnificent audacity was undermining this last sanctuary with its cardboard wings ... The whole of Mexico was there, driven by the proximity of a highly developed country to evolve in a hurry, without any transition, through a series of breathtaking acrobatic maneuvers. At that moment, I happened to meet the brother of this strange survivor who, from the top of the mast of his raft, was able to believe that he had frozen the waves of time. Completely different in appearance, without anything haughty or in any way impressive about him, he was coming home for lunch, carrying a small suitcase. That suitcase, which he obligingly opened before us, contained the least valuable of the family jewels, the ones he had not yet managed to sell while doing his daily rounds of the stores. He told us how they had given the former servants (the part-time broker who had introduced us was one of them) a small number of movable objects that they were permitted to sell for their own benefit to make up for wages that had been owed them for a long time and that it was out of the question to pay them. But those objects had little by little dragged all the others down in a gradual decline. As a result of their masters' indifference, the servants in turn had been reduced to living by their wits and, soon afterward, by plunder: constantly on the lookout for a visitor to whom they might be able to sell a lamp, a watch chain, a chess set, their reserve of spoils had spread and, without their having to leave their rooms, had led them to encroach on all sides of the old seignorial domain.

Before leaving the city, I wanted to take another look at the Tumbledown Palace, lest I should forget some part of it, lest I should lose the key that, from a distance, would enable it to open itself to me. An emotion that I had never yet experienced, that grew in intensity by the second as I felt certain I would never recapture it, was awaiting me on the other side of the living-room door. Its venetian blinds still lowered over thick curtains at this early hour, the heavily paneled room was dark and immensely empty, although it still contained an old piano. There, all alone, stood a magnificent creature, sixteen or seventeen years old, her hair disarranged in an ideal way. She had answered the door and, having laid down her broom, was smiling like the dawn of the world without showing the least sign of confusion. That girl moved with supreme gracefulness: seeing her gestures, as alluring as they were harmonious, one slowly realized that she was naked under a tattered evening gown. The spell she cast over me at that moment was such that I failed to inquire after her position: who could she be, the daughter or sister of one of the individuals who had haunted that place in the days of their splendor, or was she of the race of those who invaded it? No matter: as long as she was there, I did not care at all about her origin, I was quite content to simply render thanks for her existence. *Such is beauty.*

1938

Manifesto for

an Independent

Revolutionary Art

Without any exaggeration one can say that human civilization has never before been exposed to so many dangers. The Vandals, with means that were barbaric and relatively ineffective, destroyed the civilization of antiquity in one corner of Europe. Today, we see the whole of civilization being threatened in the integrity of its historical destiny by reactionary forces armed with the entire arsenal of modern technology. We are not only thinking of the impending war: already, while we are still at peace, art and science have been placed in an impossible situation.

Inasmuch as it comes about through the agency of an individual, inasmuch as it makes use of certain subjective skills to bring out something that will constitute an objective enrichment, any philosophical, sociological, scientific, or artistic discovery appears as the result of a lucky *chance*, that is to say a more or less spontaneous manifestation of *necessity*. Such contributions cannot be minimized, whether from the standpoint of general knowledge (which aims at furthering the interpretation of the world) or from the revolutionary standpoint (which, to achieve the transformation of the world, requires a careful analysis of the laws governing its movement). We especially cannot afford to remain indifferent to the mental conditions in which those contributions are made nor can we fail to ensure that those specific laws that govern intellectual creation are respected.

In the contemporary world, we have to acknowledge the ever more wide-spread transgression of those laws, a transgression that inevitably entails an increasingly evident degradation not only of the work of art but also of the "artistic" personality. Now that it has rid itself of all the artists whose work showed the slightest evidence of a love for freedom, even on the level of form, Hitlerian fascism has forced those who could still consent to holding a pen or a brush to become lackeys of the regime and to celebrate it by command, within the limits of the worst kind of convention. Though it has not been publicized, the same thing has been happening in the USSR during the period of violent reaction that has now reached its peak.

It goes without saying that we do not for a moment stand by the currently fashionable slogan "Neither fascism nor communism!" that perfectly suits the conservative and frightened philistine clinging to the remnants of the "democratic" past. True art—art that does not merely produce variations on ready-made models but strives to express the inner needs of man and of mankind as they are today—cannot be anything other than revolutionary: it must aspire to a complete and radical reconstruction of society, if only to free intellectual creation from the chains that bind it and to allow all mankind to climb those heights that only isolated geniuses have reached in the past. At the same time, we recognize that only social revolution can clear the way for a new culture. If, however, we reject all solidarity with the caste that is currently ruling the USSR, it is precisely because, in our eyes, it represents not communism but its most treacherous and dangerous enemy. The totalitarian regime of the USSR, through the so-called cultural organizations it controls in other countries, has spread over the entire world a heavy twilight inimical to the emergence of any sort of spiritual values. In this twilight of filth and blood, we see men disguised as intellectuals and artists who have turned servility into a stepping stone, renunciation of their own principles into a perverse game, lying-for-pay into a custom, and glorification of crime into a source of pleasure. The official art of the Stalinist era mirrors with unprecedented harshness their pathetic attempts at deception and their efforts to disguise their true mercenary role.

The muted reprobation inspired in the artistic world by this brazen negation of the principles that have always governed art and that even states built on slavery have not dared to contest must give way to a sweeping condemnation. Artistic *opposition* is right now one of the forces that can effectively help to discredit and overthrow the regimes that are stifling the right of the exploited class to aspire to a better world along with all sense of human greatness or even dignity.

The communist revolution is not afraid of art. It has learned from the study of the development of the artistic calling in the collapsing capitalist society that this calling can only be the result of a clash between the individual and various social forms that are inimical to him. This situation alone, even if he has not become fully aware of it, makes the artist the natural ally of the revolution. The process of *sublimation*, which comes into play in this instance, as psychoanalysis has shown, aims at restoring the balance between the integral "ego" and the repressed elements. This restoration works to the advantage of the "superego," which sets the forces of the inner world, of the "id," *common to all men* and constantly evolving toward self-fulfillment, against the unbearable present reality. The need for the emancipation of the mind has but to follow its natural course to be brought to reimmerse itself into this primordial necessity: the need for the emancipation of man.

Art cannot, therefore, without demeaning itself, willingly submit to any outside directive and ensconce itself obediently within the limits that some people, with extremely shortsighted pragmatic ends in view, think they can set on its activities. It is far better to rely on the gift of prefiguration with which any true artist is endowed: this is what opens the way to a (virtual) resolution of the major contradictions of his time and focuses the attention of his contemporaries on the urgent need for establishing a new order.

It is imperative, at this point in time, to go back to the idea of the role of the writer developed by Marx in his youth. Clearly this idea should be extended to cover the various categories of producers and researchers in the artistic and scientific fields. "The writer," he said, "must naturally make money in order to live and write, but he should under no circumstances live and write in order to make money. . . . The writer does not in any way look on his work as a *means*. It is an *end in itself* and represents so little a means in his own eyes and those of others that if necessary he sacrifices his existence to the existence of his work. . . . *The first condition of freedom of the press is that it should not be a money-making occupation.*" It is more than ever appropriate to set that statement against those who would force intellectual activity to pursue objectives that are foreign to its nature and who would, in defiance of all the historical determinants peculiar to it, prescribe the themes of art in accordance with alleged reasons of state. The freedom to choose those themes and the absence of all restrictions on the range of his exploration represent for the artist prerogatives that he is entitled to claim as inalienable. As regards artistic creation, what is of paramount importance is that imagination should be free of all constraints and should under no pretext let itself be channeled toward prescribed goals. To those who would urge us, whether it be today or tomorrow, to agree that art should conform to a discipline that we regard as radically incompatible with its nature, we give an absolute refusal and we reassert our deliberate intention of standing by the formula: *complete freedom for art.*

We acknowledge, of course, that the revolutionary state has a right to defend itself against the aggressive reaction of the bourgeoisie, even when it drapes itself in the flag of science or art. But there is a huge difference between these necessary and temporary measures of revolutionary self-defense and the presumption to exercise command over intellectual creation within society. Granted that, in order to develop the material forces of production, the revolution has no other choice but to build a *socialist* regime with centralized control; however, it must from the very beginning, when it comes to intellectual creativity, establish an *anarchist* system based on individual freedom. No authority, no constraint, not the slightest trace of orders from above! Only on the basis of free creative friendship, without the least constraint from outside, will it be possible to form various associations of scientists and collectives of artists who will be able to work fruitfully together and to undertake tasks that will be more far-reaching than ever before.

It should be clear by now that, in defending freedom of creation, we have no intention of justifying political indifferentism, nor do we wish to resurrect a so-called pure art that generally serves the thoroughly impure ends of the forces of reaction. No, we have too high an idea of the role of art to deny it an influence on the fate of society. We believe that the supreme task of art in this day and age is consciously to take an active part in preparing the revolution. However, the artist cannot serve the struggle for emancipation unless he has internalized its social and individual content, unless he feels its meaning and its drama in his very nerves and unless he freely seeks to give his inner world an artistic incarnation.

In the present period, characterized by the death throes of capitalism—democratic as well as fascist—the artist, even if he does not overtly display his social dissidence, is threatened with the loss of his right to make a living and to go on with his work because he is denied all means of promoting his creations. It is natural that he should then turn to the Stalinist organizations that hold out the possibility of escaping from his isolation. But, in exchange for some material advantages, he is required to renounce everything that might constitute his own message and to display a terribly degrading servility. Hence, he has no alternative but to withdraw from such organizations, provided that demoralization has not gotten the better of his *character*. From that very moment, he must understand that his place is elsewhere, not among those who betray the cause of the revolution at the same time, necessarily, as that of mankind, but among those who demonstrate their unshakable loyalty to the principles of this revolution, those who, for this reason, are the only ones who can bring it to fruition and who can subsequently ensure the free expression of the human genius in all its manifestations.

Our purpose in issuing this call is to find a ground on which all revolutionary supporters of art can come together to serve the revolution with the specific methods of art and to defend freedom of art itself against the usurpers of the revolution. We are firmly convinced that it is possible for representatives of fairly divergent aesthetic, philosophical, and political orientations to meet on this ground. Marxists can walk hand in hand with anarchists here, provided both groups uncompromisingly break away from the reactionary police mentality, whether it be represented by Joseph Stalin or by his henchman Garcia Oliver.

Thousands upon thousands of isolated artists and thinkers, whose voices are drowned out by the odious clamor of well-drilled fakers, are presently scattered throughout the world. Many small local magazines are trying to gather about them youthful forces, seeking new paths, not subsidies. Every progressive trend in art is branded by fascism as degenerate. Every free creation is labeled fascist by the Stalinists. Independent revolutionary art must gather its forces to fight against reactionary persecution and to assert out loud its right to exist. Such a union of forces is the goal of the International Federation of Independent Revolutionary Art (known as FIARI), which we deem necessary to form.

We have no intention of imposing every single idea put forth in this manifesto, which we ourselves consider only as a first step in the new direction. We urge all representatives, all friends and defenders of art, who cannot fail to realize the need for this rallying cry, to make themselves heard at once. We address the same appeal to all independent leftist publications that are prepared to join in creating the International Federation and in working out its tasks and methods of action.

When a preliminary international contact has been established through the press and by correspondence, we will proceed to the organization of local and national congresses on a modest scale. The next step will be to convene a world congress that will officially mark the foundation of the International Federation.

Our goals:

the independence of art—for the revolution;
the revolution—for the liberation of art once and for all.

André Breton, Diego Rivera[1]
Mexico, 25 July 1938

Visit

    with

        Leon Trotsky

Address given on 11 November 1938 at a meeting held
in Paris by the Parti Ouvrier Internationaliste, to
commemorate the anniversary of the October Revolution

Comrades,

I shall not give you a political lecture: that is not what you expect from me. It has been nearly three months since I came back from Mexico. During those three months, the voice of comrade Trotsky has reached us several times. His thought, which is wonderfully quick to tackle every new aspect of the political and social problem, wonderfully well equipped to turn events to best account as soon as they arise, has managed to cross the ocean to fulfill, as it found its way in the publications of the Fourth International, its role as an inspired guide, the most severely tested of any in the revolutionary movement. In view of the explosive events that have occurred over the last three months, the analysis of the international situation, which he carried out in my presence with unparalleled authority, must now take these new developments into account. It would be easy to show that Trotsky, with his predictions, came closer than anyone to what has become the concrete reality of today. But you, comrades, whose aspirations coincide with his, can demonstrate this fact as well as I can. Hence I will leave aside anything that might duplicate the presentations of our comrades in order to focus on the purely human angle of my account.

From the Marxist standpoint, we can easily understand that it is impossible in this era to make a living as an independent writer, all the more so if such a writer wants in all honesty to express his views on a series of issues that are likely to bring out his total dissidence from bourgeois society. His only alternatives are either to assuage his critics gradually so that this society can prepare to welcome him like a prodigal son, or to pledge allegiance to a form of opposition that, at least for the time being, is quite safe and also quite lucrative for an intellectual: the Stalinist opposition. Indeed, if he consents to mask the frightful historical imposture of Stalinism, such a writer is offered an almost unlimited variety of positions and jobs, each better remunerated than the next. As I did not consent to either of these two acts of surrender, of treason, I was forced two years ago by my extremely precarious financial situation to seek a position teaching abroad. The so-called competent department of the Ministry of Foreign Affairs, to which I necessarily had to submit my application, concluded, after a careful examination of my ideological position as deduced from my previous activity, that they should avoid sending me to a country living under an authoritarian regime or liable to do so at any time. Under those conditions, the possibilities were so limited—it is amusing to mention it today—that they could only offer me a choice between Czechoslovakia and Mexico. I chose Mexico, and then nothing else happened for a long time. It was only at the end of last year, after I brought myself to inquire into the reasons for this silence, that I was offered, by way of compensation, a trip to Mexico City, where I was to give a series of lectures at the university on the state of poetry and painting in Europe.

You must be wondering, comrades, why I find it necessary to detail the circumstances of that trip. The reason is, naturally, that some of our enemies have contrived to misrepresent it and are still trying to use it against me in the crudest fashion. Even before I left, a member of the "Maison de la Culture,"[1] a fairly dangerous meddler whose name is Tristan Tzara, managed to find willing ears to which he confided that I was to visit Trotsky as a Foreign Affairs representative! When I left Paris, a number of letters were sent via New York by airmail so that they might reach Mexico ahead of me: in those letters, addressed to the major Mexican writers and artists, the most brazen kind of calumny is given a free rein. Fortunately, several recipients of those letters were well aware of what I stand for and of the despicable tactics that are commonly devised in Stalinist circles. Thanks to one such person, I am able to read out to you the following document:

Dear Comrade and Friend,

We wish to inform you, and request that you spread this information among our Mexican friends, of the position of M. André Breton, who will be coming to your country to deliver a series of lectures.

Sent by the propaganda department of the Ministry of Foreign Affairs, whose reactionary policy even today is well known, M. André Breton has always sided against the Popular Front and, in so doing, has allied himself with the most suspicious political elements. His actions against the Spanish Republic have taken the most treacherous forms under the guise of a vague revolutionary discourse.

An avowed admirer of Trotsky, he has opposed every single action of the International Association of Writers and, on these grounds, he was denied the right to speak during the first Writers Congress. As we fear that misunderstandings might arise, we want to keep you informed of the real situation of literature in France.

Yours, etc. . . .

For the International Secretariat:

Signed: René Blech.

For those of you who may not be aware of this, I would like to repeat, comrades, that my attitude and that of my *surrealist* friends regarding the war in Spain has always been completely unequivocal. From the very beginning of the conflict we have condemned forever the forces of regression and darkness responsible for its unleashing; we have proclaimed our unshakable hope in the initial leap that propelled the Spanish working class forward and that aimed at forging in the crucible of danger a bloc that alone would be truly invincible, that also aimed at the primordial destruction of the entire religious apparatus and, above all, at the creation of an actively revolutionary ideology, put to the test of facts, unconcerned with reproducing any other existing or decaying ideology but able to reconcile the fundamental aspirations of our comrades of the FAI, of the CNT, of the POUM, and, as we would add at the time, of the PSUC, insofar as the latter might cease being prejudicial to the former. Is that clear enough? On every occasion, we have raised the most uncompromising objections to the policy of nonintervention. Printed and dated documents provide irrefutable proof of all this. But our real sin, that for which I personally cannot be forgiven, is that we have made the observation during these events that the USSR, in its present state, was one of the main obstacles to the victory of the Spanish proletariat, and when we stated, for instance, in January 1937: "The Moscow trials are the immediate result of the current struggle in Spain: what Stalin wants is to prevent at all costs a new revolutionary wave from surging against the world. The objective is to abort the Spanish revolution, as previously the German revolution and the Chinese revolution had been aborted. But isn't the USSR supplying arms and planes? Yes it is, first because it must save face, and then because those double-edged weapons will ultimately be used to crush all the forces presently striving in Spain, not to restore the bourgeois republic but to ensure a better world, all the forces fighting for the proletarian revolution." What cannot be tolerated is that I said: "Make no mistake: the bullets from the Moscow staircase, in January 1937, are aimed at our comrades of the POUM. The next targets will be our anarchist comrades, in the hope thereby of doing away with everything alive, everything that holds out a promise of a viable future in the Spanish antifascist struggle." In November 1938—there is still hope, comrades—Stalin lost his case against the POUM: in view of the evidence provided by the defense, the charges of espionage brought against our comrades had to be dropped, and it became most difficult to try and discredit the Spanish revolutionaries, even with the help of the allegations and oaths of that vile Jesuit named Bergamin. Proletarian Spain, revolutionary Spain, the reality for which we refuse to substitute the concept of republican Spain, is still holding its own. That reality alone is what commands our passionate brotherly solidarity. In spite of all the attempts at corruption, neither Stalin nor Franco is yet Spain's master: the verdict of October 1938 shows us that Spain has not said its last word.

To come back to my own situation: as if the letter of introduction I read out to you earlier were not sufficient, a more imperious note, which likewise failed to remain confidential, was sent to the general secretary of the LEAR [League of Revolutionary Artists and Writers] of Mexico, corresponding here to our former AEAR [Association of Revolutionary Artists and Writers]. What was asked therein was to ensure, and I quote, "the systematic sabotage of any sort of work that I might wish to undertake in Mexico." It was signed by none other than Aragon.

.　　.　　.　　.　　.

You can imagine with what emotion I approached that famous "Blue House," comrade Trotsky's residence at Coyoacán. Even though I had tried to learn as much as possible about his morale, about how he occupied his time and also about everything that makes him a living individual, as opposed to a historical figure, there was still a screen between us. What unfolded on that screen was a life more turbulent and more provocative, as well as incomparably more dramatic, than any other. I thought of the man who was leader of the 1905 revolution, one of the two leaders of the 1917 revolution—not only of the man who put his genius and all his energy at the service of the greatest cause I know of, but also of the exceptional witness, the profound historian whose works do more than educate, since they inspire men to rise up. I thought of him at Lenin's side, and later, when he continued alone to defend his theory, the theory of revolution, within rigged congresses. I saw him standing alone among his companions who had been ignominiously shot down, alone and haunted by the memory of his four murdered children. Accused of the worst crime possible for a revolutionary, living under constant threat, a prey to the blind hatred of the very people for whose sake he worked unsparingly. The dark night of opinion must be easy to organize indeed!

With beating heart, I saw the gate of the Blue House being opened. I was led through the garden and barely had time to recognize, as I went by, the bougainvillea whose pink and violet flowers littered the ground, the omnipresent cacti, the stone idols lovingly assembled along the paths by Diego Rivera, who had put the house at Trotsky's disposal. I found myself in a well-lit room filled with books. Well, comrades, the moment I saw comrade Trotsky get up and come forward—the moment the real person replaced the image I had of him—I could not repress the impulse to tell him how astonished I was to find him so young-looking. What self-control, what conviction of having, against all odds, kept his life in perfect accord with his principles, what exceptional courage, however tested, have preserved his youthful features! The deep blue eyes, the wonderful forehead, the abundant hair with barely a hint of silver, the healthy complexion combine to create a mask mirroring inner peace—an inner peace that has overcome and will continue to overcome the cruelest hardships. This could be no more than a static impression, for as soon as his face lights up and he starts using his hands to qualify this or that statement with rare subtlety, something electrifying radiates from him. You can be sure, comrades, that if the capitalist states have shown such resolve, have so unanimously decided on the proscription of comrade Trotsky, and if Stalin's government has brought continuous pressure on them to enforce that proscription, that was a perfectly natural step for them to take. Trotsky at large, Trotsky at liberty to address a meeting today in Paris, would be like a whole wall of the revolution standing before us; we would see the light of the Petrograd Soviet, of the Smolny congress rising in front of us. For this we cannot beg the consent of the exploiters of the working class. It is the working class itself that must bring it about, the working class that, when the time is right, will throw off the yoke that weighs them down, will sweep away the whole Thermidorean rottenness, and will recognize their own kin.

I was fortunate enough later on to have frequent talks with comrade Trotsky. From being the somewhat legendary figure of my imagination, he became a living and breathing person. There is hardly any picturesque site in Mexico that I do not associate with him. I remember him knitting his brows as he opened out the Paris papers in the shade of a Cuernavaca garden, hot and abuzz with hummingbirds, while comrade Natalia Trotsky, so endearing, so understanding, and so gentle, tells me the names of the strange blooms. I remember him as we climbed the pyramid of Xochicalco; on another day, as we ate lunch with hearty appetites at the edge of an icy lake, right in the crater of Popocatépetl. We spent an entire morning ferreting about on an island in Lake Pátzcuaro, where the schoolteacher, who had recognized Trotsky and Rivera, called on the children to sing in the old Tarascan language. We fished for axolotls in a rushing stream in the forest. No one shows greater interest than comrade Trotsky in everything new that comes along; no one is as enterprising, as ingenious while going on a trip. Clearly, there is something of the child in him that retains its unalterable freshness. And yet I can tell you, comrades, that no one can sustain a greater mental effort than he can: I do not know of any man capable of working with such intensity for so long. But there are already so many objective accounts of his labor that I think I can skip this and try instead to bring out the secret of his personal appeal, which is overwhelming. One evening, he agreed to receive at his home a group of about twenty intellectuals from New York, to give a short talk and then to answer their questions. I could see how, as the meeting progressed, its atmosphere grew increasingly favorable to him, how impressed his listeners were with his spirited and confident replies, how much they appreciated his lightheartedness, how delighted they were by his witticisms. I was much amused to watch those people line up, before they left, in order to thank him and shake his hand. And yet, among those most eager to do so were a state governor and an owlish-looking woman who had been minister of labor during the MacDonald administration. . . . It seems to me this attraction is due not only to the pleasure one derives from observing the workings of a superior intelligence at close range, but also to the surprising realization that the governing idea, on which this intelligence is focused, is able to subordinate all others, to use them to validate itself. But I am not telling you anything new. Sometimes I would walk or sit on a bench with comrade Trotsky in the middle of one of those Indian markets that are among the finest sights Mexico has to offer. Whether our attention was caught by the architecture of the surrounding houses, or by the many-colored stalls, or by the passing peasants draped in serapes combining the sun and the night, and by their extraordinarily noble bearing, Trotsky always managed to link this minor fact of observation to a more general phenomenon, to see in it a spark of hope for the readjustment of this world's values, to draw from it a stimulus to carry on our struggle.

There is a question that takes precedence, for comrade Trotsky, over all others, a question from which he will tolerate no diversions and to which he will always bring you back. That question is: "What prospects?" No one is better equipped than he is to be on the lookout for the future, just as no one is more fully himself than when he describes some wolf hunts in which he took part in the Caucasus. The past is something he finds rather irritating. He heaps sarcastic remarks on those who have made good on the basis of their reputations, even honorable ones. You should hear him talk of the "petty pensioners of the Revolution"!

In Mexico as elsewhere, there have been attempts to harm, to eliminate Trotsky in all sorts of ways. Since it was not enough to sentence him to death in Moscow, to tear away from him one by one, by killing those dearest to him, his best reasons for living, and to mount against him the craziest, most despicable smear campaign of all times, the GPU, who vainly tried last year to have a parcel containing a bomb delivered to him personally as if it had been sent by a friend, have resigned themselves, at least for the time being, to resort once again to a set of monstrous calumnies, all the more effective in this case since those who are being targeted know nothing at all of the political situation in Mexico. Allegations have been made, comrades, and faithfully echoed by the weekly *Marianne*, that the expropriation order issued by President Cárdenas against foreign (British and American) oil companies was Trotsky's idea, so that Hitler, Mussolini, and Franco could be supplied with Mexican oil! It has been said—in glaring contradiction with the previous allegations, but no matter—that Trotsky fomented General Cedillo's rebellion against President Cárdenas. The despicable newspapers in the pay of the GPU even went so far as to assert that comrades Trotsky and Rivera, during a trip from Mexico City to Guadalajara—a 500-mile trip during which I did not leave them for a moment—had long talks with a certain Dr. Atl, who is thought locally to be an agent of the German embassy. In fact, I was the one whom they tried to pass off as that fascist! Note, comrades, that calumny knows, when necessary, how to make itself less blatant, that it can on occasion show some subtlety. Thus it has been suggested that comrade Trotsky is on excessively good terms with the Mexican government, that he is less anxious to defend the interests of the Mexican working class than to avoid antagonizing General

Cárdenas, on account of the hospitality the latter has given him. To set the record straight once and for all, Trotsky issued the following statement:

"Let us leave the tricksters and schemers to their own fate. We are not concerned with them but with the class-conscious workers of the entire world. Without harboring illusions and without fear of calumny, progressive workers will lend their complete support to the Mexican people in their struggle against imperialist powers. The expropriation of oil is neither socialism nor communism but a profoundly progressive measure of national self-defense. Marx obviously did not consider Abraham Lincoln to be a communist. This did not prevent Marx from being in deep sympathy with the struggle that Lincoln led. The First International sent its official greetings to the Civil War president, and Lincoln's reply showed his deep appreciation of this moral support. The international proletariat has no reason to identify its program with the program of the Mexican government. There is no need for revolutionaries to disguise or falsify facts, nor to tell lies, as do the sycophants of the GPU school, who at the moment of danger double-cross and betray the weakest side. Without giving up its individuality, every honest organization of workers throughout the world, and above all in Great Britain, is duty-bound to attack mercilessly the imperialist bandits, their diplomacy, their press, and their fascist lackeys. The cause of Mexico, like the cause of Spain, like the cause of China, is the cause of the entire working class."

To do justice and homage to the Cárdenas government, it should be said that it continues to do everything possible to ensure comrade Trotsky's safety. The members of that government, some of whom played a key role in the 1910 revolution over there and fought under Zapata's command or were trained in his army, feel an unreserved admiration for a man cast in such a mold. That he must endure not being able to move about freely and that he sometimes complains that he is treated like an *object* is not their fault but is rather the consequence of the measures they have to take in order to protect him.

In conclusion, comrades, even if this should not be of equal interest to all of you, I want to deal briefly with an issue that was particularly dear to my heart and that I was dying to broach with him. For years, in matters of artistic creativity, I have defended the right of the writer, of the painter, to self-determination, the right to act, not in conformity with political slogans but in accordance with very special historical determinants that the artist alone is qualified to deal with. I have always been uncompromising on this point. In 1926, when I decided to join the Communist party, this attitude brought me before several control committees where I would be offensively asked to account for the reproductions of works by Picasso and André Masson in the journal I edited. I fought unremittingly, inside the AEAR, the inept watchword "socialist realism." There is one task to which I have applied myself continuously: this has been, regardless of what might happen, to preserve the integrity of artistic pursuits, to ensure that art continues to be an *end*, that it never becomes a *means* under any pretext. This perseverance on my part does not mean that I have not, at times, been led to despair of the outcome of the game or to think that lack of understanding, lack of goodwill would prevail. How many times have we been told, my friends and I, that this attitude we wanted to maintain at all costs was incompatible with Marxism! However convinced I was of the opposite, I could not conceal from myself that this was a sensitive issue, an object of such concern for so many people that I was quite anxious to broach the matter with comrade Trotsky.

I can tell you, comrades, that I found him extremely receptive to my concerns. Oh! Don't think we managed to reach an agreement straightaway: he is not a man to pronounce anybody right so easily. He was already fairly familiar with my books, but he insisted on reading my lectures and offered to discuss them with me. We did have a few arguments here and there: a name mentioned in passing such as Sade or Lautréamont would cause him to raise an eyebrow. Ignorant of who they were, he would ask me to clarify the influence they had on me, while adopting the only appropriate viewpoint, common to both the revolutionary and the artist, that of *human liberation*. At other times, he would challenge this or that concept I had occasionally put forward and he would proceed to pick holes in it. He thus told me one day: "Comrade Breton, I am not quite clear about your interest in phenomena of objective chance. Yes, I am well aware that Engels resorted to this idea, but I wonder if, in your case, there is not something else. I am not sure that you are not concerned with keeping open"—his hands described a small figure in the air—"a little window on the beyond." I had not finished defending my position when he interrupted me: "I am not convinced. Besides, you have written somewhere . . . oh yes, that you found these phenomena somewhat disturbing." "Pardon me," I replied, "I wrote: disturbing in the present state of knowledge, would you care to look it up?" He got up, slightly agitated, took a few steps, and turned back to me: "If you said . . . in the present state of knowledge . . . I see nothing more to dispute; I withdraw my objection."

The extreme perspicacity, even though it may tend to be slightly distrustful, and the perfect good faith I have seen him demonstrate in all circumstances have enabled us to agree fully on the timeliness of publishing a manifesto that would once and for all settle the dispute I mentioned earlier. This manifesto, signed by Diego Rivera and myself, has appeared under the title *Manifesto for an Independent Revolutionary Art*. It concludes with a call for the creation of an International Federation of Independent Revolutionary Art (FIARI), whose monthly bulletin will come out for the first time at the end of December. I may remark that the demand for total independence in artistic matters is owed to Trotsky more than to Rivera and myself. It is comrade Trotsky who, when he saw I had written: "Complete freedom for art, except against the proletarian revolution," warned us that the latter part of this sentence could lead to new abuses, and so he crossed it out unhesitatingly.

Trotsky told me many times that, in the current period, he pinned his faith on the activity of an organization such as the FIARI to facilitate a revolutionary regrouping. Moreover, twice in recent months, he saw fit to explain his personal views on artistic creation. He did so once in a letter to some American comrades, reprinted in *Quatrième Internationale* [Fourth international], and again in an interview, not yet published in France, from which I shall quote the following: "The art of the Stalinist era will go down in history as a patent expression of the severe decline of the proletarian revolution. However, the Babylonian captivity of revolutionary art cannot and will not last forever. The revolutionary party certainly cannot set itself the task of controlling art. Such a presumption could only arise in the minds of people drunk with omnipotence, like the Moscow bureaucracy. Art, and science as well, not only do not ask for orders but, by their very essence, do not tolerate them."

It seems impossible to me that all genuine artists would not receive such a declaration with relief and, if they should be revolutionaries, with enthusiasm.

Comrades, I am aware I have not been equal to the ambitious task I assigned myself, which was to make comrade Trotsky's presence among us a bit more tangible. In consolation, I remind myself of a conversation I had a few years ago with André Malraux, who had returned from a trip to the USSR. He told me how, during a welcoming banquet at which he had been invited to speak, he happened to mention Leon Trotsky, and how he instantly felt the atmosphere grow oppressive, heard glasses fall, saw some of his neighbors at the table get up and move with the obvious intention of surrounding him: *how for a moment he feared for his life.* He even told me that he thought he was saved only thanks to a sudden flash of inspiration, as sometimes comes to one confronted with danger, which dictated to him a sentence that could surprise and disconcert those who stood ready to pounce. What astonished me—and still does—is not so much that scene, which has been corroborated since by many tragic events, but rather the conclusion to which it led André Malraux. According to him, one should under no pretext, in no circumstances, utter the name of Leon Trotsky ever again. It seems that pronouncing that name entailed exclusion from revolutionary activity, such as can be engaged in under the abominable present conditions. Have you ever heard any such thing, comrades? Can the instinct of self-preservation possibly compel intellectuals to renounce their own thinking in such a manner? I know, at least I think I know, that André Malraux does not lack courage! Trotsky's name is by itself too representative and too exalting for us not to speak it or for us to merely whisper it. Nothing will stop us from brandishing it and cracking it in the ears of dogs of every breed. Over the mangled bodies of the little children of Spain and those of all men who die every day for the triumph of proletarian Spain, over the bodies of the October revolutionaries, that of our comrade Sedov, murdered in a clinic, that of our comrade Klement, whom the French police refused to recognize when he had been cut in pieces, we must raise our banner: THEY WILL NOT PASS!

I salute comrade Trotsky, wonderfully alive, and who will have his day again, I salute the victor and the great survivor of October, the immortal theorist of permanent revolution.

The

Marseilles

Deck

Various individuals involved in the surrealist movement, or in some respect associated with it, were brought together or came into contact in Marseilles at the end of 1940 and the beginning of 1941. They were Arthur Adamov, Victor Brauner, André Breton, René Char, René Daumal, Robert Delanglade, Oscar Dominguez, Marcel Duchamp, Max Ernst, Jacques Hérold, Sylvain Itkine, Wilfredo Lam, André Masson, Benjamin Péret, Tristan Tzara. Many of them were in the habit of getting together in the "Air-Bel" castle, where Victor Serge and I were staying and where they were given a warm reception by Varian Fry, president of the American Committee for Aid to Intellectuals. Let us hope that in the near future he will relate what life around him was like at that time, in the midst of those extensive grounds whose owner—a miserly old doctor obsessed by ornithology—would keep watch outside even when it was very cold for fear that someone might help himself to a dead branch. Near the greenhouse, in the fall, we were able to catch as many praying mantises as we wanted and to enjoy the exhibition of rivalries and lovemaking that they provide, which outshines by far anything that can be read in the newspapers. There also the great crystalline "nocturnals" collapsing in the morning in a profusion of white bellies and floating spread-eagled on the ponds evidenced the mysterious gestation of toads—demonstrated, in a supererogatory way, that life, in order to go on, needs death. At last, confident of his prestige, naturally, the unmentionable "marshal" had himself announced, forty-eight hours before his arrival in Marseilles, by police searches that resulted in the internment for several days aboard the *Sinaïa*, beautifully dressed with flags for the occasion, of all the people lodging in the castle. And there again, among quite a few other "suspects"—so great is the power of defiance, of scorn, and also of hope against all odds—the actors in this scene had perhaps never been more like children, singing, playing, and laughing with greater abandon.

Among the experiments that have occupied the surrealists in Marseilles—and that did not preclude any more than usual, as far as they were concerned, a spirit of inquiry and a determination to continue interpreting the world freely—there is high up on the list the design of a *deck of cards* that could be considered adapted to what is affecting our sensibility at the present time. Historiographers of the playing card are agreed that the modifications it has undergone over the centuries have always been linked with great military setbacks, but they do not provide any further explanation. What in the traditional deck is hereby dismissed by us is, in a general way, everything in it that indicates that signs outlast the things they signify. Who remembers, for instance, or cares about the symbolic signification of the "diamond," which, through the reference to the *city street cobblestone*, seems, in the final analysis, to designate tradesmen and in addition to represent historically the rising bourgeoisie? And who associates the four emblems printed on the corners of cards with the heads of *spears*, which have not been in use for four hundred years? As we set about substituting new images for the old ones, we nevertheless refrained from altering the general structure of the deck of thirty-two or fifty-two cards—with the "joker" being added to the latter one—and its division into two equal sets of red and black cards (our rationale being that in order for a new deck to come into actual use, it must not only be an incitement to new games, the rules of which should be evolved *from* it instead of being defined beforehand, but also be suitable for all the traditional games). For similar reasons—and I should mention we borrowed some of our ideas from experiments that, in this not insignificant matter, were brought about by the French revolution—we also grappled with the enduring *social* values of the court cards: we relieved the "king" and the "queen" of the authority they lost so long ago and completely released the old "knave" from his subordinate rank.

We thus came to adopt, corresponding with the four modern preoccupations we considered most important, four new emblems, namely:

Meaning:	Emblem:
Love	Flame
Dream	Star (black)
Revolution	Wheel (and blood)
Knowledge	Lock

The hierarchy from the ace up was preserved and would now be:

Genius–Mermaid–Magus–Ten–Etc. . . .

Each of the face cards bears the effigy of a historical or literary figure that we had of a common accord deemed to be the most representative in the assigned place, that is:

Flame: Baudelaire, the Portuguese Nun, Novalis
Star: Lautréamont, Alice, Freud
Wheel: Sade, Lamiel, Pancho Villa
Lock: Hegel, Hélène Smith, Paracelsus

The joker takes on the appearance of Ubu, as drawn by Jarry.

Situation of

Surrealism between

the Two Wars

Address to the French students at Yale University,
10 December 1942

I know that many of you are nearing the fork of your lifelines, that the day is fast approaching when society will ask of you an effort that differs on all counts from the one to which you are accustomed. The vast prospects of intellectual pursuits will shrink abruptly, the peaks of awareness glimpsed during the learning process will suddenly subside, the gratifications dangled by civilization will, without any transition, show their worst side. Life no longer as you would expect it to be upon leaving school—luminous, filled with endless possibilities—but life condemned to be hazarded any day, condemned to fight every inch of the way in a very real sense, without regard for what makes it individually precious, life not only threatened but also recast beforehand into anonymity, leaving aside that which, in every man, is unique in order to think of itself as an integral, infinitesimal, more or less insignificant part of a *whole* that, for reasons that are, or at least are made out to be, ideological, must now get the upper hand of another *whole*. We all know that such renunciations are the price that must be paid for human greatness, and it is an established fact, philosophically speaking, that human wretchedness is measured on the same scale as this greatness. It is nonetheless true that facing you makes me somewhat nervous: it is as if I felt quite poor, as if what the world is asking of you were out of all proportion with what I can give you. From where I stand, I can only see you as a group, not as individuals, and I feel it is audacious of me to face the agglomerate of thoughts that you comprise as you get ready to part company in order to rush toward your respective destinies. Under these circumstances, I cannot forget for a minute that the mass I am addressing is completely magnetized, that in these eyes that combine for me into a single brightness are prefigured some of those acts of self-sacrifice, even of heroism, to which the world to come will owe, to some degree, what it will be. May it be a better world! In any case, to prevent the sacrifice it demands from being even more painful, the best thing to do is to pin one's faith on it.

Why should I feel poor? Because, considering what it produced, the quarter century of existence that separates us does not confer upon my generation the least authority over yours. This legacy of those who are old enough to be your fathers (their uniforms as becoming as ever, horribly cruel duties, an increasingly evasive horizon) could provide quite reasonable arguments in support of the Oedipus complex. The slightest load of wisdom one may be tempted to attribute to age has been conspicuous by its absence in their packs since all they can pass on to you are soldiers' knapsacks. Their advice can be nothing but inadequate and totally inefficacious. I have not forgotten the state of mind of the young soldiers of World War I. Did they ever curse the old men! Not nearly enough, though, not by far, since they allowed those old men to stay in office until all of them together were able to find an outlet in the Pétain of Rethondes and elsewhere, of whom the great writer Georges Bernanos said that he is the "spit of those who died in Verdun." No, neither old age nor pontificating maturity could possibly have any rights over you: I would even be willing to say that you are the ones who should keep them at bay, recall them to a sense of decency when they volunteer to enlighten you. For how could you not feel the deepest mistrust toward them?

Not for a moment, I assure you, do I forget that Hitler *exists* and, through him, underlying the most unforgivable racial persecutions, the revival of certain myths, myths of Germanic origin it would appear, that are incompatible with the harmonious development of mankind; that Mussolini *exists* and, with the Italian brand of fascism, a hideous pruritus that requires a wire brush; that the Mikado *exists*, supported, or so we hear, by a clique so alienated that they consider fighting to be a religious necessity and an end in itself. Their will to dominate the world and the servitude that would be the result for us of their military victory must, without question, set us against them and make us accept, in all its harshness, the law of the jungle. However, even though from the standpoint of visual representation these three heads of the Beast may well meet the needs of the naive prints required by propaganda, they should not hypnotize us to the extent that we would be led to believe that by lopping them off, we would kill off *all* evil. We should realize that the evil that they indeed generate is at the same time generating them, and that regarding them as the *causes* of this evil is liable to result once again in the most tragic of disillusions if we do not also regard them as the *products* of this selfsame evil. The most urgent thing is no doubt to suppress the monstrous agitation inspired by those heads, but its resurgence will only be prevented if we realize that it is an epiphenomenon, and if we react accordingly against what made it possible (pathology teaches that, in the presence of disease, it is not enough to fight a symptom, to prescribe quinine against the fever); men are quite deluded when they hope to cure themselves of their erroneous conceptions by means of shells and firebombs. In this matter still—their propensity to band together in opposing camps so that they can destroy one another—no real cure can be effected unless the virus is properly identified and prophylactic measures are imposed the world over. My status as a refugee in the United States precludes my being more explicit on this subject.

Gentlemen, I felt it necessary to make this digression because I wanted to show you how I perceive this war and, more generally, how it is perceived from the surrealist viewpoint. By the very fact that this war will quite soon require your participation, this, I think, is what the focus of your questioning should be. My experience, not only of this war but of the previous one as well, has taught me that, because these kinds of adventures tend to be appalling and exciting at the same time, few currents of thought are able to rise above them, and even fewer are those to which they give the opportunity to find new strength. Either those currents of thought withdraw, or else—and this is even worse—they sink into a short-sighted conformism, the very same one that newspaper literature tends to propagate. It is my contention that, if today a current of thought sets about accounting for its evolution, even its prior evolution, probity requires it to demonstrate at the outset that, when dealing with crucial issues, it still operates on its own and has not been infected by contagion.

I have chosen to speak to you this afternoon about the situation of surrealism between the two wars, that is to say, necessarily in relation to them. Indeed, surrealism is the only organized intellectual movement that has managed to span the distance between them. It began in 1919 with the publication in *Littérature* of the first chapters of *Les Champs magnétiques* [*The Magnetic Fields*], a work written in collaboration by Philippe Soupault and myself, in which automatic writing as an avowed method was given free rein for the first time and reached its highest point twenty years later, on the literary level, with the appearance of *Au Château d'Argol* [*The Castle of Argol*] by Julien Gracq, in which surrealism, probably for the first time, spontaneously took stock in order to compare itself to the major emotional experiences of the past and to assess, as much from the viewpoint of emotion as from that of clear-sightedness, what had been the extent of its conquest. On another level, it culminated in the unquestionable worldwide triumph of the art of imagination and creation over the art of imitation, a triumph crowned by the unprecedented brilliance of the last International Surrealist Exhibition in Paris. I know that even during these last months at Yale you may have heard that surrealism is dead. While I was still living in France, I had promised myself I would some day put on public display everything I had been able to collect in the way of newspaper articles based on this theme: surrealism is dead. It would have been rather amusing to show that they had been appearing, one after another, almost every month since the inception of surrealism! Criticism—in reviews, in books—has, at any rate, amply compensated surrealism for those prognostications. I only mention them here to forestall your being misled by this new wave of misinformation under cover of a war during which it is always quite difficult to know who is alive and who is dead. With all due respect to some impatient gravediggers, I believe I know more than they do about what the demise of surrealism would intimate: the birth of a more emancipatory movement. Moreover, on account of that selfsame dynamic force that we continue to set above all else, my best friends and I would feel honor-bound to join such a movement forthwith. It would seem that this new movement has not yet arisen. Historically, surrealism can claim unchallenged the leading position it held between the two wars. Spanning as it did the current of sensibility flowing between them, it has unquestionably served as a bridge between the complacent oblivion into which the first war gradually sank and the blind anguish that accompanied the approach of the second one. Nothing can change the fact that it symbolizes, at least in its key manifestations, the *beam of the balance.*

Contained, for the moment still, within these limits, covering the whole emotional region that stretches between these two explosions, surrealism has been following a path that goes from the repercussions of the first catastrophe on psychological and moral life, to the rapid apprehension of the second one. In the meantime, life has nonetheless returned to normal, and it is this contradiction that surrealism has had to face in order to advocate an immediate readjustment of values.

Now that the storm is once again raging out of control, it is easier, alas, to understand how necessary such a readjustment is. Once again positivist realism, which returns in periods of dead calm to yawn above the waters, is proven guilty of impotence and, held up to derision, has no alternative but to take flight. So-called common sense, which can rightly claim it never learned anything, is requested to return at the end of the month with its invoice. What! Mankind is tearing itself apart more efficiently than it did in the early centuries of our era, and two successive generations can just see the sun of their twentieth year approaching when they are pushed headlong onto the battlefields, yet we are expected to believe that this species can control itself and that it is sacrilege to object to the principles on which its psychological nature is based! But, I ask, what is this narrow "reason" that is being taught if this reason must, from life to life, give way to the unreason of wars? Is it not the case that this alleged reason is a sham, that it usurps the rights of a genuine unyielding *reason* that we must substitute for it at all costs and toward which we can only strive if, at the outset, we make a clean sweep of conventional ways of thinking?

If I told you that I felt poor standing before you, it was less in my own name as in the name of the men of my age. From the very moment the surrealist attitude took shape, it exalted youth, urged it not to forfeit its treasures too quickly, enjoined it to count only on itself. Today the waves of youth break on things other than the shadow of the palm trees of Guadalcanal, the ruins of Stalingrad, and the sands of Libya. They have an intrinsic virtue that consists in engulfing the inadequate states of consciousness that have caused their return in a frenzy of iron and fire. Those far too embryonic states of consciousness will be swept away. Right now the future rests in the hands of youth, and of youth alone. Surrealism, I say it again, sprang from an affirmation of boundless faith in the *genius* of youth. It must be admitted that it has never recanted on this point since it has continually endowed with unequaled prestige, with a sense, one might say, of revelation—with all the unquestionable authority this word implies—the message of Lautréamont, dead at the age of twenty-three; of Rimbaud, who had completed his work by the time he was eighteen; of Chirico, for whom the gates of a world opened when he was twenty-three and closed when he was twenty-eight. This collection could be expanded to include Saint-Just, guillotined at the age of twenty-seven; Novalis, who died at thirty; Seurat, dead at thirty-two; Jarry, who wrote at the age of fifteen the great prophetic and avenging play of modern times, *Ubu roi* [*Ubu Rex*]. Won't this finally provide youth with all its credentials, this *plus* the tribute of overflowing blood that this world is in the habit of periodically exacting from it? Won't this finally empower it to have a casting vote? Will youth permit the bold solutions it would propose to obviate such redhibitory defects in organization and thinking, to be once again dismissed as childish arguments and forever deferred? Such was approximately the gist of the surrealist interrogation and, however localized, of the surrealist summons at the end of the war of 1914–1918. I would be very much surprised if, at the end of this war, that interrogation and that summons were not repeated with much greater force.

After the first war, the ideological conflict was much less the focus of attention than it is today. As fascism had not yet been formulated, the worldviews in theoretical conflict were fairly crude, and they barely concealed a growing clash of interests among European countries that was kindled by perpetual neighbors' squabbles and grudges. Yet I think I can remember that despair was widespread: the outcome of the armed struggle had long been most uncertain. Those who returned, somewhat haggard and nevertheless angry at seeing themselves so sparse, decided, after casting a suspicious look around, to turn the page. But in so doing, they were trustingly going back to a book that, for them and their sons, held the same terrible alarms. I do not hesitate to say that surrealism has questioned the very meaning of that book, that it has not shrunk from casting doubt on its premises, that it has boldly undertaken to rewrite it.

What was the intellectual situation at the time? Many intellectuals had lapsed, had let themselves—secure as they were in the civilian zone—be drawn into a bellicose blustering that rang false and for which the combatants did not forgive them. In France, this was the case with Bergson, Barrès, Claudel. Some, such as Gide, had remained silent: this was not unduly held against them. Others, few in number, had carried on with their work, which they carefully kept apart from what had just taken place; this was mostly the case with painters, such as Matisse and Picasso, who were exonerated. Valéry had confined himself to poetical exercises that were decidedly antiquated, Proust to studies of social milieus that seemed to have remained completely unaffected by the recent events; paradoxically, they were soon to be rewarded for their aloofness with the highest honors. Already a focal point for some young people, Guillaume Apollinaire, the greatest poet of our century, died on the very day of the armistice as a result of a wound received during the war. He for one had insisted on risking his life and yet, insofar as he had taken on himself to celebrate the war in song, one had to recognize that his great abilities had often failed him. Yet, I can still see this man singular among all as if it were yesterday; I have seen this man, with my own eyes, incarnate the spirit of intellectual adventure to the highest degree. Enormous, strapped up with great difficulty in the pale blue uniform of a second lieutenant, contemptuous of sidewalks—the taxis are still at the front—he makes his way along the boulevard Saint-Germain, somewhat like a balloon, from his lodgings to the café de Flore. In close-up, the look in his eyes is at once mocking and overflowing with anxiety; on his temple the round leather patch covers the trepanation scar—the same patch and the same lesion that Chirico had distinctly drawn in his portrait of Apollinaire in 1915, that is to say, by a sheer act of divination two years before the wounding occurred. If I dwell on the memory of Apollinaire, it is because he came much closer than anyone to thinking that in order to better the world it was not enough to rebuild it on a more equitable social basis but that it was also necessary to temper with the essence of the Word. That at least is the manifest meaning of his great poem "La Victoire" [Victory], one of the last ones he wrote and one of the most hermetic in its details, which may be interpreted as his spiritual testament:

> O mouths man is searching for a new idiom
> On which no grammarian anywhere will have a hold
> .   .   .   .
> The Word is sudden—a God is trembling.

Taking this literally, it is clear in hindsight that automatic writing and the various other forms of automatic expression practiced by surrealism merely fulfilled this wish of Apollinaire by providing every individual with the means of reawakening at will the god of which he spoke. But I believe that what he was asking for goes even farther if we understand the spirit in which he said it. Valéry, in a short story of twenty pages or so, "La Soirée avec Monsieur Teste" [Mr. Teste], written when he was twenty-five, which towers over his entire work, seems to have had a premonition of and to have called for something similar when he said, with great deference, of the character in the story: "Sometimes, they [his words] lost all meaning; they seemed merely to fill a vacant spot intended for a term that was still doubtful or unforeseen by language. I heard him refer to a material object by a group of abstract words and proper nouns." That which is anticipated and invoked by two such different minds deserves to hold our attention more than ever at a time when, probing the depths of the abyss created by the news we hear every day, Denis de Rougemont can write in all objectivity: "Should we assume that people kill one another over misunderstandings? Or that words no longer mean anything . . ." The more we talk, the less we understand one another. Death alone ends all disagreements. The twentieth century will appear in the future as a kind of verbal nightmare, of delirious cacophony. During that time, everybody talked more than ever before: imagine those radio sets that *can no longer* be silent, either by day or by night, from which speech spouts at so many words per second whether or not there are any listeners, whether or not there is anything to say. A time when words would wear out faster than in any other century in History, the time of the widespread prostitution of that Word that was to be the measure of truth and of which the Gospel says that, in its source, it is "the life and the light of men"! Alas, what have we done with the Word! Without mentioning the other changes that are imperative, yes, we will have to return to that source. Calling on nondirected thought provides us with the key to the first room. To enter the second one, man must be given back nothing less than the sense of his utter dependence on the community of all men. But some have sunk so low that resorting to strong remedies is unavoidable.

On the other hand, it is not impossible that an individual might come to our help amid the great distress we are facing today. He to whom it might fall to offer this succor would no doubt have difficulty in making himself known, but there is no reason to despair of his coming. At about the same time as I watched Apollinaire strolling down the boulevard Saint-Germain with the beasts of Orpheus following in his wake, I found out that a lone individual had just peered through the night of ideas, precisely where it was at its darkest—I mean Sigmund Freud. Whatever reservations one may have about some details of his vast work, and that are the smallest debt a man can pay to noninfallibility, could anyone ever have condensed more novel, striking, essential truth in the span of a theory, of a life? And tell me if the hardest rock, that of prejudices, taboos, immemorial dissimulations, did not split as soon as this finger of light was pointed at it; if from this rock the Word did not spring limpid, or better, lustral, at least until others, by harnessing it to strictly utilitarian ends, began to muddy it. And yet from the dawn of this century—*The Interpretation of Dreams* appeared in 1900—until the Nazis entered Vienna in 1938, were there many messages of paramount significance so perseveringly misunderstood?

Were there many irreplaceable lives repaid for so long with ingratitude before ending in persecution? I was twenty when, during a furlough in Paris, I tried successively to point out to Apollinaire, to Valéry, to Gide what, through the mediation of Freud (whose name was familiar in France only to a few psychiatrists), had seemed to me to have the potential to turn the mental world upside down. I inclined to enthusiasm at the time and I was extremely anxious to share my convictions with those who mattered to me—rumor has it that I am not entirely cured of that character flaw—and I remember that I held out to each of my victims the bait that I thought he could least resist: to Apollinaire, "pansexualism"; to Valéry, the key to slips of the tongue; to Gide, the Oedipus complex. Well, in spite of the pains I took, I only managed to make each of them smile or pat me on the shoulder with friendly commiseration. For here we can see from another angle the modern Tower of Babel: not only have words become dreadfully lax, not only is it true, as Rougemont also says, that "our language has come unhinged," but those who can be considered as the leading intellects of our time are expert *only in their specialty*: they have no qualms about disqualifying themselves as soon as one tries to draw them out of their fields. Observe that the situation was quite different in the so hastily disparaged period of the Middle Ages. Today we are confronted with this twofold problem: to recover the meaning of words and to rediscover, I am not mad enough to say the universality of knowledge, but rather the thirst for a universal knowledge.

We must make once again fruitful and desirable those human exchanges that today are absorbed and negate themselves in the mere exchange of bullets. This will be possible provided we fight against the widespread depreciation of that genuine currency that language is and check the growth of this malignant tumor: the fragmentation of the world into castes of increasingly specialized individuals. We must tirelessly watch out for something that may restore—as art and psychology have already done—the most general, unbiased connection between human beings. That something *will be*. Its realization only requires, beyond favorable economic conditions (but that can change), a spectacular discovery that, as some unmistakable forerunners have already indicated, will take place in the sphere of *physics*.

In 1924, I wrote at the beginning of the first *Manifeste du surréalisme* [*Manifesto of surrealism*]: "The word freedom is the only thing that can still arouse me to enthusiasm." This enthusiasm has not deserted me. Freedom: however crudely one may have tried to misuse this word, it is still completely uncorrupted. It is the only word that would burn Goebbels's tongue, it is this word that heads the inscription that his sidekick Pétain could not bear to see on the front of public monuments. Freedom: at once my mind is dazzled by the oldest, the harshest, the most exciting disputes of the theologians; at once my memory fills with some of the most meaningful phrases I know, those that carry so much farther than their words. I hear the voice of Saint-Just thundering: "No freedom for the enemies of freedom." I see the foreheads of the greatest thinkers of the nineteenth century as they bend over the crucible from which they draw this conviction that seems like nothing and that is all: "Freedom is necessity realized." Something that now sounds like a challenge, yes, it is still this brief judgment Apollinaire formulated: "The Marquis de Sade, the freest spirit that ever existed." And I see the inexorable rise, as it grows out of the ruins under which some people had sworn to smother it, of the consciousness of the working class, in which freedom is like a most delicate woman's handkerchief held in a massive work-blackened clenched fist.

From one war to the next, one may say that the passionate quest for freedom has been the constant motive of surrealist action. To those who periodically ask why certain splits have occurred within the surrealist movement, why certain individuals were suddenly debarred, I believe I can reply in all honesty that those who disqualified themselves in the process had, in some more or less obvious way, sinned against freedom. Since freedom is revered in its pure state within surrealism, that is to say, extolled in all its forms, there were of course any number of ways of sinning against it. An instance of this, in my judgment, was to return, as some former surrealists did, to *fixed forms* in poetry, when it has been proven, especially in the French language—and the exceptional influence exerted by French poetry since romanticism warrants a generalization of this viewpoint—that the quality of lyric expression has benefited from nothing as much as from the determination to break away from outworn rules: Rimbaud, Lautréamont, the Mallarmé of *Un coup de dés* [A throw of the dice], the major symbolists (Maeterlinck, Saint-Pol Roux), the Apollinaire of the "conversation-poems." And this would be equally true of painting during that same period: one could simply replace the previous names with those of Seurat, Rousseau, Matisse, Picasso, and Duchamp. It was also an unforgivable sin against freedom to renounce expressing oneself personally, and thereby always dangerously, outside the strict guidelines that a "party" wants to force upon one, whether or not one considered it to be the party of freedom (loss of the sense of uniqueness). The same can be said of those who thought they would always be so much themselves that they could with impunity associate with just anyone (loss of the sense of dependence): freedom is at once passionately desirable and extremely fragile, which gives her the right to be jealous. To incur her disfavor, there is no need to go so far as Chirico did fifteen years ago when he underscored the mediocrity of one of the paintings he did at the time with such a fascist title as *Roman Legionnaires Looking over Conquered Lands*, or to sink so low as Avida Dollars, who, more recently, daubed with obsequious academicism the portrait of the Spanish ambassador, that is to say, of the representative of Franco. Franco! The man responsible for the oppression of that painter's country, not to mention the death of the best friend of his youth, the great poet García Lorca. Franco, whose regard for life, for the mind, for freedom, is only too well known!

I insist on the fact that surrealism can only be understood historically in relation to the war, by which I mean—from 1919 to 1938—in relation at the same time to the war from which it issued and to the war to which it returned. Of course, that period was marked in France by an utter lack of awareness and foresight; it is undeniable that it has rolled along on the wheels of the worst kind of smugness and of laziness. I am thinking of nearly all the governments that have succeeded one another, made up of indifferently interchangeable personalities, having long since given the measure of their mediocrity and prolonging the lives of parties in which they no longer believed and, for that matter, in which no new blood was able to circulate for those twenty years.

While those men understood nothing, anticipated nothing—neither they nor the majority that kept them in power—I think I can say that, in the vanguard of disinterested intellectual speculation, and particularly in the surrealist movement, no one joined in their blindness, no one had any confidence in their ability either to avert a new cataclysm or to ensure that the mechanism of the republican institutions would not be tampered with. Does this mean that the surrealists had a clear intuition that we would once again drift toward the abyss, or, even better, that they were able to say approximately *when* the inevitable chasm would open up? I need but one convincing proof: this sentence from my "Lettre aux voyantes" [A letter to seers] of 1925, which can be found in the 1929 reprint of the *Manifeste du surréalisme*: "There are people who claim that the war has taught them something; even so, they have not made as much headway as I have, since I know what the year 1939 has in store for me." If, fourteen years in advance, the advent of the war is accurately foretold in this sentence, it follows that surrealism's theses in relation to this same war present both an "up to" and a "beyond." The up to consists in the affirmation of a will that is nonconformist in all regards, that aims desperately at shaking off the general inertia, and that entails some measure of frenzy. Assuredly it cannot be the expression of a return to an age of clemency or of free meditation on the ends of human existence. Man can sense that the society he has built has set a new trap for him, not far off, that the good things it holds out to him are merely transitory, that the very moral code it forces upon him is a sham, insofar as that code is known to be destined to give way to an entirely different scale of values as soon as the ceaseless perfecting and the unlimited stockpiling of engines of death demand it.

That which in surrealism's thesis can apply *beyond* this war is for you, gentlemen, rather than for me to decide. Hence it would have seemed pedantic to me, in the present circumstances, and especially at a time when you are approaching such a crucial turning point in your lives, to inflict a didactic lecture upon you. I know that you have been provided with detailed information and authoritative clarifications by Mr. Henry Peyre, who did me the honor and the solemn pleasure at a time like this of inviting me to speak to you. In the suit instituted by surrealism, it is clear that I have for too long been a "party" to be able to set myself up as a judge. I nonetheless believe that all the activity expended under the name of surrealism cannot have been *in vain*: you will grant me this point at any rate, since there is no example of the contrary case on a similar scale, with the same persistence and the same movement of men in both directions. When we come to the end of the present tunnel, we will have no choice but to try and restore man to his element. One can hope that the disastrous experience of the other "postwar" period will be remembered and that people will not simply revert to the unimaginative conceptions that then prevailed. "True life is absent," Rimbaud already said. We must not let this opportunity pass us by if we are to conquer that life. In every field I think it will be necessary to put all the daring of which man is capable into that quest. If this can happen, if at long last *this is our chance*—failing which we will simply bide our time—I doubt that one can avoid seriously reconsidering, either directly or obliquely, surrealism's propositions. It is in the face of the desperate situation of man in the twentieth century—this cannot be emphasized enough— that surrealism tried, as I said earlier, to put new keys into his hand. In conclusion, I can only state for the record this set of propositions, the way they came to be formulated within surrealism, gradually but unwaveringly:

1. One must concede to Freud that the exploration of unconscious life provides the only basis for a valid assessment of the motives by which human beings are actuated. To try and cover up those motives with so-called conscious justifications is equivalent to applying polish to muddy shoes. Taking this as a starting point, surrealism has continuously promoted *automatism*, not only as a method of expression on the literary and artistic level but also as a first step toward a general revision of the modes of knowledge.

2. What I said in 1930, I now repeat all the more justifiably: "We must test by all available means and expose at all costs the *delusive nature* of the *old antinomies* hypocritically intended to prevent any unconformable agitation on the part of man, if only by giving him an enfeebled idea of his powers, by defying him to break away in any significant manner from universal bondage. . . . Everything leads us to believe that there exists a certain point of the mind from which life and death, the real and the imaginary, past and future, the communicable and the incommunicable,

high and low, cease to be perceived as contradictions." This is not a view that was merely inherited from the occultists, it is the expression of a desire so deep that it is primarily this desire that surrealism will undoubtedly appear to have embodied. Surrealism will have stopped at nothing—and I believe this will be its greatest claim to fame someday—to reduce these oppositions that have been wrongly represented as insurmountable, that have deplorably deepened over time, and that are the true alembics of suffering: the opposition of madness and so-called reason, which refuses to allow for the irrational; the opposition of dreaming and "action," which believes it can set dreams at naught; the opposition of mental representation and physical perception, when both of them are merely products of the dissociation of a single original faculty of which primitives and children still bear the trace, which lifts the curse of an insuperable barrier between the inner world and the external world and which, if man could recover it, would be his salvation.

3. Among those contradictions that are fatal to us, the one whose resolution requires the greatest ambition—the one to which I personally devoted most of my efforts—is the one that brings man and nature into conflict from a human standpoint, since man perceives the necessity at work in nature and his own necessity to be seriously at odds with each other. Although I do not claim to have resolved it, I have at least shown that it does not stand up to the careful observation of *coincidences* and other "chance" phenomena. *Chance* is the great veil that remains to be lifted. I have said that it could be the form of manifestation of external necessity as it makes its way into the human unconscious. It is bound to become one of our foremost preoccupations because of the intrinsic nature of war in which the range of calculations appears to be constantly limited by that unknown: the oscillation of a measure of chance.

4. There are still a couple of sentences I wrote, dating back to the previous war, that I will not refrain from quoting to you, insofar as they are equally applicable to my situation then and to yours now. Here they are: "We who reached the age of twenty during this war, that is, the age at which we systematize our lives, were forced, in doing so, to take some implacable realities into account. So as not to be overly affected by this, we were led to

attach little importance to all things. We came to expect the same sacrifice from our philosophers and our poets." My contention is that these remarks are as relevant now as they were then. When I made them, they were meant as a preamble to a eulogy on Alfred Jarry and, along with him, on a sort of dramatic humor based on a succession of inspired jests in reaction against what is most tragic in the situation inflicted upon man. The human mind is so constituted that it derives pleasure from this paradoxical relaxation at times when the springs of life are stretched to the breaking point. This disposition should dissuade the mind—and sometimes surrealism has called it to account on this point—from subsequently trying at all costs to take everything seriously.

5. In its efforts to coordinate these various pursuits, surrealism was naturally brought to the very threshold of the *id*. As you know, this word is used in psychoanalytical parlance in opposition to the word *ego* to refer to the whole array of very active forces that are screened from consciousness by virtue of various reproving judgments. Freud viewed the *id* as "the arena of the struggle between Eros and the death instinct." Such a conception cannot fail to be brought into prominence in the light of current events. As soon as we return to what is called normal life, we should train searchlights on that vast and dark region of the *id* where myths swell out of all proportion at the same time as wars are hatched and then resolutely set about draining it. But, you will ask, how can we approach that region? I can tell you that surrealism alone has been concerned with finding a practical solution to this problem, that it really has set foot in the arena and charted landmarks. To all practical intents and purposes, it alone has placed here and there a few observation posts in preparation for an undertaking far exceeding our numerical strength but that appeared to us to be of prime necessity. An enduring faith in automatism as a probe; an enduring hope in the power of dialectic (that of Heraclitus, of Meister Eckhart, of Hegel) to resolve the antinomies that keep man in fetters; the recognition of objective chance as an index of the potential reconciliation between the ends of nature and the ends of man in the eyes of the latter; the intent to incorporate permanently *black humor* into the psyche since it alone can, at a certain temperature, act as a safety valve; the practical preparation for an *intervention in mythical life*

that would first proceed to a large-scale cleansing—these are, and remain to this day, the fundamental guidelines of surrealism.

Gentlemen, I keep thinking that some of you are getting ready to board that incredibly fast train whose windows are plastered with the sign "1942—Future" and that consents to make a quick stop before the platform on which we are standing, and on no account would I want to burden you with anything cumbersome. Since surrealism aspires to endure on the devastated field like an ear of wheat that is like a thing insignificant in itself and yet marvelous insofar as it holds the secret of the endless repetition of that same field, all the more reason for it to take pride in weighing as little as that ear of wheat on the scales of the wind! However great the ambition to know and the temptation to act, I know that when one nears the age of twenty, these are quite ready to bow to a woman's glance, which draws to itself all the attraction of the world. Everything that has mattered and still matters to me on another level would lose a great deal of its importance in my own eyes if I did not feel confident that surrealism, driven by the set of ideas I have just restated for your benefit, while expressing the anguish of its time, has succeeded in giving a new face to *beauty*.

Declaration VVV

VVV: that is to say V+V+V. We say · · · — · · · — · · · —

that is to say not only V as the vow—and the energy—to return to a
conceivable and habitable world, Victory over the forces of regression
and death presently unloosed on the world,

but also V beyond this initial Victory, for this world can no longer, should
no longer be the same, V over that which aims at perpetuating the
enslavement of man by man,

and beyond this VV, beyond the double Victory, V again over all that is
opposed to the emancipation of the mind, of which the first indispensable
condition is the liberation of man.

VVV: toward the emancipation of the mind through all its necessary
stages. It is only in *this* that our mind can identify its purpose

or VVV again because:

to the V that stands for viewing what is all around us, eyes turned outward,
toward the conscious surface of things,

surrealism has relentlessly opposed W, the view within, eyes turned inward
toward the inner world and the depths of the unconscious, whence

VVV toward a synthesis, in a third term, of these two Views, the first V
centered on the *Ego* and the reality principle, the second VV on the *Id*
and the pleasure principle, the resolution of their contradiction aiming
solely, of course, at the continuous and systematic expansion of the field
of consciousness.

Declaration by the journal *Triple V*, New York, 1942.

Toward a total view VVV that conveys all the reactions of the eternal upon the actual, of the mental upon the physical, and accounts for the myth evolving beneath the *veil* of events.

✸

VVV, without any sectarian bias, is open to all writers and artists who will agree with our purpose. VVV will not limit itself to being an anthological journal but will set above all else the spirit of free exploration as well as that of *adventure*. The only tradition to which VVV holds is that of such war magazines as *Les Soirées de Paris, Maintenant, Nord-Sud, La Révolution Surréaliste* in Paris, *Lacerba* in Rome, *291* in New York, *Cabaret Voltaire* in Zurich. Whatever the background of its contributors, VVV must by no means be either a station of arrival or a marshaling yard but rather a place to start out. In VVV the freest of poetic, artistic, and scientific views, no matter how daring they might be, will be brought together; through them VVV intends to bring out the spirit that will not fail to spring forth from the new human conditioning bred of this war and to draw tomorrow's main generating lines.

Golden

Silence

    The cult of an art involves necessary biases that, at the onset, ensure that the uninitiated are kept at bay, and even more so the detractor. Whatever he may say to defend himself, he will appear guilty in the eyes of the faithful: they will not even be able to grant him extenuating circumstances because his crime, the greatest of all if it were not immediately suppressed, would be that of *lèse-attraction*.

    For that matter, it is strangely disappointing, in this period of extreme specialization—a fact that, in itself, entails so many dangers—to hear even clear-minded individuals, when they come out of their specific area of experience and research, hold forth with confidence on that of which they have little knowledge or for which they feel no appreciation. I remember my embarrassment when, for instance, I would hear Paul Valéry talk about cubist painting: is it possible that intelligence, prudence—not to mention tolerance—could have found pleasure in such self-negation?

    If I think that I should disregard these cogent contra-indications, it is because I consider that, from the general standpoint of knowledge, it is of some interest to get to the root of the conflict that, to say nothing of my own reactions, alienates most of the artists of *language* from music: by those I mean poets worthy of the name and a small number of prose writers who care about verbal harmony.

    As I do not want to refer solely to my own observations, which are of doubtful impartiality, I shall call upon a testimony that could not be any more conclusive—that of the Goncourt brothers: "From that, Gautier jumped to a critique of *La Reine de Saba* [*The Queen of Sheba*]. And as we confessed our total infirmity, our musical deafness, since military music was the extent of our appreciation: 'Well, I am quite pleased to hear you say this. . . . I am just like you. I prefer silence to music. I have only managed to tell good music from bad because I have lived part of my life with a diva, but I really do not care for it . . .' All the same, it is strange that all the writers of our time are like that. Balzac detested music, Hugo cannot abide it. Even Lamartine, himself a piano for sale or for rent, loathes it. . . . Only a few painters have any taste for it!"[1] It is true that Baudelaire and Mallarmé—the latter somewhat later in life—were exceptions to the rule formulated by Gautier, but, at least in France, nothing in the overall attitude of contemporary writers (of the kind earlier specified) would seem to make it any less valid. Although few writers are openly hostile to music and assume a belligerent attitude toward it, many others are merely indifferent to it or at most treat it with a kind of polite indulgence that hardly ever extends, from what I have seen, to a desire to inquire into its current problems or to take them to heart, contrary to what happened with painting. This disfavor may have been aggravated over the last twenty years by the fact that in Paris the cause of modern music had allowed a notorious *fake poet*[2] to be its champion—in other words, one of those versifiers whose inexorable lot it is to *debase* rather than to *elevate* everything he touches and who, by definition, can only be deaf to any harmonious arrangement of words.

✳

Although my receptivity to poetry and my receptivity to music are poles apart, due to my personal makeup, I do not relinquish all objectivity in my appreciation of them. If I were to hold to the hierarchy proposed by Hegel, music, judged by its ability to express ideas and emotions, would come immediately after poetry and would rank above the visual arts. But above all I am convinced that the antagonism between poetry and music (poets are apparently much more aware of it than musicians are), which for some ears seems to have reached its peak today, should not be vainly deplored but, on the contrary, should be interpreted as *a symptom of the necessity to recombine* some of the principles of those two arts. In this instance, I am merely taking up again one of my favorite themes: that we should never miss an opportunity to take all the antinomies presented by modern thought "by the horns" in order first to protect ourselves, then to tame and *overcome* them. Along these lines, I think I have conclusively shown that, on the visual level, "physical perception and mental representation—which seem to the average adult to be diametrically opposed—are to be considered as the products of the dissociation of a *single original faculty*, traces of which can still be found in primitives and in children."[3] It is this faculty that today we should strive to re-create, since the antinomy of perception and representation is, among so many others, a source of torment and mental anguish. The painter will fail in his human mission if he continues to widen the gulf between representation and perception instead of working toward their reconciliation, their synthesis. In the same way, on the auditory level, my opinion is that music and poetry have everything to lose by not recognizing their common root and their common purpose in *song*, by letting the voice of Orpheus get farther away every day from the Thracian lyre. The poet and the musician will degenerate if they persist in acting as if these two forces were never to come together again.

Let it be understood that it is not within my intent to advocate a closer collaboration between musician and poet: of course, it would spare us all those poems "set to music" that make us regret they ever existed, even in an unopened book, and it would no doubt also rid us of the silly nonsense of opera librettos, but such a suggestion would imply a "reformist" attitude that is foreign to me. Here as elsewhere the disease is too acute, the habit of ignoring it too ingrained. Its eradication now requires radical measures. The one I am proposing, as ambitious as it may be, is this: we must aim at *unifying, reunifying the sense of hearing* to the same degree that we must aim at *unifying, reunifying the sense of sight*.

Given my total ignorance of the rules of musical composition, I am not in a position to suggest how this reunification of hearing may be effected, but I assume that anyone who possesses means of musical appreciation equivalent to mine with regard to poetry or painting could do so in my stead. Besides, the reunification process should not vary greatly from one sense to the next, so that it will be a simple matter to transfer it from the visual, where it is already at hand, to the auditory. In order to obtain the first audible diamond, it is clear that the fusion of these two elements—music and poetry—can only be achieved at a very high emotional temperature. It seems to me that nowhere as in the expression of *love* will music and poetry be better able to reach this supreme point of incandescence.

✳

Never as much as in surrealist writing have poets trusted to the *tonal* value of words. The negativist attitudes inspired by instrumental music do seem to find compensation in this fact. With regard to language, nothing has captivated, and still captivates, surrealist poets so much as this property words have to link together into singular chains and thus to shine forth at the very moment when one is least trying to find them. What they have tried to do, more than anything else, is to bring these chains out of the dark places where they form into full daylight. And what has captured their attention about these verbal combinations, what has convinced them that they should not be altered in any way, even when they seemed either to have no meaning—no immediate meaning, that is—or to do violence to meaning, thus causing the average reader great alarm, is that their structure had the compelling character of a musical progression, that the individual words of which they were made up were grouped according to unusual but much deeper affinities. "Words have stopped playing," I said when I discovered this, "words are making love." By then I had realized that thus organized, and challenging as they did to some extent shortsighted "reason" (always buried in its myopic calculations of "debit" and "credit"), they constituted the very vehicle of the emotions. Of such words Taine has said: "Our whole past life is stored up in them and through them is brought back to us."[4] The "inner speech" that surrealist poetry has been so keen to bring into the open and that, like it or not, it has successfully turned into a medium of emotional exchange between certain individuals cannot be separated from the "inner music" by which it is carried and, in all likelihood, conditioned. How could it be otherwise when the inner speech, as recorded by "automatic writing," is subject to the same acoustic conditions of rhythm, pitch, intensity, and timbre as the outer speech, although to a lesser degree? In this respect, it is the direct opposite of the expression of controlled thought that has kept no organic link with music and uses it only occasionally as a luxury. But above all, because it is free from the social and moral obligations that constrain spoken and written language, inner thought need only tune itself to inner music, *which never leaves it.* I have objected before to the label "visionary" being ever so freely applied to poets. Great poets have been "auditories," not visionaries. At any rate, in their case, vision, "illumination" is not the "cause" but the "effect." In this regard, I take Lautréamont literally when he writes: "*Let the music start.*[5] Yes, good folk, it is I who command you to burn, on a red-hot shovel, the vermouth-lipped duck of doubt with a dash of yellow sugar. . . ."[6] In my opinion, these things were only *seen* after they had been heard. This is what I meant when some time ago I wrote: "It has always seemed to me that, in poetry, verbo-auditory automatism creates for the reader visual images far more exciting than any of the visual images that may be produced by verbo-visual automatism."[7]

Thinking that for painters it might be otherwise, I tried at the time to elicit from them some comments on this point, but they are notoriously sparing of confidences. To musicians I would like to point out that poets, in spite of their ostensible lack of understanding, have gone a long way to meet them on the only path that, in this day and age, proves to be great and clear: that of a return to principles. But because we do not have a common vocabulary, I may not be able to appreciate how far they have come toward those who, in order to put new life into it, must share with them some of this sonorous and virgin land.

1944

Profanation

Chess is hand-to-hand combat between two labyrinths.

An integral weakness of chess is that it does not lend itself to divination (there is no *checkomancy*).

The Christian Church has never *banned* the game of chess, though it did ban dice and cards.

In order to be a good chess player, one should not be overly intelligent.—Jean-Jacques Rousseau: Diderot did not play very well and readily acknowledged the superiority of Rousseau, who never failed to beat him.

Modern warfare is an advanced form of chess, but most of its pieces are obsolete.

The "queen" in chess is a suspicious character. The ease with which she moves over the battlefield would have you think that she is a *general* in drag. A woman is *too lonely* with a chess player (cf. Marcel Duchamp, *Joueurs d'échecs* [Chess players], 1911). The real *Queen*, which we still await—in chess as elsewhere—is the one foreseen by Barthélemy Prosper Enfantin, the head of the Saint-Simonian religion (1796–1864).

The only legitimate game is one that would allow, for either player, only those combinations of moves that have *never* been attempted before.

Philosophical freedom is an illusion. In chess as in all other games, each move is loaded with the indefinite past of the universe.

So as to eschew any sense of greatness in competition, one would do well to acknowledge being part of a pyramid of monkey heads.

One element of ancient wisdom we might hold in mind is that deprecatory voice that the triumphant general on his chariot kept hearing.

Only *inspiration* is in control, day and night: *All in all, not every calculation is an analysis; a chess player, for instance, does the one very well without doing the other.*—Baudelaire

The real Napoleon (the killer) was a mediocre chess player. In Lenin's tomb on the Red Square, you will find a chess board (is it the beginning of a game or one left unfinished?) and fishing floats. On the other hand (it is only fair to mention it), two great artistic innovators—Marcel Duchamp, Raymond Roussel—brought new solutions to some chess problems.

The game of chess is not enough of a game; it is too serious an entertainment.— Montaigne

What must be changed is the game itself, not the pieces.

1944

A Tribute

to

Antonin Artaud

Ladies and gentlemen,

It is somewhat reluctantly that I have responded to the appeal of the organizers of tonight's event. Were it not for the pressing moral obligation to be among them in order to pay homage to a most exceptional individual and to celebrate the return of an especially dear friend to less horrific living conditions, I would have preferred not to be called upon to deliver this preamble. I have only been back in Paris a short while and I was away too long to know whether I am already once more attuned to this city, whether I am fully aware of all the emotional currents that flow through it, whether I will immediately be able to find the right *pitch*. Above all, I confess that I am somewhat troubled by this new tendency, which I am discovering, to track with a circus spotlight—or to tolerate as much—some of those intellectual investigations that we used to believe were best conducted in twilight.

Unless we let our own essence dissolve within the norm, today more unacceptable, more revolting than ever, unless we allow a series of individual defections to create the impression of a collective spiritual bankruptcy that, after so many other failures, will inflate the arrogance of what we have despised and loathed, it is my opinion that we must react in an implacable fashion. Make no mistake, it is not in the limelight that, in 1946, the movement that has been trying and is, I hope, still *genuinely* trying to find itself under the name of surrealism will come into its own. The evil spell cast upon the conditions to which thought and action are presently subjected on a universal scale, and the threat of annihilation hanging over the world, are such that we can feel but pity for those who persist in begging for public recognition or in making retrospective claims to a dubious fame. Especially in view of the events of these past few years, let me add that I find laughable any kind of so-called engagement that falls short of this indivisible threefold objective: to transform the world, to change life, to reshape the human mind.

Antonin Artaud, recklessly and on his own, has gone farther in that direction than anyone else today, and yet my previous remarks preclude my commenting openly on his most tragic message as well as my recounting his exceptionally painful social experience. If I were to do so, it seems that I would be betraying the very cause that is common to us both, that I would be disclosing sacred stakes to all and sundry. More than twenty years have elapsed, but I can still feel that burst of impossible hope that gave a few of us purpose and lifted us above ourselves. I am thinking of all that possessed us at that time, of that torrent that propelled us ahead of ourselves as its cascading laughter swept aside all the opposition with which we met. Each generation must discover for itself the secret of such energy. Each time I happen to recall—nostalgically—the surrealist rebellion as expressed in its original purity and intransigence, it is the personality of Antonin Artaud that stands out in its dark magnificence, it is a certain intonation in his voice that injects specks of gold into his whispering voice. And it is, as well, *Le Pèse-nerfs* [The nerve-scale], *L'Ombilic des limbes* [The umbilicus of limbo], and that third issue of *La Révolution Surréaliste*, for which he was solely responsible and which, among all the other issues, is the one that reaches the highest phosphorescent point: reading it always makes me feel what true life is like by showing me man braving lightning itself as he ascends the highest peaks. Antonin Artaud: I do not have to account in his stead for what he has experienced nor for what he has suffered. I do not wish to cast the blame on any particular individual, least of all on a man who is known to some of us and who, by all accounts, has been very understanding and has shown great compassion toward Artaud. The clinical methods about which our friend may have cause to complain must be ascribed to an institution that we will never cease to denounce as a barbaric anachronism, the very existence of which—with its potential for concentration camps and torture chambers—is in itself a decisive indictment against so-called civilization as we know it today.

Let us not forget that beneath skies other than the empty sky of Europe, the constantly inspired voice of Antonin Artaud would have been heard with the utmost deference, that it would likely have led the community quite far (I am thinking particularly of the welcome and the status given to extraordinary seers of his caliber by various Indian communities). I am still too far removed from the old rationalism that we decried when we were young to dismiss extraordinary accounts under the pretext that common sense goes against them. This reassurance I want to impart to Antonin Artaud himself when I see how distressed he is, because my recollections of what happened during the more or less atrocious decade we have just experienced do not exactly corroborate his own.[1] I know that Antonin Artaud *saw*, the way Rimbaud, as well as Novalis and Arnim before him, had spoken of *seeing*. It is of little consequence, ever since the publication of *Aurélia*, that what was *seen* this way does not coincide with what is *objectively visible*. The real tragedy is that the society to which we are less and less honored to belong persists in making it an inexpiable crime to have gone over to *the other side of the looking glass*. In the name of everything that is more than ever close to my heart, I cheer the return to freedom of Antonin Artaud in a world where freedom itself must be reinvented. Beyond all the mundane denials, I place all my faith in Antonin Artaud, that man of prodigies. I salute Antonin Artaud for his passionate, heroic negation of everything that causes us to be dead while alive.

1946

Before

the

Curtain

Almost ten years—which undeniably had a rather exceptional *trampling* capacity—have gone by since the last International Surrealist Exhibition. However, its opening left such a vivid memory (as one critic wrote, "We had not seen such a jostle of society people since the fire at the Bazar de la Charité") that many expect a similar evening, or worse, for the opening of the 1947 exhibition. Naturally, some people's curiosity does not extend beyond such a ceremony, which past experience has taught them to regard as a ritual, while others are already preparing to denounce the offensive, even insulting nature of such a display occurring so soon after exceedingly painful events. We find ourselves obliged to disappoint them.

Nevertheless, it would not be inappropriate today to skim with bitter satisfaction through the articles written in 1938 about the exhibition in the Galerie des Beaux-Arts.[1] Just the names of the newspapers[2] in which they were published are enough to assure us that their anger has petered out, that their venom—after a cauterization that only fell short of a more serious operation—has lost its activity. However, we confidently anticipate that it will use devious means to reappear in a thinly disguised form. Surrealism *calls* for that degrading attack against itself in the same way that man cannot do without the vulture of his shadow in full Promethean light.

Ten years later, we are in a better position not only to distinguish what, in the stir caused by that exhibition, is fairly expressive of the mental climate prevailing in 1938, but also to put into their true perspective—which, once again, is not an artistic one—those aspects of its structure that, in our minds, were intended to open to everyone that zone of agitation that lies on the borders of the poetic and of the real. The organizers had concentrated their efforts on creating an atmosphere as remote as possible from that of an "art" gallery. Let me insist on the fact that they had no other conscious intention in mind: looking back on it today, the sum total of their efforts has nevertheless transcended what they were aiming at.

About the critics of that time, who thought they could, as usual, ascribe the presentation of the 1938 exhibition to the need to astound or conciliate the "snobs" and who were almost unanimous in deploring the "gratuitousness," superficiality, and bad taste we had once demonstrated, we can say that on this occasion they went to great lengths mainly to cut their own throats. The rooms, lit only by a brazier, squeezed under a ceiling-fitting made with 1,200 coal sacks, or with their four corners weighted down by rumpled brothel beds, one of which waded in a pond edged with rushes, the street signs (Weak Street, All Devils Street, Blood Transfusion Street, etc.), all that has since then become only too meaningful, has proved to be, alas, only too premonitory, too portentous, has only been too well borne out in terms of gloom, suffocation, and shadiness. To those who, so vehemently at the time, accused us of having wallowed in that atmosphere, it will be all too easy to point out that we had stopped well short of the darkness and of the underhanded cruelty of the coming days. We did not deliberately create that atmosphere: it merely conveyed the acute sense of foreboding with which we anticipated the coming decade. Now, it may be that surrealism, by opening certain doors that rationalism boasted of having boarded up for good, had enabled us to make here and there an incursion into the future, on condition that we should not be aware at the time that it was the future we were entering, that we should become aware of this and be able to make it evident only a posteriori.[3]

Naturally these considerations are equally valid for the setting chosen for the 1942 International Surrealist Exhibition in New York. Since he had stood firm four years earlier in Paris against the opinion of the insurance agents and experts who, under the ceiling of coke-spangled sacks stuffed with straw, concluded that the risk of explosion and fire was too great, Marcel Duchamp did not find it too difficult this time to overcome the reluctance of the exhibitors whose works were to be kept at a distance from the visitors by a lacunar net of strings, as if it were made of several entangled riggings. The difficulty one had in getting closer for a better look, and the impossibility of making out from any particular angle a visual ensemble *without a crack*, if only one cares to think about it, do foreshadow in striking fashion the malaise that we feel today.

Thus it goes without saying that the 1947 exhibition will very likely be situated in the same perspective, although the intentions governing its realization do not correspond to a clear desire to prognosticate the future, any more than did the previous ones. Of course if we were to try and imagine what the years 1950–1955, for instance, will be like, we would be looking through glasses that were quite misted over and would soon become totally opaque were we to stare fixedly through them. What paralyzes us is rigor. Who knows if it will not turn out someday that, in order to sit at the royal table, one needs, to begin with, to have consented to leave in the hands of lackeys the attributes of an illusory power: impenitent "reason," pretension to rule over symbols dispassionately? And then, but only then, to have lent oneself to the *great disorientation*, this time not within a limited space as in a game of blindman's buff but in all of space and all of time, without keeping the least point of reference. The attitude we advocate in this regard is not essentially different from the one we are known to have assumed some time ago when facing the blank page: I had already at the time pointed out the extreme possibilities of its generalization.[4] In accordance with the happy turn of phrase coined by our friends in Bucharest, "knowledge by means of willful ignorance" remains the principal surrealist watchword.

> *To cast off rational demonstration by faith in [knowledge]*
> *To cast off the rotten rags of memory by inspiration.*[5]

It matters little if many of those who judge us persist in thinking that this is nothing more than laziness, a lapse into a most deplorable intellectual laxity. As for us, we maintain that spinelessness is elsewhere. We will keep on repeating that a few lines of *genuine* automatic writing (something increasingly difficult to find), an act of breadth, even a very limited one, that succeeds in breaking loose from the utilitarian, rational, aesthetic, and

moral constraints—in the same way as the "true dream" of the wonderful
Peter Ibbetson—as in the early days of surrealism, retain too many of the
gleams of the philosophers' stone not to make us call into question the
miserable shrunken world that is inflicted on us. But the exploration at
the end of which other horizons can replace those of this world is not one
that curiosity alone is able to reproduce. It begins with the unconditional
rejection of the conditions in which man is forced to live and think in
the middle of the twentieth century and can only be carried through to a
successful completion at the cost of an *ascesis*.

It is more necessary than ever to rescue "something of the grandeur
which," in Thomas De Quincey's words, "belongs *potentially* to human
dreams." And he adds: "He whose talk is of oxen, will probably dream of
oxen; and the condition of human life, which yokes so vast a majority to a
daily experience incompatible with much elevation of thought, oftentimes
neutralises the tone of grandeur in the reproductive faculty of dreaming,
even for those whose minds are populous with solemn imagery. . . . Among
the powers in man which suffer by this too intense life of the social instincts,
none suffers more than the power of dreaming. Let no man think this a trifle.
The machinery of dreaming planted in the human brain was not planted for
nothing. That faculty, in alliance with the mystery of darkness, is the one
great tube through which man communicates with the shadowy."[6] These
lines should be pondered over and over again, at a time when dreams of
oxen (oxen cut into thin slices for the most part) tend to replace all others,
when socialism itself, having forgotten that it was born of the (day)dream
of better days for all, shows the strongest mistrust toward anything that
might remind it of its origin, letting its lifeblood dry out by refusing to
reimmerse itself in it, and when a newspaper, which claims to embody the
cause of human liberation, could recently express the hope that (Soviet)
science would soon succeed in purging human life of "unproductive" sleep
and dreams that it inanely denounced as a "useless luxury."

Hardly a day goes by without surrealism being enjoined to make way
for something new, when it is not graciously invited to "turn over a new
leaf."[7] Without a doubt, the public manifestation of 1947 can only dash
the hopes of those who have a vested interest in that disappearance or

in that sweeping transformation. The surrealist undertaking, which, as we pointed out without encountering any significant refutation, had been in existence long before it became codified, could not without inviting ridicule be declared a thing of the past nor be permitted to proceed only in ways that would have nothing in common with the previous ones. In this respect, an almost immemorial past warrants our confidence in the future: consequently, it is with a light heart that we turn a deaf ear to those objurgations.

That on which we rely to preserve us from stagnation is our sensibility alone and the currents, *varying* from year to year, that it registers. I am talking about the currents of interest, curiosity, emotion that delimit for us ever new zones of attraction, away from the busy trails and especially from those that have been most recently opened to the public. Some fairly cryptic works, more exhilarating than most, do lose more and more of their vigor when banal interpretations of the author's thought keep gaining ground, supported as they are by numerous quotations—always the same ones—arbitrarily taken out of context (such is the case of a sentence like: "Poetry must be made by all, not by one," which, regardless of the entire work of Ducasse, some try to turn into a demagogic commonplace). While we must keep on doing everything we can to thwart the attempts to adulterate or bury those works, it is equally imperative that each new era—and we regard as a new era one that presents with the previous one a significant (historical) solution of continuity: this is indeed the case of the armed conflict from which we are presently recovering and of the ideological superstructure of which it is but one aspect—should find in the past specific guarantors and guides, different from those of the earlier era. Only history will tell if the figures that existentialism has recently brought to the fore are able to assume such a role or if their star is merely shining on a short transition period.[8] We are told these days that the aesthetic concerns by which people's minds were willy-nilly dominated between 1920 and 1940 are going to give precedence to ethical concerns. But that may be nothing but wishful thinking. Of far greater significance is the revived interest for works belonging to the fantastic genre as well as to what is commonly called "utopia." Nor must it be a coincidence that scholarly research has recently come to discover, at the junctions where the ideas of poets and those of visionary social thinkers meet (the great figures of the Convention, Hugo, Nerval, Fourier), the enduring vitality of an esoteric view of the world (Martinès, Saint-Martin, Fabre d'Olivet, l'abbé Constant). By neglecting until now to take this into account, academic criticism has purely and simply sunk into futility. In the light of that research, it seems probable, and the future will no doubt soon tell, that this worldview more or less directly influenced the major poets of the second half of the nineteenth century (Lautréamont, Rimbaud, Mallarmé, Jarry), while it crystallized once again in Saint-Yves d'Alveydre's writings. Thus the great movements of sensibility by which we are still affected, the emotional charter by which we are governed, seem to originate, whether we like it or not, in a tradition entirely different from the one that is taught: that tradition has been kept buried under the most disgraceful, the most vindictive silence.

Under those conditions, it can be expected that we will meet steadfastly the reprobation that will be brought upon us by the decision to design an "initiatory" setting for the 1947 exhibition. Even if, by having the aspirant to knowledge—the visitor in this case—face a cycle of ordeals (reduced practically to a minimum), the only result would be to induce him to let his mind muse over what, throughout the ages, can be strange and disturbing about certain individual and collective modes of behavior, we would already be satisfied that we were on the right track. Let me just refer, in this respect, to the invaluable observation made by no less a rationalist than Frazer: "[Magic]," he tells us in *The Golden Bough*, "has contributed to emancipate mankind from the thralldom of tradition and to elevate them into a larger, freer life, with a broader outlook on the world. . . . We are forced to admit that if the black art has done much evil, it has also been the source of much good; that if it is the child of error, it has yet been the mother of freedom and truth."

Be that as it may, we will leave it to the experts on the occult to decide, based on all the available evidence, whether a certain number of poetic works, among those that capture the attention in modern times, were conceived in close collaboration with what its followers regard as "the first *religious, ethical, and political* doctrine of mankind," or if they derive from it in a more or less conscious way, or yet if they aim—quite intuitively—at re-creating it by other means. It will be up to those experts to establish whether works like *Théorie des quatre mouvements* [Theory of the Four Movements by Fourier], *Les Chimères* [The Chimeras by Nerval], *Les Chants de Maldoror* [Maldoror by Lautréamont], *La Science de Dieu* [The science of God] by Brisset, *La Dragonne* [The Persecuted] by Jarry are rooted in traditional esoteric knowledge or whether they equip the mind with new keys, vest it with new powers of comprehension and action. "I am an end or a beginning," Kafka said. Such a judgment, which was to be repeatedly quoted in contradictory ways, is unlikely to be rendered any time soon. There will still be lengthy debates on the more or less figurative meaning that Rimbaud (who, it could not be stressed strongly enough, was an avid reader of occult writings) insisted should be ascribed to the words "Alchemy of the Word." We will keep on wondering whether the key to the passionate interest generated successively within surrealism itself by the "word games" of Marcel Duchamp, of Robert Desnos, by the discovery of the complete works of Jean-Paul Brisset, and by Raymond Roussel's last book *Comment j'ai écrit certains de mes livres* [How I Wrote Certain of My Books] is not to be found in the extraordinary spread we have recently witnessed of the activity known as "phonetic cabalism," to which these men gave the initial impetus. "It is in the tradition of the Cabala," Ambelain reminds us, "to assert that in the 'world of sounds' two words or two sounds with related resonances (and not only assonances. . .) are indisputably related in the 'world of images.'" Etc.

This is not the place to address the thorny question of whether the "absence of myth" is itself a myth and whether it must be regarded as the myth of our time. Despite rationalist protestations, *it all seems* today *as if* some relatively recent poetic and visual works exerted a fascination over people's minds quite disproportionate with that of a work of art. They receive such endorsement from the youths who open their minds to them—one wonders at their ever-increasing numbers—and they inspire them with such selfless dedication that their entire conditioning seems to be called into question.

"He spoke to his friends of a revelation, a completed ordeal." It is indeed as if those works bore the mark of revelation. And the fact that they give rise to commentaries that keep spreading like ripples created by a stone thrown into a bottomless pond strengthens this conviction. The *uplifting* nature of those works, as well as the ever more insistent questions and inquiries to which they are subjected, the resistance they put up to the modes of apprehension afforded by human understanding in its present state—and that alone should urge a complete "reshaping" of that understanding—at the same time as the intense *exhilaration*, something like a pre-ecstatic state, with which they sometimes fill us—let us take as an example "Dévotion" by Rimbaud—all this lends support to the idea that a *myth* is stemming from them, that it is entirely up to us to define and coordinate it.

What we have set out to do, within the framework of this exhibition, is merely to sketch the outline of what such a myth might be—a sort of mental "parade" before the real show.

Surrealist

Comet

The immediate relations between history and art are sufficiently enigmatic to let us concede that major causes, in many cases, produce minor effects. This is the sphere in which the anticlimax is the rule. And so we must be prepared for some astonishment if we try to determine, for the period between 1940 and 1944, what the preferred themes of modern painting in Paris were. If we refer to the special issue of *Cahiers d'Art* devoted to this topic, we discover that one object is more in evidence than all others, prevails undeniably over all the rest, is so confident of its predominance that it surrounds itself with numerous family members. This object is none other than the *kitchen pitcher*. Let us note that this utensil is less and less in use today and that, at the sight of it, nothing can explain its exceptional significance. One starts wondering about this one-handled vessel (on which everything had been said—and more—by Derain and the cubists) that is supported or supplanted here and there by pitchers with two handles and by some without any handle at all. What can this pitcher portend? I am joking, of course. Still, this *complex of the pitcher* is far from being a trivial matter. My friend Meyer Shapiro, with whom I was trying to analyze it while we were in New York, found an explanation for it in the analogy between the outline of this sort of earthenware jug and that of a man with one hand resting on his hip (or else with both hands on his hips or both arms along his sides). I have been content, since then, to adopt his interpretation.

One hand on the hip: the painter. Both hands on the hips: the street merchant. That period in our lives, I know, did not encourage in public a much more expressive mien. To maintain and to wait: that was likely to be the lot of those who were less aware or less alert but not necessarily that of those who were less sensitive or less well intentioned. Elsewhere, in the dark night of camps, the viridescent night of ambushes, in the *starry* night such as the one Van Gogh, prepared to lose it all, makes us discover in one of the marvelous paintings he did in Arles, human pots crumbled easily into dust when they were not being smashed to pieces. . . . All the same, those times are gone and everything must be done to prevent their return; the main enemy today is fatalism (the hand on the hip) and the time has come to declare: *No more pitcher-men.*

In the field of visual arts, this attitude must be denounced more mercilessly than anywhere else. The speculation that preys on the works of a number of living artists, works that have become nothing more than a medium of exchange between dealers and multimillionaires, encourages many *dabblers* throughout the world to follow shamelessly in the tracks of those artists and to offer at a discount what little they manage to steal from them. This is why, when seen from a distance, in the mercenary perspective of the majority of galleries and magazines, the art of these last few years seems to be marking time, to be stagnating.

This disease has assumed epidemic proportions and we must urgently uncover its cause. We are told ad nauseam nowadays that the first man who bought a painting by Cézanne was blind, that Van Gogh only managed to sell one painting while he lived, that Seurat would work out the price of one of his major works at the rate of seven francs per day of work (with a possible discount depending on the personality of the prospective buyer), and that a joker was able to purchase for one franc a portrait by Henri Rousseau that he used as the "chief attraction" of his "Museum of Horrors." Upon hearing such tales, everyone assumes a scandalized air and then a conceited one, as if equity, in the relations between the artist and the public, had finally prevailed. In fact, the contradiction remains, inherent as it is to the economic structure of present society. Discernment and taste have made no progress at all. The rise of a class of intermediaries who gamble on paintings and sculptures as others do on horses or stamps has only deepened this contradiction by subjecting it to an *inversion of sign.*

Already in 1931, while attending a comprehensive exhibition of Matisse's work, I was surprised to discover so many recent figures left unfinished (faces of women reduced to simple ovals, etc.), and I said so to one of the organizers: he was all too willing to explain to me that, due to the high prices already fetched by this painter's works and to a certain saturation of foreign museums and important collections with respect to them, more "elaborate" paintings would not have found any buyer. This example shows that, nowadays, artistic freedom is no less limited by a necessity of a different kind (and of the most sordid kind) than at the time when Picasso was forced to go on painting his very decent cow fields on fans in order to survive. The press keeps on feeding the dumbest sort of idle curiosity about the persona of Picasso and never tires of the idea that "the most expensive painter in the world" is a member of the Communist party, while it carefully avoids tackling this contradiction. Such is the volcano on which contemporary art is standing, and even then I am limiting myself to the works of two key artists: on the sidelines, speculators boldly overrate minor works as much as they can or even dangle shrunken windbags (like Utrillo), which they exhaust themselves puffing up from time to time.

The most serious sequel of this situation is that in art the relationship between production and consumption is completely distorted: works of art, with very few exceptions, are placed out of the reach of those who love them for what they are, and, in the hands of cynics and individuals who are indifferent to them, they become simple pretexts for capital investment. From the liberating values they should be, they are transformed into instruments of oppression insofar as they contribute—to a significant extent—to the growth of private property. It is regrettable that the more prominent contemporary artists—apart from Marcel Duchamp and Francis Picabia—have not, on this score, been more scrupulous.

As far as pure creativity is concerned, this same situation has had the effect of hindering the advancement of art by blocking, almost at the outset, the paths of great individual adventure. *Anything* to hold up to ridicule the cry "Yonder, to flee," to promote lead soles rather than "soles of wind," to tax with puerility, in someone like Gauguin, the dream of "more light."[1]

It is easy to see that the resulting productiveness in contemporary art is quite a deceptive one. Most artists are tirelessly repeating themselves with scarcely any variation. What percentage of the works of any one of them can be justified in terms of a new vision, of a turning point? In this respect, if Picasso has held his own longer than the others, everything leads us to believe that that is because he was granted a kind of *hidden exemption*: those who mold public opinion decided once and for all that he was officially to monopolize novelty, so that it could be narrowly circumscribed in the eyes of the public and so that critical rationalizations might continually keep it within bounds. It should be stressed repeatedly that the special privilege granted to Picasso serves a purpose that has nothing to do with him. It is now so well entrenched that even within the Communist party the strictest directives, which in Russia, as we well know, have resulted in the interdiction of anything that is not *state-controlled academic art*, shatter against his studio doors. Other artists, whose experiments are still more or less tolerated in those circles, are unlikely to receive the same preferential treatment for much longer.

Surrealism's grievance against the times, in the sphere of visual arts as else-where, was primarily of a social nature. What we intended—and still do—was to foil the conspiracy that keeps reappearing during uncertain times in history and strives to establish the exclusive supremacy of conservative forms. To this end, a secret brigade contrives to exalt what was done yes-terday at the expense of what is done today, to hand out dubious laurels, to belittle the experiments still being attempted by systematically ascribing base motives to them. For some twenty years, surrealism has come under its attacks—scurrilous at times—but the small bastion the few of us had erected is still standing. However debatable one may find some of the po-sitions we took, as regards painting for instance, I think surrealism has not deviated from the first prescription of its program, which is to preserve *the potential of visual arts for constant self-renewal so as to express human desire in its unceasing fluctuation*. I do not think anyone will be able to say in good faith, much less to prove convincingly, that mercenary considerations may have spoiled the quality of the surrealist mode of expression in art. How is it that, without the lure of financial reward or social success of any other kind, this mode of expression has spread to virtually all countries? The only explanation is that it was—and still is—tapping the source of one of those streams of freshness that had been stemmed until then and that are only too eager to irrigate the human mind.

Also, with surrealism, for the first time probably, poetry has continually provided its support of the visual arts. This happened in the past for some isolated works—works of the kind that surrealism favors for this very reason: Uccello, Arcimboldo, Bosch, Baldung, Goya, Blake, Meryon, Redon, Rousseau—but never before had poetry and the visual arts as a whole combined so willingly. This is a *sign of the times*, the interpretation of which will require some hindsight but which, given the force of magnetization and cohesion involved, could already indicate that the fragmentary and scattered forms of collective desire, which remains concealed from each individual, are converging toward a single point where a new myth awaits us.

When they first hear about surrealism, many people want to know what is the criterion by which to decide whether or not a visual work can be regarded as surrealist. Is it necessary to repeat that this criterion is *not an aesthetic one*? Very roughly, we can say that surrealism in art is limited by "realism" on the one hand, by "abstractionism" on the other. Nonsurrealist (and in our view regressive in this day and age) is any work that focuses on the daily spectacle of beings and things, that is, everything that inheres *immediately* in the animal, vegetable, mineral fixtures of our environment even if it should be made visually unrecognizable by means of "distortion." The surrealist work of art resolutely excludes anything that results from *simple* perception, whatever intellectual speculation may be grafted onto it in order to alter its appearance. If, in this respect, the pitcher remains enemy number one, it is understood of course that surrealism puts on the same level the little boat, the bouquet of anemones, and the accommodating lady who posed with or without her clothes on. Nonsurrealist also (and, despite its modernistic pretensions, implying, as we see it, a profound abdication of human desire on account of its arbitrary reduction to certain needs of an exclusively spatial and "musical" nature) is any work dubbed nonobjective and nonrepresentational, that is to say, at odds as well with prior physical perception as with prior mental representation (which surrealism, while emphasizing the latter, is precisely trying to *reconcile*). Naturally, these barriers are not as impenetrable as I make them out to be since, contrary to all expectations, as strict an abstractionist as Mondrian, at the end of an ascetic life, occasionally drew closer to surrealism with paintings such as *Boogie-Woogie*, and Picasso, who remains an unrepentant realist, when he gives free rein to his lyricism, sometimes verges on surrealism or even makes real incursions into it.

What makes a work of art a surrealist one is, first and foremost, the spirit in which it was conceived. In the case of a visual work, the value we place on it may depend either on the visionary powers it demonstrates, or on the sense of organic life that emanates from it (a life that cannot be reduced, on the sensory or the conceptual level, to the representation of any one of the elements it comprises), or yet on the secret it carries of a new symbolism. To cite merely the names of the better-known surrealist artists, this would be the case, respectively, of Max Ernst, of Jean Arp and Joan Miró, of the early Chirico and of Yves Tanguy. Moreover, I have stressed many times the importance of the *method* that has provided surrealism with all the others, namely *automatism*, "the only mode of graphic expression that fully satisfies the eye by achieving *rhythmic unity* (as perceptible in a drawing as it is in a melody or in the structure of a nest)."[2]

Following the International Surrealist Exhibitions of Tokyo (1933), Copenhagen and Tenerife (1935), London (1936), Paris (1938), Mexico (1940), and New York (1942), the 1947 exhibition is primarily intended to confront various works of surrealist inspiration that have been produced over the last few years. The exceptionally dramatic character of that period, the fact that the ordeals it inflicted varied greatly from one part of the world to the next and that, moreover, most intellectual contacts had broken off, all that poses a psychological problem of widespread significance. What we want to know is whether surrealism, as a mental discipline chosen by a small number of individuals scattered all over the world, has withstood that disaster and whether it was greatly disrupted by it; whether, from the most to the least affected areas of the world, the reactions within surrealism were quite different from one another; and finally, how surrealism as a whole has come out of that ordeal, to what extent the disturbing events we have just experienced have affected its unity and vigor.

There is a heated debate going on about what man can learn from this last war and its ambiguous outcome: some people maintain that the means of physical and mental destruction recently implemented necessitate a worldview totally different from the one held until then, while others refuse to regard this as a new phenomenon, at any rate not as the sort of thing that might bring conventional ideas into question and that would urgently call for a revolution in mores. This situation alone would suffice to highlight like never before the question: *How can man be saved?* Today much more than yesterday, a curse causes this noble question to divide the thinking world (from which I exclude, needless to say, exploiters and parasites), to split it up into two enemy camps paradoxically prepared to wage a new struggle that this time would result in total extermination. Above the clamor of the hostilities to come—while they are still avoidable, and warding them off in appropriate terms—the admirable and almost solitary voice of Ignazio Silone could be heard a few days ago: "The spirit roams at will. Only clerics could dream of confining it to certain paths and of blocking other ones. . . . The gravest danger to spiritual values is always to link them indissolubly to a given period, to particular economic and political patterns. . . . Whoever does not want to take part consciously in contemptible 'brainwashing' must refuse to identify the cause of truth with that of an army. Moreover, siding right now with one power group against another means, from a political standpoint, surrendering beforehand to the threat of new wars, justifying them in advance, speeding up the process that will trigger them off. Not only is it, therefore, sacrilegious with respect to the spirit, but also foolish and imprudent. . . . Salvation depends exclusively on remaining honestly, straightforwardly, directly faithful to the tragic reality of what basically is human existence."[3]

The 1947 International Exhibition was not intended to confine its program to providing such a confrontation, let alone an account of how surrealism underwent that formidable ordeal. The letter of invitation that was sent to prospective exhibitors also conveyed the desire and the intention, in relation to the previous comprehensive surrealist exhibitions, to *transcend previous accomplishments.*

This transcendence took the direction of a new myth that, as I said earlier, was still vague but the characterization of which could be expected in the near future from the increasingly perfect union of poetry and art.

Without prejudging in the least what such a myth might turn out to be, we resolved to leave these two pursuits free to come even closer together by urging them to combine, to fuse together in a common mold. The purely theoretical idea of a *cult*, with all it entails during childhood in terms of daydreams, emotions, and fervor, was naturally to appeal to us as *a means to an end.* On this point, I think we can simply ignore the protests and insults that will no doubt be sparked in *narrow-minded* materialist circles. Besides, it would be all too easy to retort that the cult surrounding the memory of Marx is one of the most *fanatical* there ever was, that if this cult has its martyrs (a fact I readily acknowledge), it also has a red pope, a remunerated clergy, and masses—I mean large-scale ceremonies where those who officiate are small in number and where no voice ever so slightly discordant can be heard without incurring the worst kind of sanctions. Surrealists, as far as they are concerned, have never ceased to adhere to *total freethinking.* While they deliberately concentrate their experiments on certain structures that are meant, in an entirely abstract way, to conjure up a ritual atmosphere, they certainly do not have the absurd and ridiculous ambition to try and promote a new myth on their own. They limit themselves to giving shape to a few *haloed beings or objects*, which were, for the most part, already born of the imagination of poets and artists and which, on account perhaps of their fuzzy contours, have excited curiosity and exerted a growing attraction. Standing next to them, a few animals, as in all Apocalypses, tend to take on a symbolic life: they have been chosen from among those that seem apt to affect modern sensibility, although their *hieroglyphic* interpretation remains, until now, quite arcane. There is nothing there that goes beyond a certain number of rights that we previously granted ourselves and that, to quote but one example, enabled us to publish the "Essais de simulation" [Attempts at simulation] of various mental disorders in 1930.

Just as those experiments did not, of course, imply that we were suffering from those disorders (nor even that we were more susceptible to them than anybody else), it must remain clear that toward the beings and objects to which we have agreed to pay tribute, this time, by granting them some of the *trappings* of the sacred, we assuredly intend to keep an attitude of *enlightened doubt*.

This observation equally applies to the entire "initiatory" layout we designed for this exhibition. It would be unforgivable to take the word "initiation" literally; in our minds, of course, it is only intended as a *guideline*. But this guideline is something *we hold on to*; indeed, we are anxious to hold on to it at a time when poetry and art, just about everywhere, long merely to toe the line, to orchestrate the most shortsighted kind of day-to-day protest, and give up trying to lead man—elsewhere occupied—through the perilous labyrinth of the mind. I know that this exploration requires a process of trial and error and that it is full of pitfalls. And yet, in my opinion, *the honor of poets and artists* depends, above all else, on their fulfilling this task. Initiation by means of poetry and art (an initiation to which the latest research on Hugo, Nerval, Rimbaud, and others gives us sound reason to adapt the patterns inherited from the esoteric tradition)—that is what surrealism intends to keep on pursuing.

The 1947 Surrealist Exhibition brings together close to one hundred exhibitors from twenty-four countries, most of which had yesterday formed coalitions against one another. After so many underhanded efforts to prevent men from understanding one another, all the more so if they do not speak the same language, to tax them with some mysterious birth defect that arouses mistrust and hatred, that stirs up envy and spreads vendetta like a plague, I think it is good, it is healthy, it is time, even on the very small scale of surrealism, for men who are fortunate enough to share, by means of the visual arts, a universal language, to unite and bring their affinities out into the open. It is to be hoped, moreover, that they will not stop at this platonic affirmation but that it will commit them to strengthen among themselves the only *indivisible* pact—the surrealist pact. Let me repeat that this pact is threefold: I believe the present situation of the world no longer allows us to establish a hierarchy among the imperatives that it includes and that must be carried out simultaneously: to contribute, as much as one can, to the social liberation of man, to work without respite toward a *total* renewal of mores, to reshape human understanding.

1947

Second Ark

Twelve years have gone by since surrealism staged a series of events in Prague[1] and half of that period—which may have been harder to endure over there than anywhere else since, when we look back to its beginning, we have to lay a finger on that *unhealed* wound that is called Munich—could not fail to blur, or even tarnish, the memory of it. Exhibitions come and go, having more or less of an impact on the world of sensation, and what traces they leave seem insignificant beside certain cataclysms that, when they turn the world upside down, confront mankind collectively with the inescapable question of its physical and mental existence. It is nonetheless true that the cataclysm has no sooner abated—or even, at worst, a truce is no sooner called—than man already feels the need to *find his bearings* and, in order to do so, begins to take stock of what has been laid to waste in the realm of ideas, of what has been undermined, and of what has successfully warded off the forces of destruction. All personal passion aside, I do think that the much greater interest that surrealism arouses in the younger generation and the increasingly animated discussions it provokes place it, objectively speaking, in the latter category. An uninterrupted flow of literary and visual works, from 1919 to this day, demonstrates its vitality on many different levels. The surrealist exhibition held quite recently in Paris, which brought together about a hundred artists from twenty-four countries, is evidence enough of its capacity for expansion as well as its *unceasing* effort to position itself on the international level.

War does not pay, not in fresh ideas, nor by scouring awareness: one need only look at the present state of the world and the solutions being offered to acknowledge this fact. "The first effect of war" (let us join Paulhan in this observation) "is that in general everybody ends up being more convinced than ever: the revolutionary more revolutionary; the believer more believing; the unbeliever more unbelieving; even the pacifist feels that events have proved him right."[2] Will surrealism—which, as its name indicates and by explicit definition, aimed at transcending these miserable conditions of thought—make a show of repentance, as its turncoats, its renegades wickedly enjoin it to do? This would indeed be the supreme paradox. On the contrary, it upholds, in all their integrity, the principles that were formulated during my stay with Eluard in Prague in 1935, and that were put on record in *Co je surrealismus*, published in Brno two years later.[3]

It is *not true* that the problem of free artistic expression should today be stated in other terms. I remain as convinced as I was then that "the elucidation of the means of expression that characterize contemporary art worthy of the name can only lead in the end to the unconditional defense of a single cause, that of the *liberation of man.*" But more than ever I intend at all costs to keep alive the meaning of that liberation so that it may be continually re-created and perfected, and not to blindly entrust its realization to an apparatus whose devious methods and absolute contempt for the human person fill me with misgivings. This is what prompts me to urge: ART MUST NEVER TAKE ORDERS, WHATEVER HAPPENS! Let us never forget that the offensive against free art, during the years immediately preceding the war, was launched concurrently by regimes claiming to have opposite ideological objectives. Artists in every country, irrespective of their leanings, not only because they are threatened by the same danger, but also because the guiding principle of their activity is being targeted, owe it to themselves to make their calumniators eat such vile expressions as "degenerate art" and "bourgeois decadent art," which are rapidly becoming synonymous. Is it at all conceivable that some of them would go along with this game of *self-slaughter* unless they were masochists or shortsighted opportunists? And how can they fail to see that with such a millstone around their necks the more general cause to which they are fanatically prepared to make this *unnatural* sacrifice is already lost?

There was a time, in France for instance, when the expression decadent art (already more "bourgeois," for sure, than proletarian, if, for want of anything better to do, one cares to play with these words on such a level) did not sound offensive to the likes of Rimbaud, Mallarmé, and Huysmans. Assuming that decadence was already a characteristic phenomenon of their time, it would, all in all, hardly have needed their prodding. Where they were neither decadent nor degenerate was in the awareness they attained of their mission as poets and artists. So much so that it is precisely the objections they met in their time—in particular the "proletarian" verbiage of Vallès and others like him—that today seem to us worn out and decadent.

TRUE DECADENCE, TRUE DEGENERATION HAS ITS ENEMY IN THE WILL TO DISCOVERY, IN ART AS ELSEWHERE. THE REASON BEING THAT IT IS A PREY TO ALL THE OBSESSIVE FEARS THAT LATCH ON TO THIS CRITICAL SYMPTOM— *THE SIGN OUTLASTING WHAT IT SIGNIFIES*—WHICH INEVITABLY BEGETS INTOLERANCE AND IS ALWAYS THAT IN WHICH ALL DOGMAS END.

It is possible that Europe (the whole world?), wounded in its vital organs, can no longer fulfill the destiny adumbrated by an irrepressible belief in a progressive "betterment." Of course, it is beyond the power of one or a handful of men to go against the tide and effectively make certain that bread will come out with a golden crust or prevent the sky from being obscured by the wings of the exterminating angel, just when we could enjoy it. But at least we should do our utmost to ensure that all will not be swept away by the next hurricane, if it is true that the appetites in conflict make it doubly inevitable. In the present circumstances, we should also *consecrate* the role of the intellectual and of the artist who, from a civilization that is coming to an end to a future civilization more impoverished at birth than any other, must *make every effort possible to hand over the powers of sensibility* and not relinquish all their prerogatives in advance in the ludicrous hope of melting into the crowd so as to pass unnoticed into the lands of suffocation.

No politicomilitary directive can be accepted or promulgated in art without treason. The sole duty of the poet, of the artist, is to reply with a categorical NO to all disciplinary slogans. The despicable word *engagement* [*commitment*], which has caught on since the war, exudes a servility that is abhorrent to art and poetry. Fortunately, the great testimony of mankind, the one that has managed to endure until now, tramples on those petty prohibitions, on those amends qualified (how ironic!) as "honorable," on those shameful compromises. Isn't that so, John Huss? Is it true, Giordano Bruno? What do you say, Jean-Jacques?

1947

Magloire-Saint-Aude

Twelve to fifteen lines, no more. I understand your wish: the philosophers' stone or close enough, the note that, being heard for the first time ever, subdues the surrounding cacophony, the unique cog that locks the wheel of anguish into ecstasy. With such constraints, who since the sphinx could have managed to hold the traveler's attention? In French poetry, at times, Scève, Nerval, Mallarmé, Apollinaire ... But you know quite well that everything nowadays is far too *slipshod*. Magloire-Saint-Aude is the exception.

When I wonder which among contemporary works would deserve to be set in the most beautiful type ever, those that come most readily to mind are the two very slim volumes published in Haiti in 1941 by Magloire-Saint-Aude: *Dialogue de mes lampes* [Dialogue of my lamps] and *Tabou* [Taboo]. In them, both the language and the poetic attitude are constantly brought to their supreme point. The fact that no French publisher has yet been tempted by the two hundred lines or so that make up these two volumes is evidence enough of a lapse in the appreciation of quality.

At last, no more silly little secrets to be heard here. At this poet's cradle, the Caribbean fairy met the "African fairy" once glimpsed by Rimbaud, and I will never forget the voice I heard one night, bearing within itself the whole fabulous island. His haughty disdain shields him propitiously from our clatter as he sits, impassive and unreachable, a bottle of rum by his side.

SILENCE

The tuff with auburn peaks, chances, clashes
Over nine towns.

※

Magdalenas in lace of yellow-weed.

※

Nothing the poet, slow doleful,
So as to die in Guadalajara.

※

The morning enters my sleeves.
I write for emotion and for Camargo.
Speak, implorers, the chatter
When Maud awaits me in the world.

※

My puppet, uncrowned in homage,
Takes aim, at my gala, at your long cool eyes,
And, as at the ball of the thirteen friends,
I listen to the Mongol with dead eyes.

Ascendant Sign

> The desire that the female feels for the male
> resembles the mists rising from the earth toward the sky.
> Once they have gathered into clouds, it is the sky
> that waters the earth.—Zohar

Only on the level of analogy have I ever experienced intellectual pleasure. For me the only *manifest truth* in the world is governed by the spontaneous, clairvoyant, insolent connection established under certain conditions between two things whose conjunction would not be permitted by common sense. As much as I abhor, more than any other, the word *therefore*, replete with vanity and sullen delectation, so do I love passionately anything that flares up suddenly out of nowhere and thus breaks the thread of discursive thinking. What comes to light at that moment is an infinitely richer network of relations whose secret, as everything suggests, was known to early mankind. It is true that the flare quickly dies out, but its glimmer is enough to help measure on their dismal scale the exchange values currently available that provide no answer except to basic questions of a utilitarian nature. Our contemporaries, indifferent to whatever does not concern them directly, are progressively more insensitive to anything that could present them with an in-depth investigation into nature: drifting on the surface of things seems enough of a task. There is an age-old conviction that nothing exists gratuitously, that quite to the contrary there is not a single being or natural phenomenon that does not carry a message to be deciphered by us. This conviction, which was at the heart of most cosmogonies, has been replaced by a numb and stupefied apathy: we have thrown in the towel. We hide in order to ask ourselves: "Where do I come from? Why do I exist? Where am I going?" But is it not absurd or even impudent to aim at "transforming" the world when one no longer cares to make sense of its more enduring aspects. The primordial links are broken. It is my contention that those links can only be restored, albeit fleetingly, through the force of analogy. Hence the importance taken on at long intervals by those brief flashes from the lost mirror.

The diamond and the pig are hieroglyphs of the thirteenth passion (harmonism), which civilized people do not experience.—Charles Fourier.

The white of the eye is a bedframe. The iris is a base for the mattress of the pupil on which a ghost of ourselves rests while we are dreaming.—Malcolm de Chazal

Poetic analogy has this in common with mystical analogy: it transgresses the rules of deduction to let the mind apprehend the interdependence of two objects of thought located on different planes. Logical thinking is incapable of establishing such a connection, which it deems a priori impossible. Poetic analogy is fundamentally different from mystical analogy in that it in no way presupposes the existence of an invisible universe that, from beyond the veil of the visible world, is trying to reveal itself. The process of poetic analogy is entirely empirical, since only empiricism can provide the complete freedom of motion required by the leap it must perform. When we consider the impression it creates, it is true that poetic analogy seems, like mystical analogy, to argue for an idea of a world branching out toward infinity and entirely permeated with the same sap. However, it remains without any effort within the sensible (even the sensual) realm and it shows no propensity to lapse into the supernatural. Poetic analogy lets us catch a glimpse of what Rimbaud named "true life" and points toward its "absence," but it does not draw its substance from metaphysics nor does it ever consider surrendering its treasures on the altar of any kind of "beyond."

The dream is a heavy ham
Hanging from the ceiling.
—Pierre Reverdy

I arrive as a hawk and come out a phoenix.
—Voice of the third soul, Egypt

At the present stage of poetic research, the purely formal distinction once established between metaphor and comparison should not receive much emphasis. The fact remains that they both serve as interchangeable vehicles of analogical thinking. Metaphor does have the ability to dazzle the mind, but comparison (think of Lautréamont's series of "as beautiful as") has the considerable advantage of *deferring*. Naturally, compared to these two, the other "figures" that rhetoric persists in enumerating are totally devoid of interest. The trigger of analogy is what fascinates us: nothing else will give us access to the motor of the world. Whether it is stated or implied, AS is the most exhilarating word at our command. It gives free rein to human imagination, and the supreme destiny of the mind depends on it. That is why we choose to dismiss rather scornfully the ignorant indictment of the poetry of our time, accused of making excessive use of the "image." On the contrary, what we expect from it in this respect is an ever growing luxuriance.

Your aggressive breast straining against the silk
Your triumphant breast is a splendid armoire.
—Charles Baudelaire

The analogical method was held in high regard throughout antiquity and the Middle Ages. Since then, it has been summarily supplanted by the "logical" method, which has led us to our familiar impasse. The primary duty of poets and artists is to restore to it all its prerogatives. To this end, analogy must be rescued from the parasitic undercurrent of spiritualism, which weakens or even cripples its potentialities.

Your teeth are like a flock of sheep even-shorn, coming back up from the washpen.—Song of Songs

Pierre Reverdy, who, thirty years ago, looked into the wellspring of the image, was led to formulate this cardinal law: "The more remote and accurate the connections between two realities that are brought together, the stronger the image—the stronger its emotional potential and its poetic reality." This condition, while absolutely necessary, cannot be deemed sufficient. It must make room for another requirement that in the final analysis could well be an ethical one. Let us beware! The analogical image, to the extent that it brings under the strongest light what are merely *partial similarities*, cannot be translated into an equation. It moves between the two confronting realities in a single direction *that can never be reversed*. From the first of these realities to the second one, it creates a vital tension straining toward health, pleasure, tranquillity, thankfulness, respect for customs. Disparagement and depressiveness are its mortal enemies. In this regard, to make up for the disappearance of noble words, some so-called poets cannot help but call attention to their sham by using vile metaphors such as the archetypal "Guitar singing bidet" from the pen of an author who is fairly prolific when it comes to such strokes of inspiration.

I saw a gathering of spirits. They wore hats on their heads.—Swedenborg

> *Your tongue*
> *A goldfish swimming in the bowl*
> *Of your voice.*
> *—Guillaume Apollinaire*

We went along that avenue lined with blue breasts where a comma is all that distinguishes night from day and a smear of itching powder a sardine from a may-bug.—Benjamin Péret

The finest light illuminating the general, compelling direction that any image worthy of its name must take is found in this apologue from the Zen tradition: "As an act of Buddhist kindness, Basho once ingeniously reversed a cruel haiku made up by his witty disciple. Kikaku had said: 'A red firefly / Tear off its wings / A pepper.' Basho substituted: 'A pepper / Give it wings / A red firefly.'"

30 December 1947

The Lamp

in the

Clock

At the far end of this foul corridor through which contemporary man is making his way, it has become morally almost impossible to catch one's breath. This corridor represents the passage between the so-called universe of concentration camps, in a drunken rat's living memory, and a quite possible nonuniverse, for the advent of which a final perforated pattern is being perfected. It would be one thing if one made sure that this could serve to edify future species, but here the myth of the message in the bottle founders like so many others. That civilizations should have reached the point where they considered themselves mortal left something for consolation and for wisdom. A beam of light remained, moving from the lid of a sarcophagus to a Peruvian pot, to a tablet from Easter Island, keeping alive the idea that the *spirit* that animated those civilizations one after another is to some extent shielded from the process of destruction that keeps piling material ruins behind us. At the most we see it *occulting* itself more and more throughout the centuries, but the enigmatic ends of this occultation did not themselves fail to test human sagacity, and therein lay the secret of a kind of greatness.

The shrinkage, the collapse of these perspectives forces those who want to continue to honor the name of man to withdraw into themselves, to examine unflinchingly the new conditions to which thought is being subjected. There is no doubt that awareness is affected, threatened in its own particular substratum. Since very few individuals are endowed with it, what works against it in the first instance is the mass of unawareness and unconcern, which is determined to ignore danger until it can no longer be averted and, meanwhile, to take advantage of what it perceives—in a confused fashion—as a general crisis of responsibility. Of course, this it can only translate in terms of license and blind pursuit of personal profit on a day-to-day basis. What also works against awareness—and this is more serious—is a whole machinery of mindless habits, running so smoothly that one may well wonder if it would not continue to motivate a handful of men, were they to be the only ones left in the world. (Who could have said that the *watchwords* of the political parties, quickly adulterated by a shortsighted opportunism, would so quickly cover the vast mental expanse so pitilessly cleared by this last war and that might have been, or so one hoped, favorable to the germination and growth of new ideas?) Each tries to defend to the bitter end, and with utter vindictiveness, a position so weak as to become untenable. What is worse, two enormous masses of men, whose grievances are inflamed by a blind or fanatical demagoguery, are defying each other and long only for the moment when they will be able to fight it out, even if it means bringing their grist to the same mill—in this case, grist that is dynamite to a mill that is a volcano. On the politicophilosophical level, materialism and idealism, whose opposition is purely formal, as the latest discoveries in physics should have sufficed to make clear, are still brandished as the two major irreconcilable doctrines, for the sake of some private or "national" interests and to provide credentials to a considerable number of fools. Corruption radiates from this conceptual corpse, automatically spreading the practices of the "black market" to the domain of ideas, and that is still an understatement since, on both sides, falsification reigns supreme. The transformation of the world, definitely more necessary and incomparably more urgent than ever, but which, in view of the common threat hanging over all men, should be entirely rethought, is claimed as an exclusive right by a party rigidly set in nineteenth-century dogmas and whose admirable original ideals have long ago succumbed to the devious and degrading ploys in which its *cadre* has involved them. Bad faith and calumny made into a way of life, patent tergiversation presented as an indisputable gesture of self-consistency, the precautions taken to wrap in secrecy everything that could be brought out in concrete terms (precautions that are still insufficient to distract from the clank of chains and the muffled reports from the staircase);

finally, the systematic obfuscation of the persistent craving for harmony and human happiness: who could possibly think that there is light at the end of those tunnels? Trapped within the appalling physical and mental misery of our times but without yet despairing, we wait for forces resisting all domestication to get down again to the task of the emancipation of man. I would be the last one to deny that such a struggle—when the very fate of mankind is at stake—has never been waged before and in such unequal conditions. It is hard, it is at times, if not discouraging, at least debilitating, to observe that history is made to depend on a roll of dice that have been *loaded* in this fashion. On this tapestry where Marx's beard is still frothing but which is no longer lit up by his magnificent all-encompassing gaze, it is no doubt a great pity to see the proletarian masses taking their allotted places and fading, just when they are reaching the end of their ascent toward a better life that is *owed* them, blindly driven as they are by florid priests who no longer condescend even to tell them which paths they are following. You were supposed to have attained freedom: you are told that this is it, but nobody leaves. Let us be quite clear! You imagined that man would be able to enjoy and openly bear witness to life, to make the most of his ability, of his genius: for a start, you will go through that room full of metallic flies and other creatures. Just take a look at that late romantic; he thought that in his lifetime—not asking much, was he—the world would come into its own: "Abandon all hope, you who enter."

Nothing can alter the fact that this is the point we have reached, and I say, everything considered, that the game is not worth the expected candle. In this context, the most clever paradoxes, the most virulent sophisms are bound to crumble in the near future. Meanwhile, everything that finds its own justification in terms of human depth and *spontaneous self-sacrifice* has not spoken its last word. Everything will put out new roots. Widespread deception will be a thing of the past. The great problems will be examined under an entirely new light as never before. We will no longer have to shudder at the sight of disfigured children. Slightly better informed audiences will no longer get excited at the prospect of scenes reminiscent of the Roman circus but which would now be played on a much larger stage, since we are told that next time the stands and the arena will be as one.

One may object that poets are odd characters—mercurial? Why, aren't there innumerable papers being published, showing that for the past hundred years they have been giving in—and through them the leading edge of modern sensibility—to the temptation of the *end of the world*? Indeed, ancient Manichaeism and Sade indisputably exerted a powerful influence on the attitudes of poets such as Nerval, Borel, Baudelaire, Cros, Rimbaud, Lautréamont, and Mallarmé—an attitude that, for the most part, has conditioned our own. It was not even the most frenetic of them who uttered this blunt statement: "To amuse myself, I try to figure out ... whether a tremendous mass of stones, marble tops, statues, walls knocking against one another, will be much soiled by that multitude of brains, of chunks of human flesh, of crushed bones. . . . "[1] It is true. And yet I have no qualms about saying that this is an end of the world that *we no longer want*. We ceased to want it when we began to see the shape it would take, which, contrary to all expectations, we find to be totally absurd. We feel nothing but loathing for that universal syncope, insofar as man's alienation alone will have been the *cause* of it. This kind of end of the world, resulting from a stupid mistake, more inexcusable because it is more critical than the previous ones, is for us devoid of any *value*—just a deplorable caricature. However much we try and guess what is being hatched under the locks of Professor Einstein or what is thriving behind the crew cut of the strange comrade Stalin, this final slaughter has nothing to do with what had been envisioned. This end of the world is not ours. As long as it remains a possibility, we have no compunction about doing an about-face with regard to this issue, to proceed deliberately to an *inversion of sign*. Only "rationalist" thought could call us to account for this, but we can be expected to disregard it from the moment it crowns itself with an annihilating meaninglessness, thereby validating and even exceeding our predictions. The possibility of this inversion of sign is in any case governed by a *pure emotional fact*, thanks to which the principle of contradiction can be overcome. There is no dearth of examples of it, especially in the works of Baudelaire, Rimbaud, and Lautréamont. It goes without saying that this has nothing to do with recantation, some instances of which have recently been widely publicized. What I am talking about is that great poetic mystery, exemplified by Sade, when, during the Terror, at the expense of his freedom and to the great dismay of his future exegetes, he spoke out against the death penalty.

There is no question, for all that, of rejecting the legacy of "black" art or of ostentatiously brushing aside the "curse" taken up by the greatest poets and artists of this last century like a burning glove. Indeed, it remains the only source of all potential ardor. Through it, as a result of the reprobation it incites, genuine poets and artists assert the absolute choice they make between, on the one hand, destitution and the enduring disrepute that directly put them in the same category as the most exploited and the most persecuted of human beings and social castes, and, on the other hand, the material benefits that, in return for a benevolent neutrality, the affluent might apportion to them. Let us note that this indicates much deeper affinities with those individuals and castes, and that it creates a bond that offers much stronger guarantees of indissolubility than the adoption of an attitude of compliance with the slogans of the "socialist realism" of yesterday or of the "antiformalism" of today. Besides, the whole question is whether the mind can renounce with impunity most of its age-old functions—whose complexity and interaction, so different from one individual to the next, are what make life worth the struggle—to turn into a simple vehicle for propaganda. On this side of the "iron curtain," some of us are still able to say no.

Although this may irk

The guardroom and kitchen riffraff [2]

who do me the remarkable honor of keeping an increasingly close watch over my slightest actions and of multiplying their provocations wherever I go, I shall add that the very conditions, the imprescriptible conditions of creative thought, which my friends and I are defending, are defined by a constant, which the mere fact of Marx's appearing on the scene was not able to turn into a variable, and which, being an untamable force, with all the more reason braves the risk of being negated. Nothing can prevent free human discovery, which existed before Marx and has outlasted him, from keeping drawn, in the darkest corner of the picture, the bow that, according to the myth, has been put in our hands by Prometheus or by Lucifer. None of the tyrannies of the past or the future can alter this fact. Even though we are now living through a period of crass ignorance when in poetry, in art, I will not even say in philosophy but in general ways of thinking, the only works turned to account are immediate ones, tied to fashion and worn down by commentaries—Rimbaud, Picasso, Lenin's "empiriocriticism"—man is bound to regain his balance on the heap of *everything* that has made him what he is. He will cease to live on an eroding hillside like a weed ashamed that its seed was brought to that place by the wind. He will once again want to shape his own destiny, as a being shaped *individually* for a purpose chosen by himself alone and that, therefore, should not duplicate any other one. Vanity is elsewhere.

The occultists are more than justified in stressing the phenomenal omnipotence of *fire* and in finding fault with the chemical formulas that are claimed to account for this or that reaction, without its essential intervention being duly specified.[3] Morally speaking, where there is no fire, there is nothing (and one cannot possibly mistake for fire the dying embers that some would use to warm their conscience). Rimbaud, even if any number of people take turns trying to cool him down, Rimbaud is still burning bright. Admittedly, the poet's attitude, when faced with the German invasion in 1870–1871, cannot be easily adapted to the use one would like to make of it as an example for a catechism of perfect public-spiritedness, bound in lead as is proper for all occasions, behind which the same people are shielding themselves and which they use to strike out at the first opportunity as the priests of old would do with their heavy crosses. But let us consider for a moment the blunder committed, during the same period, by the author of the following lines: "The French need a good thrashing. If the Prussians win, the centralization of state power will benefit the concentration of the German working class. Moreover, German supremacy will transfer the center of gravity of the European workers movement from France to Germany; and one only need compare the movement in both countries, from 1866 to the present, to see that the German working class is superior to the French, from the standpoint of theory as well as of organization. The supremacy, on the world stage, of the German proletariat over the French would mean at the same time the supremacy of our theory over that of Proudhon." Who could have uttered this statement, which, from the present point of view, is so sacrilegious? Who, moreover, could have betrayed his own fallibility by proving to be so inept, so mistaken in his predictions? This was not a poet but a man who, in all respects, should be held accountable for such predictions. For those who may not have recognized him, let me say his name was Marx.[4] To argue today in his name for resistance on the national level—let us not even talk of fire—it is a coat of ice that one must wear.

Without regard for any of the sundry threats and attempts at intimidation, we shall more than ever listen to the great isolated messages that can still reach us. We shall receive ultrafavorably any free communication that can enable us, in these "ultrasonorous" times, to spot a new way out, or that can convince us that this way out may be found at the end of a path that, if not lost, has at least not been much traveled for a long time. Nothing better can be used, at the moment, to counteract those who, so belatedly and with such exhausted words, are striving to entice us toward a deceptive "window opened onto the future" when all we can see of it are its bars. We maintain, of course, that a spiritual attitude such as this one is perfectly compatible with a firm and concerted social attitude aimed above all at uniting all those who, unaffected by incitements to hatred, are aware of an impending danger threatening the human species as a whole and who intend, *right here and now*, to do everything possible to avert it. I hereby want to make my position clear by signifying my unqualified support for the movement Front Humain [Human Front] (led with the highest authority by Robert Sarrazac), which alone seems to me to offer, at the outset, all the guarantees of lucidity and rigor that can be required of such an organization. It alone, as far as I know, draws the extreme daring and the promise of viability of its enterprise from an unshakable and contagious faith in the enduring fate of man—man whom, in circumstances almost as serious, it has never been impossible to awaken and to restore to a less grudging self-awareness. I would just refer the reader to the publications of Front Humain, the spirit and language of which are impeccable as well as within the reach of everyone, while expressing the wish that all the groups with similar aspirations may quickly unite under its banner and that, after making all due inquiries, those of us who until now have seen fit to keep aloof from such organizations may join this one forthwith.[5]

On this 26th day of February 1948, when a new coup carried out in Prague seems to reduce even more the chances of avoiding desperate solutions—when, outside any consideration of guilt, we have no choice but to admit spectacularly that Birnam Wood keeps advancing on Dunsinane Castle—I find myself rereading a letter from my friend, the great Henry Miller. Allow me this personal digression. While writing to him a few days ago, I happened to mention in passing what was being said about him, doubtlessly about the free man he is, in the less "difficult" newspapers: "Miller's books are banned from the USA? Of course! His books are intended for external consumption. Like the atom bomb."[6] Talking about this and that, I also told him about Henri Matisse, whom I had just seen in Venice, and how I marveled that, in spite of being well on in years, such an artist— even though a "formalist" if ever there was one—could live exclusively turned toward light and joy. I feel it is appropriate to quote Miller's reply because he manages to highlight two major aspects of the drama of our time: "As for that clipping, I take it in stride, like so many others in the same vein. There is no point arguing. Even if you give them your heart, people will not change. The blind lead the blind, just as they always did. . . . When you talk about Matisse, you make me think of another race of men. Among us, the old are often the younger ones, the more joyful, the more well balanced. They go on working—whistling, so to speak. Matisse belongs to another era when, if I can express this correctly, salvation was found in one's work and, moreover, when one *gave* salvation to others through that work—working in the sense of living in (or with) beauty. But work is probably not the right word, or is it? In English we say: 'a labor of love.' Love . . . I think Rimbaud said all there was to say on that topic."

Speaking of "great isolated messages," those with an entirely new ring to them, from which in this time of darkness I was suggesting we might passionately seek answers, we have to admit that we have not been overwhelmed with them since this last war. Yet those messages are of the highest value as an *index*. Moreover, this index applies in both directions. On the one hand, it expresses the convertibility of a number of signs, the harmful predominance of which is only too obvious these days, into another sign that points to the enduring and *self-renewing* nature of life. It may not be possible to express that process clearly. Its secret lies, deeply buried probably, in documents such as the series of inscriptions, copied by Fulcanelli, that comprise the "marvelous wizard's book in the Castle of Dampierre."[7] On the other hand, that index has the property of throwing light a long way back on a series of intellectual trends of which it can be considered to be the outcome. Those trends, whether they are associated with particular individuals or not, as the case may be, are thus brought to the fore and into contact and linked together by a current that leads to a closer examination of them, while other trends that prevailed over them until then are thrown back into a more or less permanent obscurity. Surrealism, for instance, was thus brought to define itself at the highest point of an ascending curve of the most sinuous kind that taxes the endurance and also the patience of critics but that the sensibility of youth innervates at the outset from one end to the other—it is also to a large extent responsible for the disregard shown by youth for a number of works that used to be held "sacred" such as those French literary works of the seventeenth century (with the notable exception of Retz, Bergerac, and Pascal). No matter what dismay this may cause in conservative circles of every kind, today as yesterday, while faced with so much devastation, it is out of the question to burden ourselves with dead weights when we are trying to recover a *free voice*. What is absolutely necessary and desperately urgent is to *forge ahead*.

Through the periscope of this era, the lenses of which we need constantly to wipe, I myself have seen only one message of the kind I was calling for, emerging and compelling recognition for being utterly real and having the requisite potential. It is found in one volume entitled *Sens plastique II* [*Plastic Sense*], review copies of which were distributed in Paris on an almost confidential basis, having been sent by the author, Malcolm de Chazal, from Mauritius, where he lives. Still, this was enough for it to reach those it was supposed to reach and to be brought to the forefront of current concerns (I am talking about genuine spiritual concerns and not about what is being passed off as such). Aimé Patri and Jean Paulhan were the first to take possession of this message and to spread it about actively, which was the right thing to do.[8] This gave us a chance to see two very different but wide open minds combining their sound and pertinent reactions, which perfectly complement each other. They seem to me to have brought out the basic points that needed to be raised *on the threshold* of this book.[9] For once, the ceremonial surrounding the reception of a great work has been, in terms of sobriety and decorum, what it should have been, and this more or less makes up for the discovery—just before this book is to be distributed in bookstores—of a photograph of the author next to that of an official figure who, in this case, can only serve as a foil.[10] Beyond a preliminary reading that is made deliberately difficult by the very structure of his book, Malcolm de Chazal calls for a thorough exploration of his thought: this process will take some time since it implies a lengthy meditation on his theses. I think that in this regard his wishes should be respected. Since we are nowhere near that point in time, I will limit myself to some provisional remarks.

First of all I want to draw aside a screen of tall grass concealing Mauritius, one that could prevent my progress. Everything in his letters seems to indicate that Malcolm de Chazal is going through a peculiar mental stage that may be the price for the "star on the forehead"[11] since it presents a striking analogy with the one Raymond Roussel was able to recount retrospectively to himself with the help of Dr. Pierre Janet.[12] What it is, if you recall, is a kind of bridge thrown from anguish to ecstasy, on which the traveler loses the awareness of his human limitations and allows himself to feel all the sensations of an eagle's flight above the summits. In the present state of human relations (primitive peoples would on the contrary honor such abilities), the bond of *understanding* that may tie this human being to those close to him quickly loosens. Precisely because of the disciplines that underlie his pursuit, I am convinced that Malcolm de Chazal gives in, in this respect, to a short-lived frenzy of divination, as remote as possible from the one that inspired Nietzsche when he wrote *Ecce Homo*.

It is appropriate, when confronted with such a work, brought into prominence by its perfect originality and the unparalleled accomplishment it represents, to wonder what vector exactly carries it toward one of the only discernible points of the future, and of what, in the past, that vector is the resultant. In other words, what force resides in it that is sufficient to pierce the unprecedented opacity of what is to come, and what precedents or antecedents more or less consciously chosen among all others have contributed to its production.

Regarding the first of these questions, I have no hesitation in answering that the very key to such a work—a key that Malcolm de Chazal has obligingly left in the door—is *pleasure*, in the less figurative meaning of the term, viewed as the supreme locus of resolution of the physical and the mental. It is astonishing that we had to wait until the middle of the twentieth century for sexual pleasure—a phenomenon that plays a unique role in the conditioning of almost any individual existence—to find a way of talking about itself without donning the veils that hypocrisy casts over it, or any licentious costume of defiance under which it manages to conceal itself just as well. The most emancipated French writers of the eighteenth century, those most determined to shake the yoke (Laclos, Sade), while putting the strongest emphasis on it, did not feel any need to analyze it. In this respect, the sad dotted line found in cheap publications is not offset by anything in those writings that would be of much greater value. Whereas the buildup of *desire* in lovemaking comes under a powerful spotlight, it seems that its parallel waning right after the climax of the sex act induces a persistent bad conscience that deters us from reverting to the supreme point that may have been reached and from where, for a moment after all slightly less brief than a flash of lightning, without being forced to be aware of it—which would mean betraying pleasure itself and accepting that it betrays us—we had the opportunity to grasp some unrevealed aspects of the world from a unique angle. What may have been needed to achieve this was an incomparably cool head such as the one we are tempted to think Chazal has, judging from photographs of him. At any rate, neither Jarry (in *Le Surmâle* [*The Supermale*]) nor Duchamp (in *La Mariée mise à nu* [*The Bride Stripped Bare*]) had managed it. Georges Bataille even less so, however much preoccupied he is known to be with describing the orbit common to a hyperbolical kind of sex and to religious ecstasy.

On this point, Malcolm de Chazal's central disquisition is of the highest significance, and I am surprised that it did not attract more notice, all the more so since it is corroborated and illustrated by sixty or so of the most beautiful aphorisms in *Sens plastique II*. I find it essential to quote this passage at length:

> *Any genuine introspection in the sphere of the senses is incomplete if the two major sensorial phenomena of life, birth and death, do not reveal their*

secrets to us to some extent. . . . And yet there is a way to "explain" these two basic phenomena of life, thanks to a field of experimentation that is open to all: sexual pleasure—that birth-death all in one, which has been far too much intellectualized until now, by pornographying or sentimentalizing it to excess. But since sexual pleasure is the universal junction of the senses, the mind, the heart, and the soul, and a locus-state where birth and death meet halfway, and where the whole man "converges" upon himself, it is also, for this very reason, the major source of knowledge and the vastest field of inquiry into the deep motivating forces within the human being.

As I enter this superlaboratory of the senses blindfolded, I try . . . to disentangle this mixed sensation . . . with the intention of discovering the relationship between pleasure and the symbolic language of nature and how, beyond this language, it connects with universal Joy, to achieve this unity, the most perfect example of which is found in the sensation of incorporation into the world of things that all lovers feel when their bliss is at its height. Then . . . I try to go all the way back to the soul, which subconsciously retains the birth experience; and I try to elicit answers from those limbos of the mind, so as to "decipher" death, since birth and death are the opposite sides of one and the same experience.

Here is a *novel* proposition, despite the sarcasms that will inevitably be heaped upon it by those who will choose to regard it as a naive development of an outdated theme (whose significance eludes them) dealing with the relationship between love and death that the beautiful title of a book by Barrès has permanently imprinted on our memories.[13] Here is the proclamation of a *revolutionary* truth—let me say, for those who may have forgotten what this word means or who might try their best to corrupt it, here is the proclamation of a truth *that both breaks with the past and goes beyond it*. Finally, here is a moving appeal, in this final hour, to everything that may constitute the *sacred* in life.

Through the voice of Malcolm de Chazal—and when it is the only one that can be heard in tragic times, such a voice is always an *oracle*—human sensibility is not merely warning so-called intelligence of the impending danger (as the voice of Fourier did in former times), it urges it to reappraise itself entirely. If it were up to me, no textbook, no anthology could dispense with reproducing the passage in *Sens plastique II* that opens with this blunt declaration: "Life is one big process of brainwashing, from birth until death" and builds up to the admirable peroration: "*But in the sphere of the mind as well, the law of the strongest prevails.* Like a tocsin, let us call out to those who are spiritually besieged: 'What are you waiting for to defend yourselves? Defend yourselves, gentlemen!'"[14] Let us beware: this commanding tone will be heard and supported by young people, who sense that someone is speaking on their behalf—they can hear it already. Nothing as resounding had been heard since Lautréamont.

But the violently iconoclastic character of those pages could not possibly mislead us to such an extent that we would concede that Chazal's attitude is without precedent in the history of human thought. On this score, we should not be any more impressed by his denials, even if they are quite sincere, than by those obviously suspicious ones uttered by Apollinaire, when he claimed, for instance, that he knew nothing—with the exception of *Ubu roi*—of Jarry's work, but pretended more speciously that he owed a great deal to *Le Magasin des enfants* [The children's store] and to *La Chute d'un ange* [The fall of an angel].[15] I repeat that the distinctive feature of works such as *Sens plastique II* is not only that they promote a novel truth by endowing it with all the force of attraction available to genius, but also that they highlight and instantly bring to the fore the *perfect* instance of a specific way of reacting to the spectacle of the world, when its significance had generally been underestimated and little effort had been made to connect its successive points of reference.

It is remarkable and highly significant that Malcolm de Chazal should incarnate and highlight a spiritual torment and a shift in direction that have steadily become more acute and more demanding over the past few years. Whether he knows it or not, his voice serves as a vehicle for a number of works that had long been stifled and that now *reappear* and demand to be heard. It has been rightly observed that the dominant one in the chorus is that of Swedenborg, which Balzac and Baudelaire had been able to hear but which, of course, could no longer reach Valéry, who had a book by Voltaire open on his deathbed. (I am saying this because to consent, at the request of the publisher, to present someone like Swedenborg in a sleight-of-hand preface is wrong; I would say the same if we were talking about Sade or Saint John of the Cross.) But, on the tiers of the mind, nothing can prevent this voice from provoking a series of *responses* with which it eventually blends. At stake is the gift of life and the tremendous efforts that have been put forth in order to discover what that gift was made of. A shameful veil of silence has been drawn over this endeavor that today is seeking redress, and, in any case, the need for that redress is *in the air*. No, with very few exceptions, we are not interested in those "great men" you are presenting to us. Their shadow only spreads over a tiny part of the world that we *recognize* as ours. It is high time you realize what you have done along the way with the major interrogation of mankind. How can you hand us those corny pictures depicting the tedious saga of your kings and the even more insipid tribulations of your wretched Sorbonne? Enough elementary history, what are you hiding from us? Gnosticism, badly misunderstood, is still today such a catchall word. Let us not even go so far back; you have decided to make us cry over André Chénier's fate: we don't care. What would interest us in that same period is to know where Martinez de Pasqually was coming from and where he was going. Even closer to our time, we hear you dwelling at length on Renan: why do you keep silent about Saint-Yves d'Alveydre?

Enough flimflam. It is desperately urgent to bring man back to a higher level of awareness of his destiny. The great poets, in touch—though they often had no inkling of this—with the *unknown superiors* (in the extended meaning of the word), some of whose names I have mentioned, have continually proclaimed this for the past hundred years.

The *Dictionnaire des idées reçues* [*Dictionary of Accepted Ideas*], which Flaubert was unable to complete, would have been even better if someone like Raymond Queneau, who has just brought out a new edition of it, had seen it through. Before making it available to the general public, it would have been a good idea to append to it a substantial excerpt from *Moeurs des diurnales* [Mores of the journalists], a new edition of which has also just come out.[16] Here is a book that deserves the best binding imaginable—a paving of leather heels.

Antibes, February 1948

Thirty

Years

Later

A peak, unquestionably the highest and most radiant one I have reached in my dreams—alas, at increasingly longer intervals—emerges from the unexpected revelation that Jacques Vaché is not dead, although everything led us to believe he was. Suddenly I hear from him or he materializes out of nowhere, shows himself in a doorway, uses some sort of all-powerful password that instantly dispels any doubt about his identity. And the resources of his dark gaiety at which I used to marvel and that had such a great impact on me are at once shared between us in all their profusion: he nips my questions in the bud before I even have time to phrase them: I am the one who is prompted to withdraw them on account of their *naïveté*. I, of course, am the only one who is moved (or who cannot manage to conceal his emotions). Even without his asking, I grant him that his leaving had been much too simple to be real (final), that all probabilities indeed favored his return. I am instantly in connivance with him: at the first knowing look, I enter his world of stratagems. Besides, it is understood that he is going to leave again: "In the present circumstances, you will concede, my dearfellow-dearfellow . . ." I think he carries a very light overnight case. The cut and color of his clothes seem meant to inspire silent complicity all around him. With great panache, he sports a *duster* folded over his arm. I feel a boundless gratitude toward him for having revealed his identity to me alone (it is taken for granted, of course, that I will not utter a word about it!). What happened to him, to me from 1918 to this day, is almost immaterial— we will have plenty of time to talk about it later. The main thing is that we have reestablished contact, that the *amusing* misunderstanding has been cleared up: there is an almost tacit agreement between us that we will meet again. But he has no sooner turned his back than a feeling of anguish grips me: I do not even have an address at which to reach him, I am waiting on his pleasure—he's abandoned me to *evasiveness*.

A strange presence, broken by interminable disappearances, a nonetheless enduring presence enjoyed by none of the other individuals who have vanished from my life, whatever prestige they had in my eyes. Without even recalling Nantes, from which at this distance in time I am alienated by certain itineraries magnetized by a magnet that, since then, has lost its poles, or by those sand mounds that must still flank the Ourcq Canal and in the shade of which Jacques Vaché's face fades at certain times like that of the sphinx, I have felt that presence, in flashes, while being fully awake this time, in many out-of-the-way places where I went for reasons completely unrelated to it. Only recently, in the middle of the Nevada desert (my wife and friends were with me), a bar standing among ruins was tended by a man surrounded by an astounding array of bottles and a whole set of girlie pinups; bare-chested, with the same corpulence as the figure in *Cerveau de l'enfant* [*Brain of the Child*] by Chirico, he told us he was more than eighty years old (he produced his birth certificate as proof) although he looked thirty years younger, precisely those thirty years he had spent in this lonely place. The hammock he used for sleeping hung from the ceiling. He contended that he had been sick when he had first arrived there and that he had cured and "preserved" himself in that shape by taking large doses of living ants, a glassful of which sparkled enticingly on the next table. There was something quite disturbing about that somewhat giddy character. No matter: even though he said that at that moment like at any other time he was alone, everything seemed ready, all the circumstances were right for Jacques Vaché to enter, coming from *inside*, from the back rooms, rather than from outside. He would not have changed since 1918.

I vainly try to sort out, as now, for instance, when a new edition of these *Lettres* [Letters] is coming out,[1] what is subjective and what is objective about the emotion that binds me to them. I acknowledged that ambiguity clearly enough when I made the remark long ago that "Jacques Vaché is surrealist in me." One must credit the timbre of certain voices and the extreme subtlety of certain attitudes with great power indeed if one is to assume that they could cross without a struggle the demarcation line that separates the private account—he who signed these letters did not intend anything else—from the public account! And even more so if, meanwhile, the return—with some different characteristics—of the events that prompted him to write them brought into play a whole new range of human reactions! In order for such obstacles to be overcome, an exemplary quick-wittedness, combined with an exceptionally rigorous style—even when writing about private matters— must undoubtedly be needed to create a *precipitate* like "umor," understood the way Jacques Vaché meant it, which does seem the result par excellence of the fusion of exacerbation and pithiness. It is definitely a question of *tone* that alone can explain the indelible impression left by the more compelling passages in these letters on select readers, shielded from all contagion and who often had almost no biographical information on the author.

In their book *Maldoror*, Marcel Jean and Arpad Mezei were the first investigators to uncover one of the major black booby traps of umor: "Jacques Vaché himself had wondered: 'Why does an alarm clock have so much umor?' The answer could be that it is because this mechanism *disrupts both systems at once, the conscious and the unconscious,* abruptly interrupting sleep and dreams, propelling the individual into waking life, while an obsessive *musical* sound goes on and on; at that point, there is no longer, in the unfortunate victim, any convergence or divergence but a totally perturbed psychological state, akin to emptiness, that takes much longer to dissipate than is commonly assumed by those who make the big mistake of using that instrument." Circumstances today are such that this state of inorganic instability goes round the clock. This cannot fail to promote to the highest rank, in terms of restorative care and first aid, these rare concentrates of total resistance that are the letters of Jacques Vaché, known as *Lettres de guerre* [War letters], and *Les Jours et les nuits* [Days and nights], the diary of a deserter, by Alfred Jarry, which have retained all their potency as antidotes.

Caught

in the

Act

Like a traveler who casts a backward glance
At the blue horizons he left in the morning

I tend to combine in my most recent memory two very distinct representations whose only common denominator is the agitation they both aroused
in me within a few days of each other. The first of these representations
is linked to the circumstances that, over the last few weeks, have turned a
spotlight on Rimbaud's work and made us look at it from another angle
(it remains to be seen to what extent this is justified). The second representation is the one I owe to the revelation of certain "Mayan" sites during
a lecture illustrated with color slides and delivered at the Ecole du Louvre
by Mr. Giles G. Healey, who recently discovered the admirable frescoes
decorating the temple of Bonampak in the state of Chiapas.

There is no doubt that the combination of my emotional reactions to
these two events was brought about by a fortuitous incident. What happened
is that, on the morning of 19 May, when I went to see M. Henri Matarasso,
who had offered to let me consult the so-called *La Chasse spirituelle* that
had just come out of the bindery (following a conversation we had had
the day before, during which Rimbaud was mentioned, since, after reading
the extracts quoted in the literary page of *Combat*, I had felt compelled to
phone and tell him that the text was forgery), there was only one person
sitting in the bookstore and he just happened to be leafing through a copy

About the apocryphal *La Chasse spirituelle* [Spiritual chase] attributed to Rimbaud.

of the book. That man to whom I was introduced was none other than Mr. Healey. Although the "few sentences" quoted in *Combat* had left no doubt in my mind, I could not refrain from pointing out to him the new and varied "impossibilities" that I discovered line after line through my perusal. It gave me some satisfaction to see him give up the idea, after he heard me, of the "long article" he had in mind, and he invited me to attend his lecture, which he was to give two weeks later. As everybody knows, those two weeks, on the literary scene, were entirely dominated by what has been called "the battle of *La Chasse spirituelle*," and by 1 June, those who had upheld the authenticity of that preposterous text were completely routed.

I now think back on the outstanding slides illustrating that lecture, thanks to which we were able to witness Mr. Healey's progress through completely unknown territory. The quality of the images was such that we found ourselves transported into that territory and that, setting aside the strain and the danger of that exploration, we embraced only the fortune by which it had been favored throughout. For that matter, all those monuments scattered far apart throughout the jungle, and whose trace was lost to whites until he came along, tended to fuse in my memory, to condense around a single one that had an elective appeal, no doubt because of its unique appearance. I do not know how the rest of the audience reacted, but my own exaltation focused, two or three days later, on a white temple with four archways, the way it appeared in that "shot": barely emerging from the heavy vegetation that concealed it and that, freshly cut, had given the whole foreground a glossy finish that stood in magnetic contrast against the matte tropical sky. I can still see the Indian guide enigmatically leaning with his back against that "ruin" that, at the very moment it reveals itself, outshines everything that can be built before our eyes in terms of freshness. The time has come when the uninitiated—Mr. Healey, each one of us—is going to step inside, when lit by sharp beams on sunlight, the interior of the edifice is going to reveal to the explorer the splendid Mayan statuettes that, when seen in full daylight, will almost appear to be barely more flesh than clay. I dwell on that moment that seems crucial to me: until then, those marvels were inaccessible to us but not to the Indian, who still knew how to find his way to them. This path leading to the hidden temples is not only the one opened up—for a brief moment—by his progress through the tall grass. It is also a "spiritual" path, the reality of which is attested by the presence, in the dwellings of all Lacandon Indians, of those ceremonial cups, one of which contains a small pre-Columbian jade god that comes from one of those temples, or, failing this, a substitute for that god. However much this ancestral worship may have degenerated since the Conquest, everything leads us to believe that the secret of that worship is not completely lost to the local Indians. A secret that is deep and to a large extent impenetrable since it is based on the persistence of faith. No external attempt at elucidating such a faith can possibly prevail against it, nor can it make up for the lack of a direct experience of a ceremony or the lack of direct contact with a plastic work of art engendered by that faith. All one can do, *from the outside*, is imperatively promote the right to search for knowledge—once again, a very relative kind of knowledge—or, and this seems to me definitely more fruitful, to foster one's ability to appreciate beauty in all its guises.

Beauty, in this respect, is the great refuge. An island where all possible enticements use their powers of fascination, but a devilishly floating island, indeed, whose course has not been plotted on any map. Most of those who talk about it only know it by hearsay. Many of those who claim to have landed on it were mistaken: how could they have hauled themselves onto it with all their luggage, including a bookish "sense of appreciation" whose weight alone is almost crushing? They think they have gone through the looking glass when in fact they have run into a row of parrots.

Nothing can remedy the lack or the loss of the sense of beauty when faced with a natural wonder or a human creation. Beauty alone can attune us to that which transcends our understanding—a butterfly's wing, the starry sky—and it alone can instantly bridge the gap between that which appeals to us today and that which may have attracted a human being similar to us hundreds or thousands of years ago.

Even though I know he is a hunter, that he will do anything if you promise him a gun and some ammunition, I am puzzled by that Indian who guides a foreigner toward the sanctuary for the first time. However well-intentioned Mr. Healey may be, once his discovery is published (and how could a man keep it to himself?), he will not be able to prevent scientific missions from taking possession of those sites that have remained inviolate until now or American planes from disgorging hordes of congenitally blasé tourists. A wind of disillusionment is crawling along the bottom of the picture; sooner or later the frescoes of Bonampak will have to put up with a patient, endless stream of gawkers. The easily transportable ceramics, which—like fruit on a tree—appear downy on the screen, will go moldy in museums unless, in defiance of all that should have forever dignified them, they have become, on the basis of the cynical compromise reached by sellers and buyers (who almost resell them), pure and simple international commodities.

There is not much difference between the fate that is in store for those objects and the one reserved for a small numbers of works from a far less distant past, quite precisely those to which modern sensibility attaches the greatest value. It is probably not by chance that those works enjoy an exceptional *aura*; they are such that they give a free rein to interpretation. This *aura* is quite similar to the intangibles sparkling around the beautiful pre-Columbian objects that are being dug out. It protects the former no better than the latter from rough handling and sordid greed. There are eyes for which this *aura* will never dissipate, but too many. Whether the fanatics of interpretation like it or not, those who are endowed with such eyes know that any speculation about a work of art is more or less futile if it fails to reveal anything about the heart of the matter: namely, the secret of the attraction exerted by that work. This is what M. Sartre did not understand at all when he set his mind to present us with his "Baudelaire." The virtue of a work at best only appears subsidiarily in the more or less learned exegeses to which it gives rise: it resides mainly in the passionate allegiance *directly* given to it by an ever increasing number of young minds. What matters, I believe, above anything else, is that crucial moment of the *approach*, when life, as it was conceived until then, takes on a new meaning, is abruptly revealed in a new light. Knowledge per se, or at least analytical knowledge, counts for little in those novel pleasures that provoke such devotion in return. At the outset, the point is not to understand but to *love*. Or at least all the gaps in comprehension do not matter, assuming they are not in fact desirable, so that the vibrations of the heart may flow through that comprehension unhindered, like clearings in the woods.

I am not advocating unintelligibility. I am simply saying that our need to understand is limited, as is everything else about us, if only by the effort it requires. Furtive gaps, turbid depths may be necessary for the re-creation of receptive faculties strained to the limit. There may also exist in the human unconscious a tendency to honor people and things in inverse ratio to their proximity, spatial or otherwise: thus the Hopi Indians of Arizona, who treat familiar animals like dogs and donkeys quite roughly, place the rattlesnake at the center of the sacred; thus the surrealist bestiary gives pride of place, above all other species, to animals that are sui generis and have an aberrant or decadent appearance such as the platypus, the praying mantis, or the anteater. Finally, there is always a corner of the veil one is expressly enjoined from lifting; no matter what dimwits may think, this is the indispensable condition of enchantment.

You will never really know[1]
the
Mayas

these are the words—themselves somewhat cryptic—that conclude the "Lettre-océan" [Ocean-letter] by Guillaume Apollinaire. They allow for the share of enigma in the emotion that a work of art affords us, a share in which, like it or not, we must recognize the lion's share—in this case, the lion-man or eagle-woman—the sphinx's share.

We could say just as well—with the same touch of regret alleviated by the obscure sense that, of necessity, the night alone can beget the day and that darkness cannot yield everything to light without causing it to die out—we could say to whoever looks into his work and his life with a view to exhaust their meaning: *You will never really know Rimbaud.*

M. Pierre Petitfils, in his recently published book, *L'Oeuvre et le visage d'Arthur Rimbaud* [The works and the face of Arthur Rimbaud], remarks that the surrealists "have been so systematically reticent in their worship [of Rimbaud] that they refuse to regard him as an individual of flesh and blood. By conjuring him away," he adds, "they made a god out of him, since to remain hidden is the nature of divinity." If "conjuring trick" there is, it is in no way an intentional one. I myself have dwelled as little as possible on the reasons why Rimbaud gave up poetry, not because I was not interested, far from it, in those reasons but because it had become almost impossible to unravel them on the basis of obviously biased accounts (Berrichon-Claudel). Ever since the discovery by M. Léon Losseau of the first printing of *Une saison en enfer* [*A Season in Hell*], which Rimbaud was thought to have destroyed, and even more so since M. Henri de Bouillane de Lacoste endeavored to prove in his dissertation that this work had been written prior to *Les Illuminations* [*Illuminations*], it has become obvious how circumspect one should be in this regard. No biography of a genius should be taken at its face value unless it can be cross-checked—especially if it has been written by relatives whose main concern was to turn it into a hagiography. Given such erroneous bases, let us congratulate ourselves on having refrained from too many conjectures.

Am I to blame (I am certainly not the one least affected) if several of those individuals who have provided us with our best reasons for being and acting present themselves with their faces completely veiled—Sade, Lautréamont—or barely uncovered—Rimbaud, Nouveau, Jarry, Roussel, Vaché, Chirico, Duchamp, Artaud? Let us concede that their life experiences, those we can more or less successfully retrace, are of little interest compared to their message, and their contribution to its decipherment is insignificant. This may be precisely what draws us to them. A new myth stems from them; its peculiarity is that it effaces their physical self or makes it uncertain. To verify the existence of this myth and to conclude that it is viable one only needs to observe the speed at which it is spreading. Willingly or not, almost all the critical speculations of today are focusing on it even before the various currents of thought from which it proceeds have had time to harmonize.

This myth was originally based on the belief that something lay beyond literature and art, and, according to Félix Fénéon, Rimbaud is the one who broke down the door leading to that "beyond." Thus it is not surprising that, as soon as the subsequent transformations of this myth are discussed, Rimbaud's work and attitude remain the primary focal point and arouse increasingly numerous controversies that, if nothing else, contribute to its reinforcement.

The *sacred* in Rimbaud's message has been underscored for quite awhile, as witness a poem such as "Loeti et errabundi" or the title of a collection such as *Reliquaire* [Reliquary]. I was merely following that tradition in 1942, when I made room for the "myth of Rimbaud" in the section entitled "De la survivance de certains mythes et de quelques autres mythes en croissance ou en formation" [Of the survival of certain myths and of some other growing or evolving myths], which was inserted in *First Papers of Surrealism*, and again in 1947, when, as my personal contribution to the International Surrealist Exhibition, I chose to set up an "altar dedicated to one of the most mysterious female figures encountered in *Les Illuminations*, Léonie Aubois d'Ashby.

I think I have made it clear enough by now how the work of someone like Rimbaud fares no differently than a Mayan work of art. Similar human categories are destined to gravitate around them. The Indians, who persist in their worship, are the only ones still to hold the spirit of the message in reverence, even if its immediate meaning partially eludes them. Moreover, they alone still attempt to behave, as best they can, in conformity with it. They are in the same position as those for whom, in their youth, the discovery of Rimbaud has been the *turning point* (their devotion may have waned at times—as with the Indians—but the embers are still smoldering and only by willfully demeaning themselves in their own eyes would they cease to acknowledge that smoldering fire; only then would it fail to set their hearts ablaze if someone threatened to take it away from them). Behind them, almost the same kind of adepts of scientism appear with devices for detecting everything, except precisely what matters to us: that which sets off the fusion of the mind and the heart in a verbal or a plastic mold that proves to be, from some angle, electively appropriate to it. (I once asked one of them what his impressions had been upon landing, when he saw the monumental statues of Easter Island: he replied that he had been careful to avoid going to see them before his third week on the island so that he could be sure he would not fall prey to any emotion. Is there any doubt that such an "intellectual" approach is anything other than a delusion and a wretched shame!) Following in their tracks comes the swarm of gawkers, a real lava flow (I remember watching in Mexico those clusters of American tourists driven only by publicity who, having had their fill of "murals," came by bus to try and see Rivera *eating* through the hedge of "candle" cacti). Not to mention the "art dealers," intent on making a living at the expense of those tourist and whose major talent consists in being able to probe a pocket seemingly worth their while and, for their own benefit, to bring it to empty itself out of sheer concession to snobbery. (Charles Fourier came too early to stigmatize this particular riffraff, thanks to whom there is nowadays virtually no painting or valuable book in the possession of anyone who might enjoy it for what it is and not for the entirely conventional repute in which it is held, or simply for its monetary value. There is no dearth of wrongly called independent painters who today abet this traffic, thus breaking with the tradition of all their immediate precursors—Gauguin, Van Gogh, Seurat, Rousseau. In the store next to the one that retails "up-to-date" modern painting [this alone says it all], the autograph dealer's gall has become such that not only can any private letter be handed over to the first ill-intentioned character that comes along, but also documents of tremendous significance for the history of ideas are deliberately made inaccessible to researchers, since the decision whether or not to divulge them is left to whoever was able to afford them.) It would be nice if my enumeration could end at this point, but this would mean ignoring the fact that the relationship we have just seen being established between the gawkers and the dealers inevitably begets the forgers.

Picasso, who—in conversation—rather enjoys this kind of jest, once assured me that one criterion prevailed in the decision he was quite often led to render with respect to paintings presumed to be his and that he was called upon to authenticate. What he said was that he would accept the authorship of those paintings or discard them according to whether or not they appealed to him. I do not deny that humor plays a role in such a remark and that, moreover, it is quite likely that this method, as long as Picasso alone applies it, and applies it to his own work, does not entail any great mistake in attribution. Nonetheless, it is unpleasantly apt to embolden all kinds of unscrupulous middlemen. Nothing can change the fact that we are wronged each time we are confronted with a forgery. Even if the abuse of confidence lasts only a second, innocence has been injured—the innocence without which no communion with the work of art is possible and that deserts us as soon as a trap is suspected.

One can deplore, with regard for the *health* of the spirit, the fact that Picasso—who denies that *La Bohémienne endormie* [*The Sleeping Gypsy*] exhibited under the name of Henri Rousseau at the Museum of Modern Art in New York is authentic, and who states that he knows who painted it and that he saw the successive stages of the painting—has failed to take steps to put an end to that imposture. It might have spared us some misgivings when we look at a painting like *Les Horreurs de la guerre* [*War*] attributed to the same artist and recently acquired by the Louvre, a painting in which I still cannot recognize his style, although its composition bears undeniable similarities with the lithograph by Rousseau reproduced in *L'Ymagier*.

By a piquant irony of fate, in the same issue of the newspaper in which M. Pascal Pia (who signed the introduction to the apocryphal text purported to be *La Chasse spirituelle*) shot off his perfectly empty last cartridges,[2] an article by Mr. Frank Elgar proclaimed the impossibility of "fabricating" masterpieces. It is true that his research had been limited to painting and mainly emphasized the conclusive character of laboratory testing as applied to works of doubtful origin. That article, a decidedly optimistic one, was not for all that completely reassuring, since the checking method proposed is a last resort and is only used to authenticate paintings that have considerable market value. One is nonetheless appalled when recollecting a particular exhibition held in Paris in June 1946, in which twenty-three out of the twenty-six paintings presented were forged (I got this information from the very individual who produced them), especially from the moment when one knows that the artist who had been wronged, or rather the pathetic puppet he has become—he is long past caring about such trifles—agreed for an "honest" compensation to withdraw his complaint so that the scandal could be hushed up and even went so far as to certify in writing that he was the actual creator of paintings that had in fact been copied by the dozen after his own style.

This is a really good story, the one of this painter and of his plagiarist whose interests, at first conflicting in the extreme, are soon reconciled and who, through the agency of some swindlers, without their having to know each other, finally become as thick as thieves at the expense of the suckers. The only reason the affair of *La Chasse spirituelle* seems more complex at the moment is that part of it still remains hidden from our sight. But we will not have to wait too long: we will force it to come to light, not by stressing the total intellectual incompetence of those who dared to place the name of Rimbaud before a text unworthy of him on the level of form as well as of content—what am I saying?—a text that should trigger an immediate protest, but by urging less discretion on those who were quite evidently to profit from this whole deal.

At the moment, those compromised to various degrees are

1. *the board of Mercure de France,*
2. *M. Maurice Nadeau,*
3. *M. Maurice Saillet,*
4. *M. Pascal Pia*

(discounting stooges).

As can be seen, I have deliberately omitted the avowed authors of the pastiche. Whether this pastiche is good or bad, the reasons that prompted them to write it are acceptable: we know that their intention was to take revenge for the disingenuous criticisms leveled at them when they took part in a performance adapted from *Une saison en enfer*. It would be in bad taste for us to quibble with them over the means that they found most expedient to achieve this, all the more so since it served its purpose and, in terms of effectiveness, went even farther. It is thanks to them that we hear that salubrious wind blow. Their alarm at the proportions the venture was taking on and the clarification the hastened to provide are to their credit in any event.

What is intolerable really begins only from the moment when the pastiche is printed and put on sale, that is, when at least unwitting fraud is committed. Those actually responsible should not be allowed any prevarication. None of them should be considered clear of their antecedents. We will not fail to point out the psychological defects *where they belong*. This must be done in order to put the most guilty among them out of action.

1. *The board of Mercure de France*: everyone concurs in deploring the unbelievable irresponsibility with which a publishing house that brought out Rimbaud's works many a time managed, without any guarantee whatsoever, to present to us under Rimbaud's name a text that is in every respect indefensible. During one of the finest rounds of blather I have ever heard on the radio (the debate of 21 May during the Tribune de Paris broadcast), when the issue of authenticity came up, M. André Chamson was heard singing the praises of Mercure as "the most honest, well-balanced publisher" and pointing out that this was a publishing firm whose "material bases" alone would preclude any possibility of a "fencing operation,," while M. André Maurois, committing himself as little as possible, confined himself to this comment: "It is only the signature that makes a text such as this valuable" (one can see what this leads to in the present case). M. Stanislas Fumet was the only one who dared express doubts based on the substance of the text. After a statement made by M. Pascal Pia (I will get back to it later on), to which he did not pay enough attention, M. Claude Mauriac aptly remarked that the persistent uncertainty about such a matter "affects criticism in its very existence" (be that as it may, criticism came out of the discussion started that evening in a fairly sorry condition).

Thus, for lack of "pro" or "con" arguments of a different order, which we had a right to expect from such personalities, it all came down for some of them to the name of a publishing house. This shows that by printing its caduceus on that fraudulent cover Mercure has staked nothing less than its reputation.

We have not given up the hope of knowing which "authorities" thought they could guarantee a previously unpublished text of such importance simply after seeing typewritten pages, the provenance of which no one cared to question (I will not go so far as to assume that the jubilation evinced by MM. Nadeau and Saillet was considered proof enough, even after it was taken under the kindly protection of such an expert as M. Pia). We are told that M. Georges Duhamel's enthusiasm smothered all thoughts of conducting an inquiry: is that true? It is at least plausible and well in keeping with the poetical discernment that can be attributed to him ever since his unspeakable review of *Alcools*, about 1913, in a *Mercure* that, aside from that, was much less unworthy of its early ideals than is the present one.

It seems that the rejuvenating treatment, a rather belated one actually, to which the firm of the rue de Condé has been subjecting itself since the end of the last war has led to increasingly unfortunate excesses. The money from the sale of 3,310 copies of a forgery, of which 310 are deluxe, is burning a few fingers right now. It is not enough to state today that the royalties have been set aside for later distributions when the situation is clarified,[3] nor to offer them to the authors of the pastiche (who are said to have seen fit to decline the offer). What happens to what is left of the profits made? Perhaps the clientele of Mercure would like to be reassured on this point? Does the board realize this, when it is rightly or wrongly rumored that it intends to publish as quickly as possible a second edition of the same text under the title "*La Chasse spirituelle* attributed to Arthur Rimbaud"—something that would permanently discredit it?[4]

2. *M. Maurice Nadeau:* everyone knows that he is the one who gave us the scoop on the forgery. In the literary section of the issue of *Combat* of 19 May 1949—a section of which he is the editor—one could read these few lines that introduced its "presentation": "It is proper that M. Pascal Pia, the first editor of Rimbaud's *Oeuvres complètes* [Complete works], whose scholarly discoveries are innumerable, should be the one who reveals to the public the existence of this previously unpublished text passed on to him as a result of several strokes of good fortune. He has agreed to present it in this column created by him, in this paper of which he was once the

editor and where everybody is his friend. We thank him wholeheartedly." Such a generous tribute to a political adversary (since M. Pia is an active member of the "Rassemblement Populaire") is not something to which we are accustomed coming from M. Nadeau, but what wouldn't a journalist do for a column of sensationalist news, at least one of the common ilk! After such a master stroke, you should see from what height of arrogance he looks down on Mme Claude-Edmonde Magny's book, *Arthur Rimbaud*, when he mentions at the bottom of the page: "We will not say anything about her essay for fear of committing a breach of chivalry and of friendship, even though her brilliant ignorance of the subject is difficult to excuse." (Meaning, you don't expect to exist compared to us and this treasure with which we are presenting the public today, do you?) The unfortunate thing is that one had to come down a peg so soon.

The haughtiness of this last quote sounds utterly laughable twenty days later, yet it is characteristic of those critics whose whole art consists in trying to convince the public that they hardly ever find anything that measures up to their standards. Those personages think it is very "chic" to assume an air of disgust when opening a "review copy" or attending a "preview." Their constant ill humor is awe-inspiring enough for them not to have to prove their *qualifications*, something a number of them would be hard put to do.

One invaluable result of the so-called affair of *La Chasse spirituelle* is that M. Nadeau—as well as M. Saillet, as we will see—has been stripped of those forbidding masks and has been proven guilty at the very least of *usurpation of authority*. I can already imagine the sardonic glance of the poets and writers whom M. Nadeau will fancy as his next "victims," assuming that they take a malicious pleasure in still reading his prose. He is going to be reminded of this escapade for a long time to come.

Those who have best known M. Nadeau in the past, and who have seen him charging at the Tarpeian Rock with disturbing stubbornness, concur in describing him as a "perverse mediocrity" who never misses an opportunity to get himself into a tricky situation. This time I think that, once and for all, he got what he asked for.

Such human specimens do not reveal their characteristics all at once. Their craft probably even requires them to feign simplicity and ingenuousness until they decide to show their hand. Since M. Nadeau forces me to recount the evolution of my personal relationship with him,[5] I will provide a summary of it. I had only met him briefly before the war, so that I had even forgotten his face when his *Histoire du surréalisme* [*The History of Surrealism*] was sent to me in New York. However mediocre this compilation, however incapable the author had been of raising the discussion above the level of anecdote, in spite of serious and inexplicable omissions that impaired a proper understanding of the overall survey, and with all due reservations about the "roguish" tone of the narration, I thought that, for want of anything better, it came at the right time and showed some measure of earnestness. It is on this latter basis that I believed I could trust its author. However, it never occurred to me, when I answered Aimé Patri's questions in *Paru* in March 1948, to include *L'Histoire du surréalisme* among those texts pertaining to the *spirit* of the movement that are worth referring to. M. Nadeau felt slighted by that omission, enough so that he straightaway opened hostilities against me. For that matter, the occasion he chose to do so is revealing enough of his character, since it was the death of Antonin Artaud[6]—who, I can prove it, virulently denied individuals of his sort any right to set us in opposition to each other.

At that juncture, having received from the Editions du Seuil the proofs of *Documents surréalistes* [Surrealist documents], which were to appear under his signature (he was the author of the foreword that comprises one *two-hundredth* of the book), I objected to a sentence in that foreword: "It [this work] would have been meaningless if I had not enjoyed the affectionate attention of André Breton" (we were to be spared the adjective when the book came out a few months later). Meanwhile, M. Nadeau had his regrets for his article in *Combat* conveyed to me (he was anxious to make amends for that "impulsive remark," etc.). I was weak enough to accept them and to utter the words needed to release him from his contrite attitude toward me. As the *Documents surréalistes* were thus able to appear without incident, he felt free to resume his wormlike activities where he had left off—these brought him, this time, right under my heel.[7]

Of course, it has long been established that "most critics talk without any discernment, knowledge, or affability, and this explains why those artists who are sensible remain indifferent to their venomous judgments."[8] It may seem pointless, under these conditions, for me to follow so closely the twists and turns of a behavior such as this one, but I think it is time to call attention to the sordid motives of certain critics. In this way, the judgments they may render will assume even less importance than they do now. Let me say in passing that M. Nadeau is strangely deluded if he thinks that such appreciations as his own, or those of his confederate at *Le Mercure de France*, can affect my well-being. If I happen to react to that sort of comment, I do so on account of those individuals alone, out of an innate distaste for hypocrisy and treachery.

In my letter of 19 May to *Combat*, I had written: "I deplore once again that the editor of that column [the literary column] could fall into such crude traps." The "once again" in connection with "crude traps," he exclaims, should be illustrated with examples.[9] There is no problem there, except for having too great a choice: if he wants to give the measure of his enlightened taste, let him dig out at random one of those panegyrics that American novels inspire him to write for *Samedi-Soir*; the measure of his professional tactfulness, the letter improperly published under the signature of M. Julien Benda, which the latter did not deign to disavow; the measure of his subtlety, not to speak of his probity, the letter attributed against all possibility to a fictitious R. P. Fougères, the original of which he was incapable of producing after its publication.[10]

Thanks to its very fast unfolding, "the affair of *La Chasse spirituelle* makes it possible to appreciate, through a few consecutive issues of *Combat*, his particular kind of shilly-shallying:

On 23 May—three days after the real authors of the pages under dispute claimed them as their own—he used intimidation: "The truth is that they have been scared by the presentation of the text in our literary column and by its publication by Mercure de France at the very moment when they realized they were going to be the instigators of a 'nasty affair' that has only just started. Dramatic new developments are no doubt to be expected. . . ."

On 24 May, he already changed his tune somewhat: "They are scared. And, according to what we know but cannot reveal, they have reason to be. . . . Could it be that they *copied* Rimbaud's text while promising the 'unknown collector' they would keep the secret? . . . They are in fact covering up for somebody or concealing something."

He remained silent on 25 May, that is to say the day after the authors of the pastiche held a "press conference" in a brasserie on the boulevard Saint-Germain.

On 26 May, while he vented his animosity against me, he began to equivocate: "I am still convinced the text is authentic. If it is a forgery or a semiforgery (a text by Rimbaud 'doctored' by those who transcribed it), enough intelligent people deem or have deemed it genuine for me to find comfort in being one of them." (We waited in vain for their names.)

He said nothing on 27 May as he waited for the meeting of the 28th during which the authors of the pastiche were to be "confronted" the next day with the three characters who in this case are acting simultaneously the parts of the deceived and the deceivers.

On 29 May, after this confrontation took place, he maintains against all the evidence that it was "inconclusive" but manages to "take a French leave": "Pascal Pia and Maurice Saillet maintain that *La Chasse* was indeed written by Rimbaud." Pascal Pia and Maurice Saillet? Where has the courageous M. Nadeau gone?

3. *M. Maurice Saillet*: in Jarry's work, which he feverishly exploits and the sole ownership of which he tries to secure, M. Saillet seems to have been mostly impressed, to the extent of wanting to model himself on them, by "certain double characters." Thus he writes under two names (Maurice Saillet and Justin Saget), and he deemed it extremely witty to have one of his characters publicly disown the other without suspecting that these two pseudo-distinct personalities would sooner or later, even in the eyes of the most nearsighted, recombine into a single identity—that of a swine.

I will let the reader be the judge of his method:

> *I know of nothing more stirring than this poem written by André Breton in his prime. With the Ode à Charles Fourier [Ode to Charles Fourier], his personality and his work—and this changing landscape of*

their "coincidence" that surrealism has been since its inception—are tri-
umphing today over a protracted skepticism.

... This book, which, by its form as well as by its content, conjures
up the image of an aerolite, does not belong only in the corner of our
libraries reserved for "rare books." It also belongs in our hearts, continually
vitalized by the swell of a great emotion as it goes, "raising its weighty
wings," toward freedom.

Justin Saget
Mercure de France,
August 1947

The Ode à Charles Fourier ... completes André Breton's image by drawing
out his similarities with the theoretician of the phalanstery. The meeting
between those two princes of Utopia ... throws into sharp relief this trait
they have in common, which could be called the genius for disproportion.
We are thinking less here of that kind of disproportion that appears in
the works of the founder of Surrealism (where one can see just as well a
molehill turning into a mountain as a mountain turning into a molehill)
than of a disproportion of the mind, in the character of the person. . . . A
druid whose bill has neither handle nor blade ... he walks straight ahead
with an unblinking gaze and tirelessly performs the rite of the mistletoe.

Maurice Saillet
Mercure de France,
1 April 1949

I think that no sensible person will be inclined to see in this an acceptable evolution. If the individual who committed those lines aims at creating an ultradynamic impression of his emotional reactions, let us deprive him of the illusion that he is fooling anybody. Although Baudelaire is the one who legitimized the right to contradict oneself, as we are rather inopportunely reminded in the introduction to the forgery published under Rimbaud's name by Mercure, no self-respecting individual would confess that right with a license to play a double game. Fortunately a lasting stigma identifies the *double agent*, the one who keeps in favor with both sides so that he can make a living by testifying either way and whose services are available, from one hour to the next, to the highest bidder. Is there, from the social viewpoint, any running sore more nauseating than this? The transfer of such a conduct to the intellectual sphere must be denounced with the utmost energy. M. Saillet's tergiversations, which he would like us to perceive as stunning changes of mind, will merely make it possible to infer his sexual preferences. M. Saillet writes his secrets on the walls of a public washroom. With him, the dihedral angle no longer conceals Dricarpe's "golden revolver" but an intellectual canker. I do not think I should be less severe toward a professional denigrator of the qualified writers of our times, one who wants to "vomit" when he reads M. Paul Eluard's poems, one who, with his eye shaped like a keyhole, tries, at the expense of M. Jean Paulhan, to entertain the other lackeys in the basement where he belongs, and who states in the last issue of *Le Mercure de France* that "we have no need of M. Francis Ponge," adding in a priceless burst of self-conceit, "let it be said once and for all."

If only M. Saillet-Saget could content himself with those identifies alone! Of course those two garish vests could never suffice to satisfy his partiality for liveries. In the now famous literary page of *Combat* of 19 May, M. Pia's "presentation" was supported, if I may put it that way, by an article entitled "the saga of *La Chasse spirituelle*, by Gabriel Gros." We were soon to learn that under this last pseudonym "a well-known critic, M. Maurice Saillet, had taken cover" (I would be curious to know why, since it did not even occur to him to wonder whether the text was authentic, M. Saillet felt the need to *take cover*).[11]

In "the affair of *La Chasse spirituelle*" M. Saillet, shielded by his protective coloring, was only implicated by name at a late date, but then, from the start, in a much more serious way than anyone else. M. Billot, a bookstore clerk, recounted the following at the press conference of 24 May: "Last May, my friend Nicolas Bataille brought me a text: he told me under the seal of secrecy that an admirer of *Une saison en enfer* had allowed him, still under the seal of secrecy, to look at that text and even to make a copy of it. Two days later, I nonetheless took the text to Maurice Saillet and told him, under the seal of secrecy, that it was the famous unpublished *Chasse spirituelle* by Rimbaud. About ten days later, Saillet informed me that the text was to be published by Mercure de France . . ."—"There is one thing still unclear," M. Benjamin Péret asked. "How did your text get from Saillet to Mercure?"—"It is M. Maurice Saillet who handed it over to M. Pascal Pia," then said M. Billot.[12]

From that moment on, M. Saillet, with no way out left to him, kept a very low profile: after requesting an obviously superfluous "arbitration," he confined himself, when answering M. André Rousseaux, to recounting the events in chronological order and contended "that the royalties of *La Chasse* have been set aside."[13] One had never seen a more complete debacle. Mercure, which, in the issue of 1 June, kept shamefully silent on the publication of the forgery, has not seen the worst of it yet with such a "poetic" editor for a publishing consultant.

If the recent events have led me to form a low opinion of M. Nadeau's courage, in M. Saillet's case, the truth is that I have long known just the sort of man he is; to be precise, ever since the day I heard of his reaction to M. Henri Pichette, about whom he had passed intolerable remarks in *Combat*, when the latter, accompanied by two friends, had gone to his den him the thrashing he deserved. Not only did he at once profusely apologize, but he had no objection to making a public apology, even if it meant devoting his next columns to just that.

Even though it appears in its simplest form, what comes out of this whole affair, from a strictly objective standpoint, is the criminal collusion there has been between MM. Nadeau and Saillet. What could they possibly have hoped to achieve by conniving with each other in that scam? I was still wondering about that only yesterday when I saw the title M. Nadeau gave to his last "article," "To call everything into question and to start from scratch"[14]: what was this sentence of mine doing there, put in quotation marks by him? Does it mean that he was hoping to weasel out of that recent tight spot by insinuating that in this case—counterfeiting Rimbaud or objecting to that forgery—it was I who had fallen short of my principle and that he was the one who had, when all is said and done, conformed to it? This very specious argument would be no less daring since it allows for the premeditation of that *coup*. If everything is to be called into question, it goes without saying that those who promote nonconformism and doubt are not the ones who must urgently come under attack. The methods used—the forgery and the skunklike spray of ink protecting the escape—would be enough to invalidate the operation and would result in the opposite of what was expected. There could not possibly be any way out in that direction.

4. *M. Pascal Pia*: in his case, we are dealing with an intellect of a very different class. With respect to his role in the affair in question, I am greatly disappointed to see him sponsoring a text that is so far beneath anything that might create an illusion. Anyone who knows anything about the publishing business of the last twenty-five to thirty years is aware that the guarantee of origin is not the main quality of the various publications that came out under his patronage. For easily understood reasons, I will naturally refrain from listing them. *Combat* tells us that his scholarly discoveries are innumerable but, for the purpose in hand, fails to mention of course that some of them are more than questionable. Indeed, M. Pascal Pia has speculated with great zeal on the craving for unpublished texts and the regret for lost manuscripts with which we are left after the demise of illustrious poets. Am I to blame if he is rumored to have had a hand in a number of those, either by padding them with writings of his own or by fabricating them entirely? One will eventually be able to distinguish what is authentic in his contribution from what is not, but this will not happen with any degree of precision as long as he is alive. Let me add that I am not fundamentally hostile to the activity to which M. Pascal Pia seems to be partial. I do not think it is a bad thing once in awhile to test the culture, the sensitivity, and the taste of certain devotees of a consecrated work—all the more vociferous as they are deaf to the unique voice flowing through it. As long as this only involves deluxe limited editions, I find it rather entertaining to see most of the bibliophiles who behave like sheep losing a few tufts of wool on those invisible barbed wires. The prospect of having a well-known forgery incorporated into "complete works" is another matter altogether, because this reduces the *value* of those works, impairs their interpretation, and lessens their effectiveness.

"May the publication of this text, which was made possible by a series of coincidences," M. Pascal Pia said in his introduction, "encourage them [those who may be in possession of the manuscript] to be less secretive from now on about their hoard of Rimbaud manuscripts."

On 21 May, that it to say the day after the authors of the pastiche came clean, he stated in a telephone interview to *Le Figaro*: "If this affair is a hoax, I have had no hand in it. . . . The text I am presenting here came to me as copy of the original, which I have known for thirty years." During the debate on the radio that took place on the evening of 21 May, he added a not insignificant rectification: "The text I am presenting here came to me as a copy of the original, *which I have known to exist* for thirty years." (In other words, he has been aware of the existence of that text but does not know its content any more than we do.)

On 23 May: "I think it may be useful to remind people that, out of the five texts by Rimbaud that have been made available to the public over the past thirty years, there are at least three (*Les Stupra* [Debaucheries], *Un coeur sous une soutane* [A heart under a cassock], and the poems included in the *Album zutique*) whose authenticity has only been acknowledged after it had been questioned. Let us wait and see . . ."[15]—"Yes," he admits for the first time on 26 May, "I got the text from Maurice Saillet."

We had to wait until 1 June to read, under M. Pascal Pia's signature, a detailed account of the affair.[16] After recounting at length the alleged tribulations of the manuscript he had never seen and, for form's sake, questioning the version given by the authors of the pastiche one last time, he got around to the sticky question: "Why a preface?": "It remains for me to state why, despite the fact that Rimbaud's manuscript was still unavailable, I agreed to write a preface to *La Chasse spirituelle*. For the simple reason that various presumptions support its authenticity: (1) The text is written in prose. (2) It comprises five parts [a fact that, according to him, fits the description supposedly included in the Carrington catalog "about 1905 or 1908." Here again there is a lack of precision]. (3) It is closer to *Une saison en enfer* than to *Les Illuminations*, whereas a hoaxer relying on the biographies of Rimbaud that *incorrectly* mention 1872 as the year when *Les Illuminations* was written would have been more inclined to draw his inspiration from the latter." I am sorry, but these are very weak arguments: (1) If *Les Illuminations* (namely, only those prose poems that M. de Bouillane de Lacoste will agree to include in a collection under this title) were thought to have been written in 1872, why would the hoaxer not have chosen to write in prose? (2) In a book published in 1947 (with which the person who wrote the pastiche is accordingly supposed to be especially familiar), *La Symbolique de Rimbaud* [Rimbaud's symbolic system] by M. Jacques Gengoux, the works of the major period (from "Bateau ivre" [Drunken ship] to *Une saison en enfer* included) are characterized as follows: "Each of those texts is divided (I do say 'is divided' because the division is indicated by marks) into five parts, to which I shall refer by the five letters (without talking as yet about what these mean) [A], [E], [I], [U], [O] in the order in which Rimbaud set the vowels in his famous sonnet." It is easy to see that, by adopting the five-part division, the authors of the pastiche were playing their hand well and that there was every chance their text would conform to the catalog description to which M. Pia referred in support of his statement. (3) One wonders why they would not have found it easier to prefigure *Une saison en enfer*, as if Rimbaud had been trying to find the tone of the latter (hence taking advantage of a ready-made explanation to justify the awkwardness of their text), rather than to "go beyond" *Les Illuminations*, most of which were believed to have been written prior to the *Saison*. It is clear that this final attempt at self-justification does not stand up to examination.

Since M. Pia alludes to those texts by Rimbaud (or attributed to him) whose publication over the last thirty years has aroused controversies, it is only proper to state who was responsible for what.

1. In June 1919, *Littérature* (the journal of which I was the editor, along with Aragon and Soupault) revealed "Les Mains de Jeanne-Marie" [Jeanne-Marie's hands]: a facsimile of the manuscript was later to appear at the beginning of the critical edition of *Poésies* (Mercure de France, 1939).

2. In May 1922, *Littérature* (I was by then its sole editor) opened with the free-form sonnet "Obscur et froncé" [Dark and puckered], until then buried in Verlaine's collection *Hombres*, and called particular attention to the two tercets, written by Rimbaud as proven by the autograph that used to be in M. G.-E. Lang's possession.

3. In February–March 1923, *Littérature*, under the title "Deux sonnets inconnus de Rimbaud" [Two unknown sonnets by Rimbaud], published

"Les Anciens animaux" [The ancient animals] and "Nos fesses" [Our butts], other free-form poems that, along with the previous sonnet, were published that same year, 1923, in a limited edition entitled *Les Stupra* and retrospectively dated 1871. The manuscripts remained undiscovered.

4. In September–October 1923, the journal *Les Feuilles Libres* presented under Rimbaud's name an allegedly hitherto unpublished sonnet, "Poison perdu" [Lost poison], which I expressly contested in a letter to *L'Intransigeant* on 20 October and in a letter to *L'Eclair* on 25 October.[17] The expert examination of the handwriting, made in 1926, established that it was not authentic.

5. In June 1924, *Littérature* published extensive excerpts from *Un coeur sous une soutane*, the complete text of which was to appear several months later with a preface by Aragon and myself. The manuscript was discovered at a later date (a facsimile can be found in Henri de Bouillane de Lacoste's *Rimbaud et le problème des Illuminations* [Rimbaud and the problem of *Illuminations*]).

6. At the beginning of February 1925, M. Marcel Coulon presented "Ce qu'on dit au poète à propos de fleurs" [What we tell the poet about flowers] and authenticated it with a facsimile of the manuscript inserted into the deluxe edition of his book, *Au coeur de Verlaine et de Rimbaud* [At the heart of Verlaine and Rimbaud].

7. During that same year, 1925, *Les Stupra* was once again published, this time in a clandestine "enlarged" edition including a "hitherto unpublished poem" entitled "La Serveuse" [The waitress] (a poem without any indication of origin and so different from Rimbaud's style that MM. Rolland de Renéville and Jules Mouquet discarded it from the *Oeuvres complètes*). It is worth mentioning that the preface to this second edition of *Les Stupra* was signed Marcelle La Pompe. "As a matter of fact," M. Jules Mouquet told me in writing, "Marcelle La Pompe is a pseudonym of Pascal Pia, as listed in the catalog of the books in print in the Bibliothèque Nationale."

8. In 1943, it fell to M. Pascal Pia to present in an original edition entitled *Poèmes* a collection of fourteen texts excerpted, he said, from the *Album zutique*. His introduction to those poems was soon to appear, marred by serious flaws. He said he had "chanced upon a whole batch of texts that came from the 'Maison de Bois,' a drinking establishment on the rue de Rennes

that disappeared long ago and where the Cercle Zutiste used to meet, that is to say Rimbaud, Verlaine, Albert Mérat, Léon Valade, Charles Cros and his brothers, Jean Richepin, Raoul Ponchon, André Gill, and the musician Cabaner." In fact, M. Petitfils, on the one hand, and MM. de Renéville and Mouquet, on the other, ascertained that the Cercle Zutiste was only formed in 1883 on Charles Cros's initiative; namely, at a time when Rimbaud, as far from those preoccupations as it is possible to be, was in Harer. Upon rectification—a significant one—MM. de Renéville and Mouquet were inclined to think that the album incorrectly named "zutique" could be none other than the *Album des vilains bonshommes* [Album of the nasty fellows], to which Verlaine alluded in a letter of 1871; but they themselves were mistaken, as M. Mouquet freely admits today when he attributes, based on the Blaizot catalog of 1936, seven texts from that collection, as well as its decorative presentation, to Germain Nouveau, who was not to meet Rimbaud before 1874 and Verlaine even later. Hence they were not familiar with the *actual* album, a fact that is rather worrisome considering they had concluded, based on their having seen facsimiles of four of them, that the fourteen texts attributed to Rimbaud were authentic. In any cause, these are of secondary interest at best, since they are parodies; the ones that capture our attention are "Lys" [Lilies] and "Les Remembrances du vieillard idiot" [Remembrances of the old idiot], which, according to M. Pia, "deserve to be inclined among Rimbaud's best works." But MM. de Renéville and Mouquet have warned us that "MM. Bonnet and Pascal Pia were the last persons to have had the album in their possession before sale held by the bookseller Blaizot on 12 March 1936," that the *Album zutique* was sold in 1940 to a collector who is now deceased, and that in spite of their efforts, it has proven "impossible for them to have another look at it and to collate Pascal Pia's text with the original." We have thus been reduced to trusting our instinct.

This is no longer the same situation as the one in which we were placed by the sonnets "Obscur et froncé" and "Nos fesses," which had also been published without an absolutely satisfactory guarantee. The existence of two sonnets that might have been those was attested by letters from Delahaye to Verlaine (1876–1877) and to Charles Morice (1884), as well as by a letter written by Vittorio Pica to the editor of *La Cravache Parisienne* (1888).[18] We know, however, that Verlaine had the opportunity to use, as epigraphs to poems included in *Parallèlement* [On a parallel line] and in *Femmes* [Women], Rimbaud's phrase "Ange ou Pource" [Angel or Swine] and the beginning of the line that read: "Nos fesses ne sont pas les leurs ..." [Our butts are not theirs ...]. These extremely original and wonderfully constructed poems could be presumed authentic on internal evidence alone, but that presumption was strengthened by the greatest number of probabilities (I do not think, for example, that a forger would have ventured to use the word *pource* as a rhyme, unless he wanted to overtax himself). I do not think their attribution can be invalidated. Only the title *Les Stupra* may be apocryphal.

I do not feel nearly as confident when it comes to "Lys" and "Les Remembrances."

LYS

O balançoire! O lys! Clysopompes d'argent!
Dédaigneux des travaux, dédaigneux des famines!
L'aurore vous emplit d'un amour détergent!
Une douceur de ciel beurre vos étamines!

[LILIES

O swing! O lilies! Silver clyster-pipes!
Disdainful of labors, disdainful of famines!
Dawn fills you up with a detergent love!
A heavenly sweetness butters your stamens!]

Already the first line is questionable. In "Ce qu'on dit au poète," the lines

Que les lilas,—ô balançoires!

.   .   .   .   .

Les lys, ces clystères d'extases!

[Only the lilac, o swings!

.   .   .   .   .

The lilies, those clysters of ecstasies!]

have a far superior "finish." *D'argent* is weak. The author seems to want to glorify the lily, thus contradicting the sentiment in "Ce qu'on dit. . . . " *Une douceur de ciel beurre* . . . is far beneath most of Rimbaud's "visual" feats. Finally, the quatrain makes very little *sense* by itself: could it be an isolated "fragment" and nothing else? Was it part of a preliminary draft of the poem dedicated to Banville? There is no other example of the switch, from one version to the other, from the Alexandrine to the octosyllabic verse.

I must confess that I find "Les Remembrances" more perplexing. Its "structure" is rich and complex, its palette is reminiscent of the one in "Les Poètes de sept ans" [The seven-year-old poets]; even better, one can almost recognize Rimbaud's unique tonality:

> *Une honte plus crue et plus calme, c'était . . .*
>
> > *. . . Oh! personne*
> *Ne fut plus fréquemment troublé, comme étonné!*

> [*A more raw and quiet shame, it was . . .*
>
> > *. . . Oh! no one*
> *Was ever more frequently disconcerted, as if surprised!*]

Yet the overall poem and especially the last few lines far from dispel all doubts. The text is a bit too prematurely "Freudian," and its ending seems to be more an excessive purple patch than a natural closure. The last four lines, filled with "disjunctions" as they are, seem particularly contrived. The last verb is vile and, to my mind, could not have been chosen as such, on account of its ineffectiveness from a lyrical standpoint.

One is tempted to regard "Les Remembrances" as a "fabricated" poem. There is nothing implausible about such an assumption, considering that a free-form work entitled *Les Silènes* [Silenes] and signed by Alfred Jarry (adapted from a play by Christian-Dietrich Grabbe) was clandestinely published in 1926. In his introduction to a new translation of that play published in 1946, M. Robert Valançay provided the following explanation about that previous version: "The introductory poem and the erotic passages with which that work is peppered do not appear in any German edition of

Grabbe. Did Jarry write them? I am inclined to believe, rather, that we owe them to the publisher, a skillful author of pastiches who added them for the purpose in hand."

If the existence of the manuscript of the genuine *La Chasse spirituelle* remains most problematical, at least the existence of the manuscript of "Lys" and of "Les Remembrances" has been established. The so-called *Album zutique* is said by some to be in the possession of M. Latécoère, by others in the possession of Picasso. The only way to settle the dispute is to get hold of it so that it can be submitted to an expert in graphology. At the same time, the sonnet entitled "Propos du cercle" [Remarks at the circle], which was communicated to *Combat* by M. Pascal Pia on 28 March 1947, should be closely examined. (One may appreciate, in passing, the extent of his generosity toward a newspaper that is no longer his, even less so since he is the editor in chief of *Carrefour*.) This sonnet, which is thought to be the product of the collaboration of fourteen authors, is remarkably disappointing. (Charles Cros's contribution in particular is far beneath him.) It is only interesting because the existence of a Cercle Zutiste in 1871 is therein explicitly mentioned by Antoine Cros, a fact that, if the sonnet is not suspect, *and only if that is the case*, would tend to authenticate the whole album.

A superficial examination of the handwriting, such as can be conducted by people who are not experts, is naturally inconclusive. When it comes to a forgery of this kind, there is every reason to expect the handwriting to have been imitated. For that matter, it is easy to be deceived even if one is in good faith: witness the publication in 1919, under the supervision of Paterne Berrichon, of forty-one poems presented as facsimiles of Rimbaud's manuscripts, ten of which, though they were gathered in a notebook, will only be recognized several years later as "copies" made by Verlaine. It is just as astounding to see M. de Bouillane de Lacoste, after the expert analysis that put an end to the "dispute over 'Poison perdu,'" reexamining the manuscript letter by letter, even though he reaches the same conclusions (let us hope that professional graphologists have more sophisticated means of verification at their disposal).

Before resorting to those laboratory methods, I think one should have exhausted the internal exegesis of a text and formed a considered opinion about whether or not its structure is consistent with the work of the author. If "Les Remembrances," in my opinion, requires additional research, it is obvious at first glance that "Poison perdu" was not written by Rimbaud and the only use of the analysis of the manuscript is to help confound the charlatans who proclaim its authenticity. The same holds true, even more so, for the fake *La Chasse spirituelle*, to which any expert on Rimbaud raises an uninterrupted series of objections at the outset. In my letter to *Combat*, I had to limit myself to only a few of those. The best proof that we are dealing with strictly objective criticism in this instance is that I found many of the objections I had to omit excellently stated by M. Jean Marcenac in *Les Lettres françaises*.[19]

In the "affair of *La Chasse spirituelle*," those accountable to public opinion, driven back into an untenable position in just a few days, were reduced to relying on the confused agitation they could stir up around the dissertation written by M. de Bouillane de Lacoste on *Rimbaud et le problème des Illuminations*, which was about to appear in print and which came as a providential diversion. "Pascal Pia," M. Nadeau told us as early as 24 May, "will no doubt find unexpected support in the dissertation that M. de Bouillane de Lacoste defended in the Sorbonne just last Saturday: *Les Illuminations* were written after *Une saison en enfer* and not prior to it as was generally believed. *La Chasse spirituelle* should thus be considered to be a preliminary draft of *Une saison en enfer*." But M. de Bouillane de Lacoste spurned those overtures and wrote to *Combat*: "I do not wish to be asked about *La Chasse spirituelle*, given that I have had no involvement in that affair." Under those conditions, M. Pia was only able to take minimal advantage of the opportunity. M. Nadeau has no other choice now but to try and find others with whom he might share his misfortune. According to him, that dissertation is apt to invalidate all previous speculations on Rimbaud. "Comic or tragic consequences: all the critics who have been talking about Rimbaud for the past fifty years seem to have been wide of the mark; famous conversions were based on a factual error; a poetic movement like surrealism, insofar as it claims to have its roots in Rimbaud's work, evolved from a misunderstanding." The stratagem is an obvious one:

since everybody was "wide of the mark," no one could blame M. Nadeau for having made a mistake, even if it was a more serious one than anybody else's.

It remains to be shown, however, that everybody was actually completely mistaken and, more particularly, that surrealism is based on an error fraught with consequences and brings back into question the very principle of its program. (I quite understand how much M. Nadeau, having just been run over by a truck, would want to spit out his venom wherever he can.) Still, such an allegation is totally groundless. The surrealist view—I call on everybody in a position to do so to bear me out—has always been that *Les Illuminations* were superior to *Une saison en enfer*. By the same token, we were always convinced that Rimbaud's technical evolution went from verse to prose, the transition occurring in the poems "Marine" [Seascape] and "Mouvement" [Motion]. The vector of this evolution matters greatly, first because it provides us with an index of Rimbaud's spiritual development, and second because, as it combined with other convergent elements (Lautréamont, Jarry), it acted as a *historical determinant* that was going to make a return to fixed forms, for instance in poetry, appear regressive (and therefore illicit). I myself have always been so unwilling to accept the idea of Rimbaud's work coming to an end, as if by "disenchantment," in 1873 that I have never ceased to attach extreme importance to the poem "Rêve" [Dream] inserted in the letter of 14 September 1875 to Delahaye[20] or to demand an explanation for its being left out of the *Oeuvres poétiques*, in which it should be included just like any other poem. If, as we have been told, "the best expert on Rimbaud in the Sorbonne, M. Jean-Marie Carré, who supervised M. de Bouillane's dissertation, did not hesitate to say that the discovery set out in that work demolishes everything that has been written on Rimbaud until now, including the book M. Carré himself published about twenty years ago,"[21] I think he is going out on a limb. One would almost think that the worth of Rimbaud's work depended only on the fact that it was completed by 1873 rather than by 1875, and this under the sole pretext that sheeplike critics are seeing the *edifying* glosses under which they have buried *Une saison en enfer* being reduced to ashes. In any case, I imagine that poets will be least affected by this chronological correction. Besides, it would be excessive to incriminate all experts on Rimbaud in this regard: without being aware of M. de Bouillane's research, M. Jacques Gengoux wrote in 1947: "This letter [of 14 September 1875], combined with that of February 1875, will make it possible to solve the well-known problem of *Les Illuminations*. The accounts of Verlaine and Delahaye are quite definite, and they were written at a time when there was absolutely no reason to concoct a story about the manuscript being handed over. Rimbaud simply took advantage of an opportunity to leave his texts with Verlaine. He could very well have written several of those after *Une saison en enfer*, given that there is absolutely nothing about the latter that might be interpreted as a farewell to literature."

It should be said that in many respects M. de Bouillane de Lacoste's study is no more authoritative than any other. While leaving it to real experts in graphology to verify his observations on the manuscripts that, along with the deductions he felt justified in drawing from them, make up his personal contribution, I am concerned by the fact that his approach to Rimbaud leaves something to be desired in terms of sympathy for the man he was and in terms of understanding his work. It is extremely disappointing to read, for instance: "This senseless way of life [the existence he led with Verlaine] turned him into a wreck in just a few months. To verify this (*sic*), it is enough to take a look at the two drawings made in London that year by Félix Régamey and reproduced in his book *Verlaine dessinateur* [Verlaine and his drawings] on pages 23 and 25. They speak for themselves. The first one shows Rimbaud slouching in a chair with drooping arms and his head on his chest like some poor stupefied wretch. . . . The other one is a sketch of Rimbaud wandering the streets with wobbly legs behind Verlaine, with an idiotic expression on his face and a pipe in his hand (*sic*). . . . This is what he had come to after a year devoted to the famous 'disordering of all the senses.' One can feel that the painter was impressed"(!). The limits of his understanding of Rimbaud's writings are made repeatedly apparent: he considers "Bruxelles" [Brussels] and "Fêtes de la faim" [Feasts of hunger] to be "raving" poems; in his opinion, in "Larme" [Tear], "poetry verges on insanity"; reading *Les Illuminations* wears him out ("One should savor them only in small doses"). Elsewhere, one is astounded to read that in *Une saison en enfer* "slang words are used alongside learned nouns" when he quotes as instances of the latter the words "idolatry, churl, sabbath, hallucinations, visionary, sleepwalker, etc." What is rather revealing about his frame of mind is this sentence, which he kept for the end of his book: "But is it really the main function of art to capture moments of vertigo?" It shows that its author was never in deep communication with Rimbaud, that he is not among those who *love* Rimbaud and who will always know more about him than those who decipher his message with a magnifying glass.

M. de Bouillane de Lacoste is not so clever that we cannot see the schoolteacher in him showing through. In his case, we are dealing with a new onslaught of the "moralizing" sort of criticism that has not done yet with using Rimbaud as a touchstone (I do not think that even the most malicious will dream of suggesting that I am bringing grist to that mill by defending the *integrity* of Rimbaud's work and by making sure that it does not get undermined or wrecked through devious means). Since M. de Bouillane is devoting himself with such perseverance to Rimbaud,[22] in spite of the fact that he is not yielding to an irresistible attraction, we have reason to wonder what could have motivated this choice on his part and to stay on our guard. It is easy enough to see what kind of interest may guide him here. His interest is above all a class interest, a "bourgeois" interest. He intends nothing less than to convince us that in London, in 1874, under the "salutary influence of Germain Nouveau, Rimbaud discovered 'music' and was introduced to art" (probably in museums). M. de Bouillane is not afraid of remarking with utter priggishness that this was "an experience of great interest, and consequently a powerful stimulus that greatly contributed to his taking up his pen again to write *Les Illuminations*." This would need no comment if, raising absurdity and provocation to a peak, he had not added: "Thus came to be realized, in a way the author may not have foreseen, this sentence from *Une saison en enfer*: 'I am now able to greet beauty.'" So, the beauty he greets is accordingly nothing other than conventional—who knows, academic?—beauty. It is in attaining that beauty that he finds the equilibrium he never had until then.

Is M. de Bouillane joking? Perhaps M. de Bouillane wants us to crown him with the champagne bucket? Between the interpretations of that sibylline sentence that have been hazarded and his own, there is indeed quite a significant gap; with him at least, nothing is gained in terms of the exaltation of the mind. From the lofty height of his superb two-arched name, does M. de Bouillane de Lacoste hope to confuse the "Bateau ivre" with a mere bauble?

Well, what can we expect from someone who maintains that in order to write the word *wasserfall* one must have spent time in Germany, and who calls it a spoof when he reads, "The bloody meat flag flying above the silky Arctic seas and flowers (they do not exist)." Such poverty of intellect, which goes beyond a basic insensitivity to any form of poetry, obviously does not make the demonstration he has in mind easier. What is intended, let us make it clear, is to have us acknowledge that *Les Illuminations* are the record of a "return to life and to health" (life and health as understood by this well-bred gentleman, that is). Thereafter, giving up poetry and getting involved in business activities should make it fairly easy to return to the fold.

For the trick to have any chance of working, M. de Bouillane would have had to come up with at least a semblance of evidence to back up such a moronic opinion. But in spite of his jollity, he cannot quite convince us that there is more exhilaration, more "euphoria" in *Les Illuminations* than in such prior poems as "Ce qu'on dit au poète." "Les Mains de Jeanne-Marie," or "Bonne pensée du matin" [Happy thought for the morning]. What is even more damaging is that, although he contends that Rimbaud, in 1874, ceased to indulge in "the intentional inconsistency of words," he himself is incapable of proposing an interpretation of the so-called difficult texts that are among the fascinating ones in the collection: "H," "Dévotion," etc. We have, therefore, good grounds for stating that everything he suggests in this regard is unwarranted.

In spite of all this, one should not a priori dismiss all of his conclusions. Until there is evidence to the contrary, some of them are no doubt worth taking into consideration, at least those that do not too far exceed the rights of chronological rectification, based on the analysis of the handwriting. But even so, nothing conclusive will be achieved in this regard as long as it has not been established that the manuscripts put forward—which show almost no deletions or alterations—are not *copies* that were made of the original at some later date.

The way Lacoste's thesis was received by the newspapers, which were unanimous in praising his "scientific," "meticulous" work, would be enough to arouse the strongest suspicions. Strictly in terms of exegesis, nothing as weak as this had ever been seen. The worst kind of priggish pedantry, serving the pathetic designs earlier mentioned, only manages here to make the most of some rudimentary notions of arithmetic. It would be comical and *we would simply dismiss the matter* if it were not to be expected that all those who pride themselves on their spurious erudition will immediately pounce on this choice morsel, and if the Decerebrating Machine, so "well trained" nowadays that it will indiscriminately obey the reactionary as well as the Stalinist commands, were not to feed on it very soon. At M. Nadeau's pressing invitation, there is still hope that, on the Stalinist side, they will grasp this opportunity (just in case) to "revise" Rimbaud's message and to take their revenge for the hand time he gave them with "Le Coeur volé" [The stolen heart] and the rest. No doubt there will be some drudge, desperate for promotion, who will argue that the "Rimbaud problem" was contrived from start to finish by the surrealists, that it is the product of their social and economic conditioning and their "refusal to face up to it," etc. (always the same old tune). This way, Rimbaud can finally be cut down to the size of a "communard" who eventually "turned out" to be more or less acceptable—for the greater Mithridatism of some.

It would be unfair not to mention one good point—quite a fortuitous one for that matter—about a study with so many flaws. Thanks to this book, at least, the researchers' attention is called to the year 1874—the year Rimbaud turned twenty, which some of us have always considered to be the key year to his thought and to his life. There is admittedly a dearth of biographical information regarding that particular year, and the handwritten pages— inconsequential in terms of content—provided by Cazals do not help us gain much insight into that span of time. All they prove is that Rimbaud spent at least the first few months in London in the company of Germain Nouveau. How is it that we have been unable to shed light on that period? In my opinion, this will not happen before we free ourselves of that deep-seated literary bias that induces us to view Rimbaud *in relation to Verlaine* and that rests on the unquestioning overestimation of the latter's importance. There is no one today, among those *to be reckoned with*, who takes the slightest interest in Verlaine's work or in his attitude (to be more exact, his work and attitude still arouse interest, but only to the extent that they relate to Rimbaud). This overestimation, which was, in my opinion, the major mistake of the symbolist generation—a mistake that the laziness of textbook authors has helped spread until this very day—is matched only by the even more deplorable, nay scandalous, underestimation of Germain Nouveau's message (it is astonishing, for instance, to see that Germain Nouveau's name does not even appear in the book entitled *Cinquantenaire du symbolisme* [Fiftieth anniversary of symbolism] and published under the patronage of the Bibliothèque Nationale in 1936, which manages, however, to dwell at length on individuals like Raynaud, Ajalbert, and Mortier!). There is no doubt Germain Nouveau was in on Rimbaud's great secret (Verlaine could never have been: he was hopelessly doomed to search for it). The selfsame Nouveau who *got up* when Rimbaud entered Tabourey's café, quite willing to wander with him to the end of the world—the end of the world turned out to be England, but the wandering went on until his death (which occurred thirty years after Rimbaud's) and may have led him, where his mind was concerned, even farther. Nouveau, who—under Rimbaud's gaze, Rimbaud whom we cannot see and whom, at that moment, he was *seeing*—copies "Villes" [Cities] and "Métropolitain" [Metropolitan]. The man who, more than anyone, proved worthy to be his friend and, even without a single word being exchanged, his mystical confidant. Will we ever know what degree of reciprocity existed in the relationship between those tow geniuses? What happened during their stay at 178 Stamford Street, Waterloo Road, remains one of the great mysteries of our time. As I go on talking about Germain Nouveau, I conjure up the wonderful poet who wrote *Savoir aimer* [Knowing how to love]: each time I happen to utter his name, I come under his spell; with delight I listen to Gregorian chant blossoming anew in his poems. Germain Nouveau who wrote that "ghost-letter," a letter dated from Algiers, 12 December 1893, and addressed to Rimbaud, who was by then *over-hidden* in his grave, a heartrending letter because it is worded as if he were still grappling, as was Germain Nouveau at the time and as we all are, with the nothingness of ordinary life only. The shining beggar by the portal in Aix. The man I could still have reached, had I hurried, while he was alive and whom I could have *embraced* (it is one of my regrets). The one who, in an idle moment, did that small painting I held in my hands a few days ago at M. Jules Mouquet's: nothing more than a cut-up apple near a clasp knife that was probably his, but the space is still filled with the cry of the fruit under the blade when one is thirsty and hungry. Rimbaud-Nouveau, Nouveau-Rimbaud: nothing will have been learned, nothing will have been discovered in terms of poetry as long as this relationship has not been elucidated, as long as the significance of the exceptional conjunction of these two "characters" and also of these two stars has not been brought out.

The following information was recently reported in the press:

Cairo, 12 June. A batch of manuscripts on papyrus dating from the third century A.D. *and written in Coptic has just been discovered in a jar, fifteen kilometers north of Luxor. They compromise a dozen thick volumes whose leather bindings are still intact. They include numerous religious treatises and sacred books used for worship by the Gnostic sect. These documents are extremely interesting in that they shed an entirely new light on the history of late paganism and early Christianity. They prove that Gnosticism was not a Christian heresy but a separate religion established throughout the Nile Valley, with its own dogmas, its own followers, and its own ritual practices, long before Christianity ever appeared. Dr. Etienne Drioton, director of the Egyptian Antiquities Department, stated in this regard: "We must now reappraise everything we thought we knew about the Coptic language. Contrary to what we had assumed, it was not the language spoken by the early Egyptians transcribed in Greek characters when it became necessary to translate the Christian Gospels. The Coptic language, with its writing borrowed from the Greeks, was in existence long before Christianity came to the Nile Valley, and it was the religious idiom of the Gnostics."*

Should it be confirmed, such a discovery—beside which the one claimed by M. de Bouillane pales into insignificance—would open up an entirely new vista to the mind, one of unprecedented scope. It is a well-known fact that the esoteric tradition, which is thought to have been handed all the way down to us, not without suffering a gradual decline and a partial deterioration over the centuries, originated with the Gnostics. (The Templars are believed to have gotten its precepts in Asia, at the time of the early crusades, from a group of remaining Manichaeans they found living there.) Bearing this in mind, one cannot help noticing that all the genuinely qualified critics of our time, without any mutual consultation whatsoever, have been led to the conclusion that those poets who have had the most lasting influence over us, those who have had the greatest impact on the modern sensibility (Hugo, Nerval, Baudelaire, Rimbaud, Lautréamont, Mallarmé, Jarry), were inspired to a greater or lesser extent by this tradition. Of course, they should not be regarded, strictly speaking, as "initiates," but all of them have at the very least felt drawn by its attraction and have never ceased to hold it in the highest regard. Better still, when they communed in complete solitude with their inner voice, without giving the least thought to this tradition, it seems they often chanced to "connect" with it, to go in the same direction along a different path. This poses a great mystery, which a few of us are still pondering. Should we subscribe to the idea that poets unknowingly draw their inspiration from depths common to all men, from a unique swamp teeming with life where the residues and the products of earlier cosmogonies ferment and recombine in an endless process largely impervious to scientific progress? This is what M. Denis Saurat suggests we do in his exceedingly thought provoking book *Les Dieux du peuple* [The gods of the common people]. His "Hyde Park ragged man" seems to know more than we do about the higher truths. *Les Textes anonymes du XXe siècle* [The twentieth-century anonymous texts], from which M. Saurat has excerpted long and extremely compelling passages, are apt to convince us that these ways of feeling, which follow their subterranean course in the mind of the underprivileged class, are continually codified, and that *expert hands keep a perfectly up-to-date record of the whole process.*

The attraction exerted by the works I have quoted (M. Denis Saurat finds echoes of that mysterious popular tradition more particularly in Spenser, Milton, Blake, and Hugo) seems due to the osmotic and parasomnambulistic kind of absorption power of those conceptions, which are considered aberrant from a rational standpoint, a power that goes hand in hand with the ability to propel them forward with a burst of fresh energy. Here, we come very near the realm of the "Mothers" glimpsed in the second *Faust*. We have to go back in time as far as possible to get some idea of the impregnations undergone by the human subconscious and to identify the most determining ones. In that virgin forest of the mind, which stretches on all sides beyond the region where man has succeeded in putting up signposts, beasts and monsters, barely less awe inspiring than in their apocalyptic roles, keep on prowling. This goes to show how anxious we may be to see Gnosticism put back in its rightful place, after it has been so long decried as a Christian heresy.

I am convinced that many a problem will thereby come to be elucidated and that, if the expected revelations do come about, we will be able to confirm the *reality* and to grasp for the first time the *nature* of those dazzling connections that have enabled M. Jules Monnerot to take in, at one and the same glance, the Gnostic approach and the surrealist approach.[23] This is, I repeat, the only angle from which Rimbaud's enterprise should be viewed. There is nothing in what links us to Rimbaud that could possibly be at the mercy of one of those latitude adjustments that from time to time warrant the publication of new maps. Deep-sea navigators will gladly take them into account, but they have not marked time waiting for them.

Appended Documents

THE "POISON PERDU" AFFAIR

I.   Letter to *L'Intransigeant* (20 October 1923)
II.   Letter to *L'Eclair* (25 October 1923)
III. The Dispute over "Poison perdu" (P. Petitfils)

THE "CHASSE SPIRITUELLE" AFFAIR

IV.   Letter to *Combat* (19 May 1949)

I.   Letter to *L'Intransigeant* (20 October 1923)

In today's *Le Courier des Treize*, I was greatly surprised to read about the discovery of a sonnet allegedly written by Rimbaud and hitherto unpublished. Irrespective of the stratagems used to deceive us, I would like to point out right now that the poem in question, which is not even a pastiche (*resté* used twice as a rhyme, the pin *comme un gross insecte* [like a big insect], five lines ending with a preterit form, *sois-moi préparée*, etc.), is one of the apocryphal texts that have seriously discredited *Reliquaire*, that collection published under Rimbaud's name with a preface by Darzens. Thus, this joke, a fairly bad one at that, is not even new, and Verlaine had already exposed it as such a long time ago. When a journal recently published a similar "previously unpublished" poem entitled "Les Internés," it was one that could be dismissed with a smile; but today, when better-intentioned people make such a mistake, it would perhaps be appropriate to call them to order.

André Breton

II.   Letter to *L'Eclair* (25 October 1923)

1. Verlaine, in a letter dated 1 November 1888, deems "Poison perdu" to be one of those poems Rimbaud wrote "late in the day": this tallies with the possibility that Rimbaud had given it to Forain in 1874. If this is the case, one would have to acknowledge that "Poison perdu" is contemporaneous with the last *Illuminations* most of the free-verse poems in that collection were written before 1873). But such a proposition is quite untenable. Rimbaud wrote no more sonnets after 1870, and we realize the full importance of this observation when we talk about a poet whose evolution, even on the level of form, is so characteristic.

2. How could M. Delahaye not have been aware of the publication of "Poison perdu" in *La Cravache* and of Verlaine's testimony when he brought out an edition of Rimbaud's *Oeuvres complètes* in 1898? I cannot believe that M. Delahaye, when he took on the responsibility of the first definitive edition of Rimbaud, did not take the trouble to leaf through *Reliquaire*, in which that poem and that testimony appear on page 147. M. Delahaye is honor bound to account for such an obvious oversight. What value can we attach to his work if he should acknowledge that he neglected his sources to such an extent? I ask M. Delahaye, since he was aware of his omission as early as 1905, why he did not find a way to rectify it in the next editions (published by Mercure de France in 1918 and quite recently by La Banderole).

3. I feel the deepest admiration for that great poet who wrote *Valentines*. I find it incredibly unfair that his work should now be ignored, but Germain Nouveau and his immense detachment will forever elude literary history. Germain Nouveau—and I believe that this is the meaning of his entire conduct—could not have cared less whether this or that was attributed to any particular individual, *himself* included.

4. I say it is impossible that Rimbaud ever wrote:

> *Et sur le balcon où le thé*
> *Se prend aux heures de la lune*
>
> .   .   .   .   .   .
>
> *Luit une épingle à tête d'or*
> *Comme un gros insecte qui dort.*
>
> [*And on the balcony where tea*
> *Is served in the moonlight*
>
> .   .   .   .   .
>
> *A pin with a golden head glows*
> *Like a big sleeping insect.*]

or that he would have replaced *Brille* [shines] with *Luit* [glows], or *Pas un souvenir* [not a single memory] with *Aucun souvenir* [no memory] as suggested by the variants presented to us. Show me anything in Rimbaud's work that might come close to such weakness of expression.

5. Why doesn't M. Forain show us the manuscript in his possession?

André Breton

III.   The Dispute over "Poison perdu"

In 1923, a heated dispute broke out over a sonnet attributed to Rimbaud and entitled "Poison perdu" that was reprinted in a journal edited by M. Marcel Raval, *Les Feuilles Libres* (September–October, p. 143).[24]

Let us recall that this sonnet, first published in *La Cravache Parisienne* on 3 November 1888, had later been included in *Reliquaire* in 1891 and in the Vanier edition in 1895. Verlaine had vouched for its authenticity in a letter to the editor of that journal (3 November 1888), but E. Delahaye has definitely excluded it from Rimbaud's work in 1898. Hence it was far from being a hitherto unpublished text.

Here is how the episodes of that dispute can be pieced together:

This joke, a fairly bad one at that, is not even new (A. Breton, in *L'Eclair* and *L'Intransigeant*, 21 October).

This sonnet is authentic: it was among Forain's papers (Marcel Raval in ibid., 22 October).

The sonnet is authentic (Ernest Raynaud, in ibid., 23 October).

After Verlaine's testimony came Germain Nouveau's, as reported by E. Delahaye. The author of *Valentines*, questioned around 1905, was convinced that "Poison perdu," which he used to enjoy singing, along with "Ophélie," was indeed written by Rimbaud (A. Lods, in *L'Eclair*, 24 October).

This argument is most questionable (A. Breton, in *L'Eclair*, 25 October).

The sonnet is authentic (Marcel Raval, in *L'Intransigeant*, 25 October).

In that case, let the manuscript be photographed! (A. Breton, in ibid., 26 October).

In 1897 I was not sure, but today I believe the sonnet to be authentic (Ernest Delahaye, in *Le Figaro*, 2 November).

Then, a letter written by Verlaine in Coulommes on 17 November 1883 was made available by Louis Barthou. In it, Verlaine voices a new opinion: he is much less positive than he was in 1883 and does not dismiss the hypothesis of a hoax (A. Lods, in *Le Figaro*, 17 November).

The sonnet is authentic; it was included among the poems by Rimbaud that Forain had entrusted some time ago to his friend Millanvoye. Moreover, M. Canqueteau's expert report concluded that it was authentic (M. Raval and J. Porel, in *Le Figaro*, 24 November). This particular article entitled "Le Point final" [The last word] was illustrated with photographic reproduction of the manuscript.

The sonnet in question was not included among those of Rimbaud's manuscripts that Forain had handed over to Millanvoye and that the latter had entrusted to me (G. Maurevert, in *Le Mercure de France*, 15 February 1924, pp. 236–246).

This is how the proofs of authenticity collapsed one after another. There remained one that was based on the handwriting. It did not stand up to the scrutiny of an expert in graphology, M. Charavay, who withdrew that document from the public sale of M. G.-E. Lang's collection in January 1926.

P. Petitfils

(*L'Oeuvre et le visage d'Arthur Rimbaud*

[Paris, Nizet, 1949])

IV.   Letter to *Combat*

Paris, 19 May 1949

Dear Sirs,

There is not a single genuine expert on Rimbaud whose shock at seeing the literary page of *Combat* this morning must not have turned almost immediately to disbelief and soon afterward to indignation. As for me, I once again find it deplorable that the editor of that page can fall into such crude traps. Indeed, one must never have understood the first thing about Rimbaud to dare maintain that the "few lines" quoted were written by him. The extreme mediocrity of expression, which the laborious attempt at pastiche is unable to mask, gives rise at the outset to the most serious doubts about the authenticity of the document. Although I did not need to do so to be clear in my own mind, I took it upon myself to get hold of the book announced under the title *La Chasse spirituelle* and I had the patience to read it. There is absolutely nothing there that could leave the slightest doubt: the consistently awkward paraphrasing of the themes as well as the characteristic wordings of Rimbaud, the total lack of spark throughout those twenty-five or so pages (and that is an understatement!)— above all, the unbearable vulgarity in "tone"—would alone stifle any desire to keep on arguing. Literary hoaxes are not always devoid of charm, and I remember, in particular, those *Poèmes libres d'Apollinaire* [Free-form poems by Apollinaire], which, though they were not written by that author, did nevertheless brilliantly mimic his style. But this time M. Pascal Pia is going too far. To look no farther that the attributive adjectives and the images used, who—among persons the least bit sensitive and knowledgeable—is going to believe that Rimbaud could have indulged in such associations as *chats griffus, mariées hypocrites, mammouths furieux* [cats with claws, hypocritical brides, furious mammoths], or that he could have been at such a loss for analogies to have been satisfied with *la tête sonore comme un coquillage géant* [the head as resounding as a giant shell], with *une terre chaude comme un oiseau* [a land as warm as a bird]? The verbs used here (*Des chansons niaises groupaient des rondes dans ma tête* [Foolish songs gathered dances in my head]), sometimes without any awareness of proper usage (*Je titube les soixante vies du cycle* [I reel the sixty lives of the cycle]), are only second, in terms of insipidity, to the representations that strive to be the height of luxury: *Je vois ans hésitation (sic) des falaises de quartz* [I see without hesitation cliffs of quartz], etc. . . . I need hardly remark that Rimbaud, such as he was in 1872—at the height of his genius—could not have experienced such serious and continual lapses without our having to give up the principle of identity.

I think that it would be a credit to *Combat* if you were to declare without delay that your good faith has been betrayed and that the book published under the title *La Chasse spirituelle* is a forgery of the most contemptible kind.

André Breton

V. A Note to André Breton

I do not think that the affair of *La Chasse spirituelle* was a "crude trap." On the other hand, I do see one in which Breton fell headlong: Pascal Pia. I am still convinced that the text is authentic. If it is a forgery or semiforgery (a text by Rimbaud "doctored" by those who transcribed it), enough intelligent people deem or have deemed it genuine for me to find comfort in being one of them. Mlle Akakia and M. Bataille have provided no evidence of the work they allegedly did in creating a pastiche, even though, as our readers may recall, I asked them in an article published in this very paper last Tuesday to produce the most simple and obvious proofs in support of their claim.

When, in connection with this "crude trap," Breton writes "once again," he should illustrate what he means with some examples. I hope he will take the trouble of listing them in an article that I will be delighted to publish in this section, of which, much to his resentment, I am the editor. Since when has he resented this? Since a particular article about his unfortunate "Poèmes," with which he was none too pleased, whereas a few months earlier he had told me he owed me one "of the greatest joys of his life." But didn't Prévert already write in 1930: "A mere critique in a newspaper is enough to make him take to his bed"?

There is therefore only one "trap" in which I acknowledge today I once got caught: the one set by that man whom I still love and admire in spite of everything, when he tried to have me believe that he was cast in a mold much different from the very common one of the "man of letters."

Maurice Nadeau
(*Combat*, 26 May 1949

VI. Letter to *Le Figaro*

Paris, 27 May 1949

I cannot understand why M. Pascal Pia would have people think that I refer to him as the author of the text improperly published under the title *La Chasse spirituelle* and that I persist in doing so after two theater performers have claimed sole responsibility for writing it.

In the letter of protest I sent to *Combat* on 19 May—the very same day the text was "revealed" in that newspaper—I merely wrote that, in terms of literary hoax, "this time M. Pascal Pia is going too far." At that particular moment M. Pascal Pia was indeed the only culprit I could implicate. Being the one who signed the introduction, he was vouching for the authenticity of the "work" he was presenting. Since that work is quite obviously a forgery, it is logical that he should be held accountable for it, particularly in view of other apocryphal books, such as those *Poèmes libres d'Apollinaire*, in the publication of which he is rumored to have had a hand. Such feats show a predilection for a rather peculiar type of activity, so peculiar that we might do well to stay on our guard when presented by M. Pascal Pia with a new "find" of his. Having said this—and allowing for the good taste and humor from which he has seldom departed—I have never for a moment assumed that he was the author of the text in question: I have kept saying all along that if it had been written by him, it would almost certainly be a better one.

In any case, this issue is no long of prime interest to those who have followed the developments of the "Rimbaud affair." Today, what really matters is to know what kinds of deals, commercial or otherwise, it took for Mercure de France to publish under Rimbaud's name 3,310 numbered copies of a text about which Jean Paulhan could objectively say that it is a sample of "modern poetry the way it is imagined to be in the most outlying provinces." Who was involved in those deals? Hoping, quite in vain, to confuse the issue, M. Nadeau tries to spread the idea that I have found an outlet for the grudge I hold against him. My retort is that in 1923, when I asserted against Forain himself, that the sonnet "Poison perdu" could not have been written by Rimbaud—something that has now been established—I was already prompted by the same loathing for imposture. It is only human for me to consider myself amply compensated for MM. Nadeau and Saillet's recent attacks against me by the blatant evidence of their utter lack of critical competence. The only thing that remains for them to try and salvage is their "respectability."

André Breton

VII.   The Rimbaud Affair Comes to a Close

The affair of *La Chasse spirituelle*, to which extensive coverage was given in *Le Figaro* and *Le Figaro Littéraire*, has just been brought to a conclusion. It ends on a happy note, since we have been told that the publisher of that famous pastiche will donate the profits from that edition to the Rimbaud Museum.

In his letter to the curator of the Charleville Museum, M. Hartmann mentions that it is "a fairly substantial amount."

Le Figaro Littéraire
2 July 1949

Oceania

Brothers who find beautiful all that comes
from afar!—Charles Baudelaire

From one period to the next, a quite observable shift in tastes induces us to
imagine the art of various lands and eras as if it were etched on a constantly
rotating sphere of which one well-localized aspect will, throughout our lives,
appeal to us more than any other. It would be useful to get some idea
of how this circling motion follows the unfolding of certain larger cycles
and meets, at the present time, such and such specific needs. Be that as
it may, writers and artists in the last third of the nineteenth century came
electively under the influence of Japanese art, whereas at the beginning of the
twentieth they turned toward an inquiry into African art. It is well known
that Impressionism accounts objectively for the first of these solicitations,
Fauvism and cubism for the second. Actually, the lack of information
regarding the provenance and original function of so-called savage objects
with which early collectors of those objects had to contend, as well as the
unmethodical way in which they brought them together, did not exclude
from their collections pieces that were fundamentally foreign to the African
continent and yet more or less assimilated to the other ones under the crude
designation of masks or "fetishes." For those collectors, it was primarily an
instinctive quest in which no hierarchy of values came into play, with the
exception of the interest for a certain nobility, of *skin* rather than blood,

Foreword to an Oceanic art exhibition held in Paris in 1948.

attested by the "patina." Picasso is probably the only one who got something else out of it: not only the driving factors of the spatial revolution that occurs in his work between 1907 and 1914, but also the secret of a dramatic apprehension of the world that has never failed him since. Between those objects, which had long been lumped together incongruously, we should note that the first indication of a choice, leaving no doubt as to its deliberate nature, appears around 1913 in Apollinaire's poetry:

> . . . you want to walk home and
> Sleep among your fetishes from Oceania and Guinea.[1]

Here the emphasis is squarely placed on Oceania taken as a whole at the expense of Africa—aside from Guinea, whose statuary does present, with that of some South Sea Islands, at least fortuitous similarities (Southern Rivers area). From that moment, the opposition between African and Oceanic art deepened, and in interested circles, which kept on growing, a contest got under way: the issue, for modern sensibility, was the establishment of the preeminence of the one over the other. Although the spectators in the stadium are in limited number, that contest is still to this very day a passionate one.

As an instance of this, two texts came out one after the other in the last few weeks: "The Oceanic mask, as revealing as the African one, as strange albeit less deep, manages at times to reach the abstract transposition of plastic elements achieved by black artists, but most often falls short,"[2] and "I only really found what I hoped for when I discovered those Oceanic fetishes that are seemingly shapeless, antiplastic at any rate, but that have a tremendous secondary potential and a sustained effectiveness precisely because of their *formal elusiveness.*"[3] As you can see, the conflict is still in full swing and the time has not yet come for arbitration.

Do not worry. I have been far too much of a *party* to this dispute to dare play the judge. A party, yes, always. What was and still is at stake as far as I am concerned is the necessity to ensure that one form of awareness of the world will prevail over another, which, in any case, I reject as such, in spite of its pretensions. The latter, in broad outline at least, could be said to correspond to the realist vision and the other one to the poetic (surrealist) vision of things. Nothing in common, once we are out of the *wood* of compromise. On one side of the barricade (in my eyes) we find the perpetual variations on the *external* appearances of man and animals, which naturally can attain to *style* through a gradual refinement of those appearances (but the themes remain weighty, material: the structure ascribable to the physical being— face, body—fertility, housework, livestock). On the other side, we find the expression of the greatest effort ever to account for the interpenetration of mind and matter, to overcome the dualism of perception and representation, not to stop at the bark but to return to the sap (and the themes are ethereal, the richest in spirituality I have ever known, also the most poignant: they lay bare the primordial fears that civilized life, or what passes as such, has masked—although they have not become any less pernicious, far from it, as a result of being repressed).

Oceania . . . this word has enjoyed a tremendous prestige in surrealism. It will have been one of the great sluices of our hearts. Not only has it been inspiring enough to hurl our reverie into the most vertiginous bankless stream, but also so many objects bearing its trademark will have supremely aroused our desires. There was a time, for some people who used to be my friends and for myself, when our trips, out of France for instance, were entirely guided by the hope to discover some rare Oceanic object for which we would hunt all day long without respite. It brought out in us a compelling need to possess that we otherwise hardly ever experienced, and, like none other, it fanned the flame of our greed: none of the things that others might list among worldly goods could hold its own beside it. I talk about this in the past tense to avoid offending anyone. I am guilty, it seems, in some people's eyes, of continuing to be moved by the resources of the primitive soul and of having recently conveyed that feeling while talking about specimens of Indian art or of the art of polar regions, for which we had a common predilection—the most narrow rationalism has nowadays attracted fresh converts: no doubt they have lost the memory and the grace of that as of the rest.

I am still as captivated by these objects as I was in my youth, when a few of us were instantly enthralled at the sight of them. The surrealist adventure, at the outset, is inseparable from the seduction, the fascination they exerted over us.

First there is the astounding diversity of the art of those islands due to the way they spread out, like the leaves of a palm tree. Only timid dotted lines between their shores attempt to account for the ancient migrations, only thin washes try to attest ethnic fusions. The world of the imagination takes advantage of this to supply its most exuberant products, which, in the eyes of the observer as well as of the native, to a great extent eclipse the real world. Never has it yielded such sumptuous flowers as when cultivated like these, in seclusion. One is tempted against all possibility to pass through them the thread from Ariadne's clew, which cannot be found on another level. Once one has been singed by the otherworldly fragrance of some of those flowers, one longs to know them all. Several of us experienced that fever: here is a *tino* from Ponape or Nokuor in the Carolines: there the nose, the eyes, the ears, the human mouth were slowly disappearing. Halfway between those islands and the Bismarck Archipelago, for instance, some will not rest until they know how the human figure was represented in the Greenwich islands. Whoever judges that he has other fish to fry has never been poetically hooked on the Oceanic mystery.

There is also the fact that the marvelous, with all it implies in terms of surprise, splendor, and dazzling outlook onto something other than what we are able to know, has never enjoyed, in visual art, the triumphs it scores with some first-rate Oceanic objects. One would wish to bring together under an auspicious light the masks of the Hawaiian war god—his fearsome mother-of-pearl eyes blazing among the feathers of the *ii*—some of the large open-work constructions from New Ireland with fish and birds teeming around the man in a trance, the most beautiful masks made of shell and bird of paradise feathers from the Torres Strait, the sea gods sprouting human beings all over from the Cook and Tubuai Islands. . . . Still dominating all those, in a garden of Sulka masks strewn with the butterfly proboscises of the Baining masks, there would stand the great mask from New Britain, its magnificence unequaled, which one can discover in the Chicago Museum— a conical mask like so many others but crowned with a large parasol on top of which a six-foot-long praying mantis, made of pink elder pith like the rest of the mask, sits like a ghost. Whoever has not stood in front of that object does not know the limits of the poetic *sublime*.

Since, however, many of those objects are large and brittle, it is highly unlikely that they will ever be brought together in one place. We must therefore be able to insert them mentally into the tapestry in order to enter into physical communication with other, more accessible ones that are worth our while. Those gathered here partake of the same sparkle as the others. For us, they fit the pattern of those *haloed* objects by which we are enthralled, and we have not done paying them the tribute they deserve. As for me, I often need to come back to them, to watch them as I am waking up, to take them in my hands, to talk to them, to escort them back to their place of origin so as to reconcile myself to where I am.

Fronton-Virage

Some works that at first baffle understanding, reckon on the repulsion or the discouragement of the common herd, and, at the same time, it should be said, on the attraction that, sooner or later, on account of their subversive, or unusual, or simply "difficult" character they cannot fail to exert on a very small number of minds *outside the norm*: theirs is the only enviable destiny. Such works, I repeat, are bound sooner or later to overshadow most of those other works that shone brightest when their authors were alive and even to make their brilliance appear transient and superficial. It all seems as if, in terms of influence over other minds, the finishing list of the speed race tended to be in reverse order to the finishing list of the endurance race; the latter being, when all is said and done, the only one worth running. It is a question of trajectory, whereby "underground and long" is the opposite of "high and short" (the way one gets to hang from the gallows).

"In terms of destiny," as the expression goes nowadays—albeit in somewhat disquieting contexts—it is puzzling to observe that those works that have been neglected for so long and that are apt to be promoted someday to the rank of *perpetual lamps* should need an elective hand to unearth them and pull them out of the grave. I have shaken some of those hands: one of them, its glove quickly taken off, quivering and displaying its arabesque

About Jean Ferry's study of Raymond Roussel. [First published in *Cahiers de la Pléiade* in 1948, this text was later used as the preface to Ferry's book *Une etude sur Raymond Roussel* (Paris: Arcanes, 1953). The title ("pediment-curve") is presumably a riddle. (Trans.)]

only on vellum, was the hand of Maurice Heine. Maurice Heine, who did not live long enough to witness the dramatic vindication of Sade against which last-minute jesuitical sophistries are of no avail. The other one, warm and sparing of gestures but, as soon as Roussel is mentioned, glimmering like one of those "fighting fish" that he likes to keep and that the proximity of a mirror is enough to drive wild, is that of Jean Ferry.

I have often wondered, with regard to such individuals ready to devote themselves heart and soul to the dissemination of a great message that has been ignored or buried—as if nothing worthwhile could exist before it is rehabilitated and proclaimed—what attributes enable them to remove the interdict and to bring this message into the open so that it may wield its rightful influence. Did the original work lack those attributes, wherefore it is a "queen" among works (the way the word applies to insects) that calls for a kind of fertilization in the more or less distant future? I cannot put this idea out of my mind when I recall Maurice Heine and when I try to account for what tied him so intimately to Sade, both in terms of similarities and of dissimilarities. That man, who definitely belonged in the eighteenth century, so lost among us; that encyclopedic culture he had, virtually the last of its kind; that unique emancipation from all prejudices; and also that impassioned heart always ready to drive the mind to the limits of human aspirations and demands (as a result, he was excluded from the Communist party by Trotsky around 1922 on account of "leftist extremism"!). And, on the other hand, that supreme discretion; and that concern for the unassailable, for the impeccable in matters of documentation, of judgment, of expression; and that gift, at which I still marvel nine years after his death, for re-creating the ultrasociable from pure unsociability in the closed vessel of his voice. What was that relationship based on? How is it that, thanks to that relationship, the torrent of Sade, cleared of its monumental impurities, could suddenly burst into a cascade of *daylight*? What was that belated, transmuting flight above it which proved capable of drawing a panacea from the most slippery of all pitcher plants?

What interplay of virtues, some common to two minds, some complementary from one of those minds to the other, is needed to achieve this! Wherein lies the secret of that double-entry maieutic, which requires an intercession of this kind so that a thought may release all its power and strike as far as possible in time? Without claiming in any way that I can resolve it, I am led to pose the question once again about the duo Raymond Roussel–Jean Ferry.

I see Roussel's world the way I perceived it before seeing it through Ferry's eyes and the way it appeared to me afterward. I did indeed perceive it at first as a complete world and one of the very few of its kind that had been offered to us in the twentieth century (by complete world, I mean a world entirely re-created by a man who is quite determined to follow only the unique bent of his own mind and to be guided only by that which he deems exceptional about his specific needs). Some great contemporary artists may have experienced that temptation, but, because of some unexplained infirmity of purpose, they have only managed to reveal to us hopelessly fragmentary aspects of that world, their own, of which we had been able to catch some glimpses: a woman and a bouquet by a window, both flooded in sunlight, or a human being, feverishly agitated and painstakingly detailed but unable nonetheless to extricate himself from the spider's web that convention spins around him, between a musical instrument and a fruit dish. With them it is impossible, or nearly so, to *see* beyond those limits. It is obvious that the exploration comes to a dead end: they merely keep on indefinitely raising the same corner of the veil. Where visual arts are concerned—with the exception of Duchamp—who can claim nowadays to have gone beyond that point, who has shown himself able to shift the sights at will until we were made to "loop the loop" of vision? Under the leadership of the others—follow the guide—one may well reach a certain altitude, but there is no panorama to be seen.

With Roussel, I knew right away that I was indeed faced with one of those complete worlds, even though I was at first (and for a long time) bedazzled by it. Jean Ferry, at one point in his study—no doubt to "give some rope" to the reader—shows himself so sure of his facts that he ventures a teasing remark about Roussel's supporters, who, struggling along as they did to keep up with him from line to line, and however little enlightened they may have been about his intentions, held out nonetheless against a raging audience during the premieres of *L'Etoile au front* [The star on the forehead] or *La Poussière de soleils* [Sun-dust]. I was one of them, and I certainly do not pretend that my own enthusiastic response to the performance was based on an immediate and completely satisfactory understanding of the text. Still, most of my friends and I had read (and reread) *Impressions d'Afrique* [*Impressions of Africa*] and *Locus Solus* [*Locus Solus*], and that was enough for us to feel that we could place our trust in the author. The reactions of the audience, despicably echoed by the articles and testimonies in the name of "public morality" that can be found at the end of Jean Ferry's book, greatly contributed to strengthen our sentiments. Besides, the deliberate use of surprise (Apollinaire) and shock (Jarry, Cravan) had long been regarded by us as the surest means of conquest. Unquestionably, from that point of view, Roussel left nothing to be desired. Finally, even without such adequate preparation, let us suppose that at age seventeen, without being in any way prepossessed, I had attended the performance of *Impressions d'Afrique*, I am convinced that I would have been able to unravel its tangled threads, just as two years earlier, without making either head or tail of it, I had let myself fall beneath the spell of one of Mallarmé's little sonnets that someone had read to me on the spur of the moment.

It is a total mistake to think that comprehension should play a major role in those pleasures that are ill defined from the outset, and this is not the first time I come into conflict with the rationalists on this issue. They seem to me so overtaken by events that it is out of sheer condescension that I feel the need, in passing, to rectify an erroneous version that may have been, and may still be given, of my behavior, presented as symptomatic, on one very particular occasion.

One evening years ago, while Roger Caillois and Dr. Jacques Lacan were at my place, a lady who had just come in set down, on a piece of furniture, a handful of those "jumping beans," which can easily—I have seen it since—be bought in New York's Chinatown shops. Those jumping beans, though they are quite real, do not seem to me—any more than my long digression—

out of place in the Rousselian world. They are little white seeds, the size of a pea, with nothing special about them at first sight. But if one just keeps looking at them, something quite unusual occurs. After a time that can vary but that can be measured in seconds, some of those seeds start making short jerky movements, completely unexpected, ranging from a slight lateral jump all the way to a complete flip. I think I can safely say that the three impartial observers gathered there, to whom nothing like it had ever been described, shared the same amazement at first. It is only after awhile, measured in minutes this time, that they recovered, each reacting according to his particular disposition. Caillois was, from then on, in favor of splitting the jumping bean open right away; Lacan wanted us to refrain from ever doing so, since what mattered was that the irrationality—at least on the surface—of this phenomenon had been enough to make us suspect our usual frame of reference; myself (I insist on this characteristic difference where I am concerned), I suggested that we should only do it after the three of us had exhausted the discussion on the *probable* cause of the movements we had witnessed (this would have required less than a few additional minutes). I still believe to this day that there is nothing obscurantist about such an attitude and I want to put an end to the story that Caillois has been telling since then, and that Etiemble has circulated: "I thought (when I met him a few years later) that the time was over when Breton, in order to preserve its magical character, would refuse to open those hopping seeds well known to Mexicans and that are indeed *animated* by an insect trapped inside."[1] This is not true. I was not at all opposed to that investigation and, if I was inclined to delay it awhile, I nonetheless considered it necessary. It is obvious that my idea of magic—as it was then and still is now—would have prevented me from wanting to "preserve" it at such little cost. We were adults, after all: all I asked for was a slightly more sizable contribution of the mind before appealing to the dull arbitration of the eyes.[2]

I have always maintained that the essential value of a certain number of poetical and other kinds of works resided in their ability to appeal to a faculty *other* than the intellect. Beauty demands that we enjoy, most often before we understand, and its links with clarity are only tenuous and secondary. Not that beauty rebels against all elucidation but it only puts up with such elucidation a posteriori and outside of itself, as it were. Nothing could be more fatal to it than instantly to attain a clear awareness of the intellectual and sensible elements it brings into play and to strive, in the process of self-manifestation, to make all its resources manifest as well.

Hegel's assertion that aesthetic pleasure depends exclusively "on the way in which the imagination represents itself and nothing but itself" calls for and heralds like no other the work of Raymond Roussel. A work free of all concessions that consents to provide a few explanations about its methods only when it has reached the end of its unfolding, that is to say just before its author *chose* to disappear.[3] Why those explanations nevertheless? Perhaps because no man, in whichever "solitary place" he may have decided, or resigned himself, to live, forgoes at the last moment—not even Sade— casting a glance over his destiny and appealing more or less pathetically against the verdict of his time to the judgment of future periods. Great spiritual testaments, over the meaning of which we are still pondering; half-black, half-phosphorescent milestones the likes of which I have seldom encountered in the countryside (but there are not that many travelers who go that way). Enacting a rather beautiful phrase, unfortunately more hackneyed than any other one, this gesture, which consists in putting into good hands, *without seeing them*, the legacy of a life that is henceforth impossible, is what used to be called "passing the torch" (where Sade is concerned, it was perhaps necessary that he be the first one to trample it underfoot in order to show that its flame would not go out).

The torch in question never fails, in any case, to go through several hands before it reaches the individual whose role it is to express and to spread all the light it contains. In this way Borel, Swinburne, Charles Henry, Duehren, Apollinaire relayed it one to the other before safely handing it on to Maurice Heine; in this way, Leiris and Brunius willingly entrust it to Jean Ferry.

For I am coming to him and I would be neglecting all my duties if I did not try, when talking about him, to point out what affinities and what dissimilarities between him and Roussel contribute to the formation of that harmonic state thanks to which it becomes possible to let the diamond glitter before the countless eyes of those who had disdained it in its gangue. One of Fourier's most inspired ideas will have been to show that the principle of the only fruitful associations consisted in a skillful well-balanced mixing of analogies and contrasts. Roussel's patience in toiling for a whole day over each line of *Nouvelles impressions d'Afrique* [New impressions of Africa]: we know this patience has outlived him, since Jean Ferry admits he tried for ten years to uncover the meaning of three of those lines. We can be thankful for the time that some individuals, *for our benefit*, accept to devote unsparingly to arduous tasks. The main thing is that *Nouvelles impressions* was finally completed and we now have a quite unassailable literal commentary of that book. But it should be clear that this ideal conjunction in an effort that allows for the same fulcrum, either as a starting point or as an end product, is possible only if there exists the rarest community of aspirations. With Roussel, with Ferry, the latter seems to be centered above all on the exorbitant need for the free, the versatile, and the *new*. In return, this need necessarily entails an exacerbated rejection of "realist" or similar conventions, expressed with the same harshness by each of them but strengthened, between them, by differences of generation and of class (in the social sense of the word). Before it was taken apart and put back together with outstanding skill under our very eyes, we would circle round Roussel's work as we would around a fascinating machine we did not know how to use. It is this machine that Jean Ferry delivers to us ready for operation.

What was probably needed to achieve this was the mediation of a kind of humor that comes from faraway places, carefully packaged to prevent staleness—a novel spice to make those marvelous otherworldly dishes that called for red salt palatable to us. What was needed was the spontaneous affirmation of a kind of partiality that can only be explained by an allergy to more or less ordinary dishes, carried to its extreme limits: Jean Ferry, in his essay on Roussel, gives vent to his aversions quite liberally. This fixation on a work persistently deemed a pure and simple extravagance by public opinion and that dim-witted critics have done everything to isolate or to expel like a foreign body from the literary account of our times, while proclaiming its lack of consistency, testifies to Ferry's irresistible vocation as a franc-tireur (one wonders what would happen without such individuals on the battlefield of the mind). What was also needed, with respect to

Roussel's work, in order to initiate reparations, the extent of which can only be conjectured at this point, was for Jean Ferry to be exceptionally gifted in two different respects, since the rara avis is born of the combination of those two kinds of talents, of their fusion in one and the same mind.

The first kind of talents includes those that are presumably required of individuals who specialize in *figures*—those personages who definitely enjoy great prestige although their anonymity and the raison d'être of their work tend to incorporate them into the world of the *Trial* rather than into the world of the *Gold-Bug*. In that area, Jean Ferry, through his interpretations of some six hundred lines of *Nouvelles impressions d'Afrique*, has ample time to give us the measure of his perspicacity. And make no mistake: the modest and casual way in which he presents them, his rapidity in jumping from one to the next, this sort of "obviously" he enjoys dropping sotto voce after each of them, should not make us forget that the major part of those interpretations constitute genuine discoveries. That, moreover, they bear the stamp of a definitive irrefutability that modern exegesis had made us forget existed. Even if some minor quibble were to be raised here or there, it could not in any way compromise the solidity of the construction. One could argue that Jean Ferry did not go beyond this impeccable version: he is the first to acknowledge this and to regret that he cannot, for the time being, take us any further. But if the riddle set by the message he studies remains unsolved, and even if, thanks to him, it becomes incomparably more urgent to solve it, future researchers will nonetheless have cause to be grateful to him for this scholarly and indispensable sketch map.

That which overqualifies Jean Ferry for his role as a pioneer are talents of a different kind that lead me to imagine his emotional universe as a place of apprehensions, of suspense, and of anxieties dominated by a star of prey, incomprehensibly subjugated (until when?), and that, for me, is identified with the most disquieting clawless-looking paw ever offered in human memory.[4] A world of superior curiosity where the big cats of boredom pace up and down behind bars neither more nor less vertical than Jean Ferry's hair, the way he wears it, and that opens only onto panic. The only source of light is a lone woman-flame—Matilda from *The Monk*, the heroine from *Le Bonheur dans le crime* [Happiness in crime]? The mind, kept in this way at the height of its excitement, seems able, in relation to another mind of its own choosing, to act as an accumulator by producing or intensifying the current of which it had run out. This, at any rate, is what we see happening between Ferry and Roussel, on a level of continuous reciprocity. This is probably possible only between minds that present striking analogies of structure and at the same time, on the level of reactions, contrasts that are sharp enough—in this instance, between a repressed anger and a radical indifference that spares only a very narrow field of interest—for the process of compensation to ensure a continuous exchange between them.

Having said this, my fingers are itching to touch the printed work of Raymond Roussel before I go back to Paris. I feel frustrated and somewhat frustrating, all the more so since the wonderful mechanical toy train that used to go round all my childhood dreams (I am still talking about the same work), due to circumstances about which the least one can say is that they were beyond my control, several years ago disappeared into a tunnel. That tunnel is far from being one of oblivion but, all the same, I would have liked, on such an occasion, to shorten the distance between Roussel and myself, the way one starts by rubbing one's eyes before raising the blind. Since there is no possibility for me to do so, I must limit myself to a few remarks in the margin of Jean Ferry's text that will deliberately focus on his contribution alone.

And yet, this is precisely the paradox: inspired as I am both by his passion for Roussel's work—which I have good reason to suppose to be a jealous one—and the dissatisfaction he expresses with his inability to give us the total interpretation at which he had aimed, I stop on the threshold of the comments I feel prompted to make for fear of antagonizing Jean Ferry, for fear of unleashing against me that severely tamed fierceness of spirit that I so like about him. God forbid that I should spoil his idol for him! I am referring to these intentionally peremptory concluding sentences: "I know now that Roussel is not at risk. He is invulnerable to bastards. He is that dazzling water ball hovering, untouchable, above the realm of birds." I have no difficulty ascertaining that the bastards, for him as for me, today as yesterday, are indeed the same ones (they may have increased in number, they may have assumed a different corporate name, but that is all). When I say that I stop, whoever knows me knows that it can only be for a moment—the time to take a deep breath. What I believe to be true (or likely) is too close to my heart for me to resign myself not to say it.

"Roussel is not at risk." Who knows, after all, whether Jean Ferry is not being too confident when he ventures such an opinion? As long as no one succeeds in forcing the last door open, in bringing out the deep meaning of the message before us—"the real one, the third one" for which Jean Ferry entreats others to search with him—it will worry me to see him stake his life on it. For that matter, I understand his position very well, since I myself have made a number of equally impulsive gestures. In the presence of certain deliberately obscure works, one dreams, upon completing their analysis, of coming into possession of a secret that owes nothing to any preexistent knowledge, whether or not such knowledge has been widely disseminated. I admit that this may betoken a messianic tendency and also that one often needs to come off one's high horse. Some twenty years ago,[5] this proven possibility of using eminent works for utterly detestable purposes induced me to turn against those very works. Since then I have had to retract that excessive judgment that would lead us to relinquish, one after the other, the values on which we have chosen to model ourselves. Today I think that the original stand we took with regard to those values must, on the contrary, be defended every inch of the way. Whatever ground we may thereby have to yield to our adversaries, I am convinced that we will draw enough strength from those values to confound and eventually to corner them. To try at all costs to shield these values from our adversaries' tactics would imply a lack of confidence in them, a refusal to get to know them better by testing their resilience, and the adoption of the most pathetic kind of pragmatic attitude.

Nothing could be more moving than the momentary fit of depression to which Jean Ferry succumbs when, having completed his already extremely fruitful research, he laments over the fact that they nevertheless have not been crowned with success. "There is probably nothing to find," he tells us like a somewhat petulant child who has been reduced to asking for the answer to a riddle. But it is true that he pulls himself together right away, as if he were talking to himself again: "How? Where should one look? What can one rely on?" At this point, I will venture not to formulate an objectively admissible hypothesis but at least to put forward a few conjectures. I hope, once again, that Jean Ferry will not see anything vexatious about them. I am well aware that, at least until further information is available, we are led here to venture onto uncertain ground and that we would be quickly swallowed up if we were to let go of the rope. But don't we have enough confidence in our intrinsic stamina to walk surefootedly?

Some will say that they could see what I was leading up to and that what remains for me to add completes a series of theses I have adopted and coordinated so as to try and formulate a law proclaiming the deep unity of the pursuits of so-called high magic and of what I am not afraid to call high poetry, as opposed to those other activities that are nothing more than conjuring tricks or dubious hocus-pocus borrowed from *Le Petit Albert* [The shorter Albert].[6] More spiteful individuals will not fail to pity me or to call it an obsession: I take no notice.

What engaged my attention first of all were those lines Jean Ferry wrote: "Most of Roussel's fictions, twisted or not by his self-imposed use of certain phonetic combinations, center on this idea: how to hide something so that it will subsequently be difficult, but not impossible, to find?" Further on he insists once more, with some evidence to support his argument: "He told us how it was done; better, he discreetly encouraged us to follow suit." Like it or not, this half-disappointing, half-engaging attitude is entirely in keeping with that of hermetic philosophers. It is not up to me to decide whether this attitude on their part is justified or not, I am merely pointing out that it is consonant with their observance of a strict discipline to which all of them conformed. Should the rest of my analysis show that Roussel may well have been in secret communication with them, Jean Ferry would have no more grounds for saying that "if *Nouvelles impressions d'Afrique* concealed a secret, Roussel would probably have revealed it to us, along with the other ones, in his literary testament." This final secret is the *only one* that, just like those other secrets, he would not have been permitted to divulge. The whole of occult literature teaches that this secret is not hidden forever: whoever is in possession of it is not only allowed but apparently obliged to pass it on: to do so, he is to plant along the way leading to it a certain number of markers, each of which requires, in order to be recognized as such, a specific qualification.

The "how to hide something . . ." that Jean Ferry attributes to Roussel inevitably entails a "why should it be hidden?" The latter question, with regard to the alchemical secret, for instance, comes up against a wall of silence. Is it really conceivable that a man not tied to any esoteric tradition should feel duty-bound to take to his grave a secret of a different kind (which, after all, would be his alone), while providing clues that seem to indicate a keen desire to have that secret uncovered? I think this would be an unprecedented case, and I cannot even fathom what mental pathology might have to say about it. Is it not more tempting to acknowledge that Roussel, being an *adept*, observes an imprescriptible ordinance? Or else that he transposes that ordinance from one sphere to another (as Rimbaud had started to do in *Alchimie du verbe* [*Alchemy of the Word*]), which would imply in any case that he had to be aware of that ordinance and thus constitutes a far less satisfactory explanation?

However risky this thesis may seem, it does not meet with any serious objection that could be based on Roussel's behavior, about which any information of any significance is strangely lacking. From my few and very brief encounters with him, the most distinct memory I retain is that of a man *hidden*. He remained that way with all of the members of our group, say between 1922 and 1928, even though one of us—Michel Leiris (whose brother, I believe, was Roussel's stockbroker)—did not lack opportunities to approach him, and another one—Robert Desnos—encouraged by Roussel's appreciation of his rejoinder during the performance of *L'Etoile au front*,[7] felt confident that he could lift the veil of secrecy with which Roussel had surrounded himself. But when he was with him, Leiris could not manage, in spite of his efforts, to divert the conversation from its banal course, and Desnos, even though he would be given a courteous welcome, would always come back from his visits discouraged. Whatever has become of Raymond Roussel's manuscripts and library, and whatever additional darkness in which his close relatives apparently wish to envelop him, one can hope that the mystery in which the greatest part of his existence is shrouded will someday be at least partially uncovered.

There is a more compelling line of argument that may buttress my theory. "His self-imposed use of certain phonetic combinations": here is something on which we should dwell at length. No musical whimsy, for sure, and even less of a concern for "spinning" words as Mallarmé would do (from that standpoint, the lines in *Nouvelles impressions* are written in the worst convoluted style ever; the logographs that used to be found in newspapers would seem a sensuous relaxation compared to them!), but, how should I say, a kind of obscure hope to set the thinking process going again by systematically compromising language, using the ambiguity residing in its very sounds to achieve this. In poetry, this is not a new temptation, and one of the greater appeals of this device is that it grates on those ears that pride themselves on being the most delicately rimmed. It was used and, it is good form to say, abused by Hugo. At the very most, in that genre, one likes to quote this distich by Charles Cros: "*Dans ces meubles laqués, rideaux et dais moroses,—Danse, aime, bleu laquais, ris d'oser des mots roses!*"[8]—much less for its intrinsic qualities than because Impressionism is fashionable. The important thing is that this family tree, whose roots are quite old, grew its main branches in the early twentieth century: those were Jean-Pierre Brisset and Raymond Roussel.[9] These two individuals who, in all probability, knew nothing of each other, aside from their extreme predilection for those phonetic combinations pointed out by Jean Ferry and the fact that both spent their entire lives being decried and derided, have in common another characteristic that I find quite thought provoking. Brisset—whose work should be reconsidered at length as soon as possible—continually refers to the seven seals of the Apocalypse, and Jean Ferry points out, without, I think, drawing from this fact the logical conclusion, that "Roussel must have loved sealed envelopes" (that is, closed with five seals—I will come back to this number 5, which may well be of some significance in Roussel's work). Could this really be the expression of Roussel's partiality for things nobiliary? I do not think so at all. I think he likes the seal for the fact of sealing (and of concealing), and that "the smartly dressed man" who is supposed to be the subject of the twenty-sixth drawing in *Nouvelles impressions* is none other than himself.

But, in spite of the extraordinary display we observe in Roussel's or in Brisset's work, the "play on words" should not, by a long shot, be viewed as an exclusively poetic device. Let us, in this connection, open a book on the esoteric tradition and see what it tells us on the subject: "During that period (the last three hundred years of the Middle Ages), the popular mind, imbued with oriental mysticism, took delight in rebuses, symbolic veils, allegorical expressions. . . . The 'hostelries' often displayed a golden lion depicted in a heraldic pose, which, to the peregrinator looking for lodgings, meant that one 'could spend the night there,' thanks to the double meaning of the image: *au lit on dort.*[10] . . . (Nowadays) one hardly notices, from time to time, that this debased art is used regularly, but most often for advertising purposes. For instance, a large modern corporation, which specialized in manufacturing sewing machines, chose an advertising poster that is now quite familiar. It shows a woman sitting in front of her machine, in the center of an imposing S. What is most prominent is the initial of the manufacturer, but the rebus is clear and its meaning transparent: *this woman sews during her pregnancy*[11]—an allusion to the machine's easy operation."[12] Midway between that sign and that poster, a newspaper recently displayed an advertisement in the form of a drawing of the Napoleon-to-be with one arm missing (*bon appartement chaud*).[13] From there to the *règles de lard* and the *taies d'eau rayées*[14] . . .

We have come to the heart of what is called *the language of birds*, "a phonetic idiom based only on assonance." It is important to note that this language is used primarily for cabalistic purposes: one resorts to it to disguise a message one wants to send to certain privileged individuals while befuddling the common run of people.[15] It is worth mentioning in passing that one of Roussel's possible sources is Cyrano de Bergerac, and particularly his *Histoire des oiseaux* [History of birds]: the apparently frequent contacts between Roussel and Rostand—who painted a gaudy and ridiculous portrait of the author of *L'Autre monde* [Voyages to the moon and the sun]—could have led him to seek answers about the hermetic Cabala from the "naked little man, sitting on a stone" whom Bergerac entrusted with the task of teaching it.

It is thus possible that Roussel's preoccupation with seals is less frivolous than Jean Ferry would have us think.

But I have saved till last, as you well imagine, an argument that seems to me far more conclusive. However, in order to follow this line of reasoning, you should already have read Jean Ferry's essay and, moreover, you should be willing to carefully reexamine the chapter entitled "La Chaîne de *La Poussière de soleils.*"[16]

In his study, Jean Ferry mentions the problem of the "treasure hunt" in Roussel's work but immediately launches into a digression on Jules Verne and quickly dismisses that which he deems to be nothing more than a "commonplace." And yet he specifies in a footnote, of the utmost importance in my view, that Roussel intended to come back to the theme of the treasure hunt, that he felt the need to develop it from another angle. What does this mean? That Roussel was haunted by that childhood myth? Or else that he sought through it to reveal to the wise something deep and invaluable?[17] In view particularly of the last sentence in that note, the latter opinion is the one I shall take up.

Although this was more than twenty years ago, I can still see us one afternoon, Aragon and myself, sitting side by side while we watched the performance of *La Poussière de soleils* and, after exiting the Renaissance theater, walking toward the porte Saint-Denis while we excitedly confronted our impressions. We had no difficulty agreeing on the desperately dull character of the action that Roussel, in skimping less than ever on the scenery, seemed nevertheless to have done his utmost to make interesting. In this respect, the play as such has undeniably fewer qualities than *Locus Solus* and *L'Etoile au front*, which, from a conventional theatrical standpoint, were already hardly defensible. Because of the "absurd" manner in which the dialogues proceeded, as if the changes of voices had been decided solely by haphazard cuts in a strictly anecdotal text, it had not taken much longer for us to "lose the thread" than for the rest of the audience. Of course we were not going to lose our admiration for Roussel nor the faith we had much earlier placed in him over such a trifling matter, but we had to confess, much to our chagrin, that a certain disproportion between the *seen* and the mentally *assimilated* left us panting for breath even more than a variety show would have. Still . . . Still I myself clung to an episode that especially struck me as being highly significant—although I could not have said in what way—and that, thanks to a kind of retrospective television, I can see even today being replayed with the same clarity as when, from my seat, I saw it performed on stage. That episode, which, in hindsight, seems to stand out noticeably from the rest of the play, to have been quite deliberately given prominence, is that of the subscription—a fund started in memory of an anonymous hero—in the vicinity of a cross engraved with three stones. One learns that Blache (the master of the secret), thereby observing a strict clause, contributed the sum of one hundred and twenty-five francs (125 being nothing other than the *cube* of 5).

On the basis of that recollection—of the peculiar, unjustifiable emotion that took hold of me at that moment, when I first saw the play—and of what has just come to my mind as I was reading "the chain in *La Poussière de soleils*," I think I can request Jean Ferry's permission to borrow his pattern and to superimpose on it, while being solely responsible for this, one of those sheets of tracing paper that make it possible, by covering a reproduction of a painting and using a system of arrows, captions, or anything else, to bring out a certain category of nonobvious connections between its elements. It is important not to lose sight of the pattern presented by Jean Ferry. Since I have no way of referring directly to Roussel's work, I ask the reader to kindly disregard a few oversights.

For a demonstration such as the one I have in mind, it would most certainly be ideal to be able to proceed in an entirely analytical way and, from one deduction to the next, to bring the reader to a point where on his own he can find the solution I have reached. But there is one insurmountable obstacle to this: the solution in question can be found *only* by those who will have been steered in its direction because they have read some very special books.

Under these conditions, I have no choice but to present the solution first and then to put forward some insights that will validate it and point toward those links that are still missing.

As I ponder "the chain in *La Poussière de soleils*," as reconstructed by Jean Ferry, I am nearly certain that *Raymond Roussel endeavored, at least in this instance, to provide us with the rudiments necessary for undertaking what the alchemists mean by the Great Work, and that he did so, after so many others, in the only way traditionally allowed.* Again I quote Fulcanelli, whom I find to be the highest modern authority on the subject: "Our intention is merely to arouse the sagacity of the inquirer and to enable him to assimilate, through personal effort, those secret teachings the principles of which the most sincere authors have never been willing to disclose. Since all their treatises are acroamatic, there is no point in hoping to find in them the slightest bit of information regarding the basis and foundation of the art. This is why we are endeavoring, as far as possible, to make those sealed works useful by supplying the gist of what used to make up the first initiation; namely, the verbal revelation necessary for understanding them."[18] I shall now quickly turn to the grounds on which my argument is based.

Let us observe first of all that the stage directions for *La Poussière de soleils* provide for twenty-two scene changes (22: that is to say, the number of signs of the Hebrew alphabet, or of paths linking the Sephiroth of the Cabala, or of the major arcana of the tarot). But let us go back to the beginning of the chain itself, while keeping in mind that the few suggestions that follow are in no way restrictive (for that matter, they are definitely incomplete and undoubtedly awkward at times).

Ambrosi's skull (*le crâne d'Ambrosi*): I think the emphasis should be placed here on the words *death* (death's-head) and *Renaissance*.[19]

✳

The word sepia (*le mot sépia*): it is impossible to avoid the association with the cuttlefish, which hides behind a cloud of black liquid.[20] Are we not getting close to the phase in the alchemical process called *sublimation* that begins with the "separation of the gross" and leads up to the "ascension of the subtle"?

✳

The pterodactyl's stone (*la pierre au ptérodactyle*): just these words, *la pierre au*, would be enough to conjure up the expression *la pierre au noir*, or *au blanc*, or *au rouge*, which recur so often in the alchemical vocabulary.[21] But I wager that the pterodactyl is not merely added here as a colorful detail. We should remember in this respect that the primitive material from which the Great Work proceeds "is generally represented by a *black dragon* covered with scales, which the Chinese call *lóng*, and which is perfectly analogous to the Hermetic monster. It is also a kind of winged serpent with a horned head, breathing fire and flame through its nostrils."[22]

✳

The swallow (*l'hirondelle*): many hermetic authors have prescribed, in these very words, that at this stage the original solvent should be "made to fly," and behold, here is the "subtle" itself. The ambiguity of its second name, *martinet*, brings to mind an idea of mortification, which is quite appropriate in this particular regard.[23]

✳

I must leave it to more qualified researchers to elucidate the reasons requiring a detour via d'Urfé[24] before coming upon:

The albino shepherdess (*la bergère albinos*): one cannot possibly doubt that this refers to the "White Work." I will not weary so soon of quoting Fulcanelli: "Arthepius, Nicolas Flamel, Philaleles, and many other masters teach that, at this stage of the coction, the *Rebis* takes on the appearance of fine silky threads, of *hair* spread on the surface and progressing from the periphery to the center. Hence the name *capillary whiteness* used to refer to this coloration."[25] *Albino*: we understand that. But why the *shepherdess*? Quite probably because she stands for the emblematic ermine "represented inside a small pen enclosed within a circular hurdle"[26] that is found on the coat of arms of Anne de Bretagne along with the motto "Sooner death than defilement" and in which we are asked to recognize the "proximate mercury" or "Pontic water" of alchemy. This supposition is also supported by the discovery, in the hands of the shepherdess, of a *Breton* prayer.

❋

The sunny spell (*l'embellie*): here again, Roussel is playing wonderfully, and no doubt quite cleverly, on the literal and figurative meanings of this word, which can refer to a ray of sunshine in the sky as well as in the human soul.

❋

Dr. Flurian (*le docteur Flurian*): I still cannot figure him out, nor his little game (the original text will have to be consulted on this point).

❋

The caricature (*la caricature*): I think its primary function is to introduce King Louis-Philippe, who appears later on and is commonly known to have been portrayed in the shape of a pear. This being said without mentioning the alchemical meaning that could be extracted in addition.

❋

The dried lily sprinkled with gold powder (*le lys séché tout imprégné de poudre d'or*): once more Fulcanelli comes to our rescue. The gold powder is quite obviously "the gold of projection, that is to say alchemically produced," which is, as he also tells us, the "third form of the Stone."[27] As for the lily, it corresponds "to the Hermetic Rose. Combined with the cross, it is used, like the rose, as a device and a blazon by the practicing knight who, with God's blessing, has produced the Philosophers' Stone."[28] Combined with the cross? Indeed, the cross will soon appear.

❋

The subscription raised to the cube, in the vicinity of a cross engraved with three stars (*la souscription au cube, à proximité d'une croix gravée de trois étoiles*): here it is! The cube in question—here Jean Ferry corroborates the vague intuition I had long ago—definitely represents not only one of the central points of Roussel's preoccupation and one of the major keys to his play, but also one of the crucial operations of the Great Work. It is clear, if we refer once again to the same source, that this cube is none other than the "cubic Stone," that is to say with its six sides already cut and that now only needs to be perfectly set in the "Hermetic Vase" and thus brought to completion. Fulcanelli shows us a picture of this stone solidly set, as it appears on a bas-relief decorating the Saint-Martin fountain, located on rue Saint-Martin in Paris, right near the theater where *La Poussière de soleils* was performed. I refer those interested to his admirable and numerous commentaries on this subject: I will simply mention that the cube, the symbol of quintessence, is here necessarily linked to the cross, the symbol of the Passion. The three stars may refer to the fact that the die had to be cast three times ("the Stone must be thrice dissolved"), but they also emphasize the anonymity the seeker must preserve.

✳

The Phrygian cap (*le bonnet phrygien*): it could, on account of the number 5 (which, as suggested earlier,[29] should be raised to its various powers), be an allusion to the "pope," the fifth arcanum of the tarot. Indeed, Roussel appears to have been oddly preoccupied with the latter's headgear, which is not necessarily a tiara, as Jean Ferry seems to think, but which was originally the "*mitre* or *camelauque*, the plain Phrygian cap."[30] My friend Gaston Puel, whom I had asked, concerning an entirely different matter, what emblematic meaning he ascribed to the Phrygian cap, has just replied to my query—I received his letter yesterday—with a long quotation, which reads in part as follows: "Its magic (that of the cult of Mithra) was linked to totemism, it included a baptism in blood and extremely esoteric ritual formulas involving animal spirits. The bull, which, according to occult principles, represents the genital energy and the radiations of the solar plexus, was at the center of that Mystery. . . . The mystes had to combat the beast, to fell it, and to cut its throat; thereby he had overcome the sexual principle, he was proclaimed FREE and the red Phrygian cap was placed on his head. According to the old gnostic Rosicrucian tradition, this red Phrygian cap is the symbol of the bloody foreskin."[31]

*

Louis-Philippe: the pear, as earlier mentioned. The color changing to yellow? This is precisely the fruit that has been recognized with one accord in the coffer described by Fulcanelli as coffer number 2 of the second series, which came from the castle of Dampierre. With it, the inscription: DIGNA, MERCES, LABORE. *Justly rewarded work.*[32] "This symbolic fruit," he tells us, "is none other than the Hermetic Gem, the Philosophers' Stone of the Great Work," which we are going to see even more clearly in

The strawberry mark (*la fraise*): "The expression *Philosophers' Stone* means, in the sacred language, *the stone that bears the sign of the Sun.*" (Thereby, not only does the name Magès, the name of the character with the strawberry mark, become clear but also the title of Raymond Roussel's play.) "The *solar sign* is characterized by the red coloration, which can vary in intensity, as Basil Valentine said: 'Its color varies from cherry red to crimson, or from the red of a ruby to the red of a pomegranate, . . .' and this redness—Khunrath concurs—is the *signature* of the perfect fixation and of the fixed perfection, and it makes it, he adds, 'everlasting, indestructible, . . . permanent and judging all things justly (for it abides solely by its own rule), and proclaiming: I shall renew all things.'"[33]

Thanks to Jean Ferry, who made it possible, I think that Raymond Roussel's work should now be entirely reexamined in this light.

Antibes, 12–19 March 1948

The Night

of the

Rose-Hotel

Just as for some Indians in British Columbia the day is symbolized
by a small piece of redwood that a crow (representing the night) carries
in its beak, so am I surprised that this stanza from *Poésies* [*Poems*] by
Lautréamont has not attracted attention: "At the break of day, maidens go
and pick roses. A wind of innocence blows through vales and capitals, braces
the intelligence of the more inspired poets, shields the cradles, crowns the
youth, rouses beliefs in immortality in the old."

In spite of the utilitarian interpretations given by some commentators
to a number of other propositions found in a book the purport of which
remains most enigmatic,[1] this stanza contrasts sharply with the rest, which
remains extremely tense throughout and, even when taken literally—leaving
aside the humor, as evident here as in the *Chants* [*Maldoror*]—seems to
have great difficulty in reaching pragmatic conclusions on the moral and
social levels. The few lines quoted above convey a feeling of peacefulness:
the sky has completely cleared up, the luminous stick in the black bird's
beak shines forth—more to the point, a bay window has suddenly opened,
allowing us to catch a glimpse of Eden, even if it closes just as quickly. When
it does, we are back in a schoolroom where only dazzling strokes of chalk
alternate with the furious sweeps of a sponge on a board that has reverted
to black. Still, during that flash, rational knowledge has been transcended,
a gap has opened up: even better, a seed has slipped through, perhaps the
seed of all the light we will ever know, that can only sprout and grow in an

Introduction to Maurice Fourré's book *La Nuit du Rose-Hôtel* (Paris: Gallimard, 1950).

environment that must be in total obscurity. Thus it is within the "darkest" kind of poetry that the bud of dazzling light was able to open, that, in a cellular state, the nucleus of "yang" with the potential to compensate for all "yin," as Chinese thought would have it, was able to come into being. While we wait for this compensating process to unfold, it is quite true historically that "yin" prevails, that the Western world goes through a protracted season of yin—winter, "whose symbol is a closed door," according to M. Marcel Granet. And he adds: "Scholars maintain that, during the freezing season, yang is confined to an underground lair, surrounded on all sides by yin. . . . For the whole winter, yang, surrounded by yin, undergoes, at the bottom of subterranean Springs, under the frozen ground, a kind of annual ordeal whence he comes out invigorated. Yang escapes from his prison at the beginning of spring by hitting the ground with his heel: then the ice breaks by itself and the springs awaken."[2] It will come as no surprise to anybody if I remark that here we have been experiencing a protracted winter for many years. Patches of sunlight, clearings, heralding mosses have occupied for too long too little space in our lives. Whoever is not on the lookout for a genuine "new spirit"—having nothing in common with the old one—sees nothing that might point to the beginning of the "change of sign" required, in my opinion,[3] by the discovery of nuclear fission and the unprecedented threat that this constitutes for the world. However, one only need pay close attention to them to realize that the symptoms of *mutation* are far from being totally absent: there is enough evidence of this in the reception given to the work of Malcolm de Chazal, which celebrates a total reconciliation of men with nature, or in the burst of enthusiasm aroused by Garry Davis's gesture and in the rapid growth of the constructive movement supporting him. I do not think that the word *Revelation* is too strong to convey what these harbingers of health regained represent for the widespread desire and expectations present in the hearts of men. With this in mind, I did not feel too presumptuous when I urged M. Gaston Gallimard to publish a series with this word as a title. That series would not merely duplicate the one edited by our friend Albert Camus under the title *Espoir* [*Hope*]. His aspirations are ultimately similar to mine, but while I intend to give pride of place to spiritual adventure and to leave it a clear field, his own purpose seems to be to influence the conscience specific to our time and to restore it as quickly as possible. My objective is to bring to light a number of truly *exceptional* works that are not always easy to understand but that have the power to make us see *beyond* the horizon of the life we think we lead, thereby preventing stereotypy and sclerosis of the living forces of the mind. There will be room in such a series for some works of the past that did not obtain the resonance they deserved in their time, either because for one reason or another they were privately circulated, or because they were intended to go against the current, or yet because they included, out of necessity, a wide array of visionary ideas. It seems that the word "revelation" applies equally to such unobtainable works, which had to wait until now to appear in a favorable light. In my view, it is only by confronting those belatedly topical works with new as yet unpublished ones that we can expect to develop a new way of looking at the situation of man in the world and to find the means to free him from the constraints inherent in the increasingly standardized methods used for shaping his mind.

✳

I could not think of a more auspicious beginning for this series than the publication of a book such as *La Nuit du Rose-Hôtel*. This is a work that is free at last of any bitterness and that seems at the onset to borrow its substance from the very reflection of the Loire castles. A work designed with the least opaque materials in mind and so deliberately lacelike that some of its peaks make the outlines of the carved stone indistinguishable from the figures drawn by the birds flying to and fro. A work whose novel—and most wonderfully confounding—property is to compound the "Songs of Innocence and Experience." A work pervaded with a fervor and effusion focused on what makes each moment unique and that succeeds in extracting a liqueur of the most subtle kind from the still of memory in which the privileged moments of a life have accumulated. Finally, a work that could not be freer of the parasitical aspirations that vitiate most others: the wish to be noticed, to impress the people around, to find a place in the sun for oneself. Here, that place is readily found within man himself, and I do not know of a more enviable one.

Like it or not, it is somewhat frustrating to provide an introduction to such a book, not only because one must refrain from pointing out its beauties so as not to spoil the reader's pleasure, but also because one must avoid offering an interpretation that might restrict the right of anyone who cares to do so to prefer a different one. I do not think that the choice between those various interpretations is much more limited than it is with respect to Kafka, who could be considered his dark counterpart, and this choice seems to me likely to arouse no less heated controversies. The epigraph of *La Nuit du Rose-Hôtel*, borrowed from Teresa of Avila, "Life is but a night spent in a bad inn"—if we put it in its true perspective—would already be enough to place this book at a level seldom reached by works of fiction. It is explicitly confirmed that this way of looking at things dominates all others since in chapter 10 ("Supper will be at Rose's Inn"), which is particularly interesting in that it occupies the central position in the book and was written, so M. Maurice Fourré told me, after the eighteen other chapters (he thus wanted it to be the backbone of his construction), we hear the following dialogue: "Will you always think, dear Rose, about the famous apothegm by the very great Spanish mystic, which drops from her cloisters onto the Inn of Our Lives?—Always, Governor." It is clear enough that we are meant to be raised to a level of experience far above the state where the "slices of life" dear to certain authors are being cut. The characters gravitating here, if they leave nothing to be desired in terms of concrete intensity, do not in fact really exist independently of their author: they are truly *at long last* the children that Flaubert could have acknowledged without so much ambiguity as the offspring of his affair with Madame Bovary. Even so, far from being without antecedents, they are not in essence different from Henry von Ofterdingen and the heirs in Arnim's tale.[4]

One of the author's charming affectations—and not the least of them—is to remind people that he is seventy-two years old and that, about forty-six years ago, he faced, for the first and until now for the last time, the dreadful *spotlights* that turn the writer and more generally any public figure into a vassal of opinion, which at once swoops down on him and lies in wait for him to come out into the open a second time so that it may set the limits of the field in which he is free to play. Between the year 1903, when René

Bazin (of pleasant memory for the generations that follow his) introduced a short story by M. Maurice Fourré in *La Revue des Deux-Mondes* and this year, 1949, just when *La Nuit du Rose-Hôtel* is coming out, the events that have made their way over a fairly bumpy terrain—and have maimed all of us to some extent—have left intact this enduring idea, upheld by M. René Guénon, among others, that "historical facts are only relevant as symbols of spiritual realities"—an assertion that today requires some courage if it is to be set against the fanatical, matter-of-fact views of history that are disseminated or even imposed by terror. In a world where spiritual and material realities have long ceased to counterbalance and to engender one another, one man had to endeavor to set them apart and to be strong enough not to retract, so that the ultimate human testimony—the only one that matters—might recover its original meaning. And so M. Maurice Fourré still wears to this day the mask of a man indistinguishable from the other notables of Angers, aside from the fact that, as he says, "I was far too detached ... from the circumstances of day-to-day reality, where my external self played its mechanical part in the economy of the community, to set store by my bourgeois existence: it meant nothing to me, even though I think I was putting to good use the choicest possibilities of an efficient system within the guidelines of a transcendent activity." A certain myth originating with Rimbaud (who is thought, against all possibility, to have remained a poet, despite the transactions that occupied him body and soul, as shown by his letters from Abyssinia) happens to be confronted here with a deliberately different side of itself: a freedom that, with some help from humor—taking fully into account the limits of human existence—succeeds in making its way though the obstacles of necessity. This is also, within the closest approximation, the case of those inventors dreamt up by Paul Valéry at the beginning of "La Soirée avec Monsieur Teste" [Mr. Teste], who are all the more impressive for having managed to keep their secret to themselves. (The author of *La Nuit du Rose-Hôtel* was not planning to get his work published: it is only because Julien Gracq and Michel Carrouges lived in the same area as the author or had acquaintances in common with him that they chanced upon his manuscript and spoke to me about it.) It is not without some emotion that, when I consider the ways by which it has reached us, I once again *test*—in contrast to the vanity of the name, which by and large taints literary and artistic expression—the value of the criterion of rare and undeniable authenticity that made us, Jean Dubuffet, Jean Paulhan, and myself, search avidly for works of "Art Brut," as they came to be known, from which so mediocre a concern is excluded. I am all the more attentive to it in this case as it involves a work of art of the most highly and patiently elaborated kind. For it is all too obvious that, if *La Nuit du Rose-Hôtel* originated in the events of 1940—which in particular affected a region like Anjou, less inured to war than others—it is based on and brings into play the amazingly rich accumulation of emotions and the peak vibration of an entire life.

*

It is not my place to point out the exceptional resources of language that M. Maurice Fourré has built up in order to communicate at a deeper level not so much with others as with himself. I believe, however, that no one has ever better walked hand in hand with the most ductile and sensitive thought while "the call of the paddle steamer rises with the evening tide coming in up the Loire estuary." I shall only remark that this language—which, in the descriptive mode, with its strikingly excessive precision, involves us in complex relationships with familiar objects or everyday occurrences— bears similarities from time to time with that of Lautréamont, just as, in the meditative mode, I cannot find for it any other lyrical precedent than the best of Forneret. The alternation of prose and verse—the latter giving free rein to affective outpourings—is here as justified, as natural as it is in Novalis or in works that follow the old patterns of improvisation. I am only mentioning this to give an idea of the *class* in which such a language, in my opinion, belongs, while I intentionally set aside the narrative mode in which I think that, in view of the liberty and luxuriance displayed in his use of storytelling devices, which children find so delightful, he is unequaled to this day.

The message conveyed by M. Maurice Fourré, "paralyzed with emotion, under the crystalline arches of language," may compel respect at first because of the distinction of its formal qualities, but its deep meaning remains entirely to be deciphered. The keys needed to penetrate it are probably not on every ring, as is the case with works that conceal more or less conscious parabolical intentions under the guise of a fiction in which they enwrap the most dynamic aspects of everyday reality. The primary problem concerning M. Fourré, as in Kafka's case, is to know whether in his work, as someone said about Flaubert, "language invents its object at the same time as it unveils it"[5] or whether we are facing a clearly premeditated design. If such a design could be shown to exist, it would still remain to be seen whether it is a religious or an initiatory one. If I may quote an expert opinion in this respect: "Religion is only concerned with the self within the individual human condition and does not aim at all at pulling the self out of it ... whereas the main goal of initiation is to transcend the possibilities of that condition and to make it effectively possible to reach superior states of being and even to lead the self eventually beyond any conditioned state of being whatsoever."[6] In order to settle this delicate question, it is important not to overlook any of the pointers that the author seems to have intentionally provided. This Night of the Rose-Hotel coincides with the night of 21 June 1921: one might as well say that its relation begins at the time of the summer solstice (of a specifically chosen year), in the same way that in the traditional Chinese calendar the solar year began with the autumn equinox, which was considered "the starting point of a liturgical cycle."[7] Let us observe that it is precisely on the back of an official calendar of the Postal and Telegraph Service (that is to say, undoubtedly, contrary to its very nature) that we can discover the annotation that best accounts for that night in its plenitude: "NIGHT of the Rose of Love—NIGHT of the Mystical Staircase—NIGHT of the Celestial Attics—NIGHT of the Farandole—NIGHT of the Southern Cross." It is up to us to reconcile the barely whispered allusion to those higher disciplines ("The time has not yet come, and it is not part of our duties to tell you everything. . . . One must tread with great caution on the burning edges that fringe those dark abysses") with the exquisite and deliberately picturesque image presented to us by the one who urges: "Let us make haste. . . . When the proud sun comes up, we will no longer have anything but our bodies," as soon as he lets us recognize him in the deceptive light of high noon—I cannot do any better than to quote him: "I am a man of the West,[8] full of gentleness and strength hidden under the pleasantries of congenial evasion, of self-effacement concealed behind smiles and dreams, and of a *victorious stubbornness.*"

Isle of Sein—Paimpont Forest, August 1949.

Predescription

When I was quite young—around 1915—I went briefly through spells of furious impatience with the general structure of the human body, especially that of the head. Leaving aside what could make the face of one of my fellow creatures extremely precious—or valueless—and taking only characteristics of the species into account, I would then inwardly pity and deride the *pattern* on which physical man is built. From that angle, I could not see anything that mixed in a more inharmonious fashion features of a stubborn root and of a cheap skittle pin. Ah! one had to admit that the Botcher demon was pretty ill inspired that day! Those approximate solids, miserably jointed, endowed—almost as an afterthought, haphazardly—with attributes that jar with the whole as well as with one another, filled me with commiseration. The head seemed particularly stupid, nodding as it does like a half-peeled coconut, with the measly space occupied on the same side by the eyes, the nostrils, the ears (two of each as a minimum warranty for replacement purposes): the workman had to be mad to thus install the electricity meter—and moreover, what an indecent one—plumb in the middle of the chimney. Human taste, the sense of beauty based on the humble criterion we share, were thereby definitely flouted and defied to the utmost. That head, which arrogated to itself the faculty of understanding, of judging, of praising, that head, with what it shares with any other of its kind, only had to catch a glimpse of itself in the mirror: its only salvation was to burst out laughing.

Since then, though I have made the effort to read books that might reconcile me to that spasmodic way of feeling (from *Analysis of Beauty* by

William Hogarth to *Construction de l'homme* [Construction of man] by Pierre Mabille), I am afraid I remain obscurely jealous of the appearance of radiolarians, in all their variety. An anti-Narcissus stands next to his brother, leaning over the spring. In the metamorphosis whereby the latter is punished, the former has won.

The regret to take on a human appearance rather than some other is, to tell the truth, the most cunning form of defiance I can think of, since it makes use of the sense of the relationships that the human eye claims to bring out and wants to codify while it can be immediately challenged for being both the judge of and a party to the dispute.

The fact remains that the sense of that defect inherent to the whole species is in practice denied and overcome for the benefit of the interest we take in the individual physical image as something unique. By virtue of the fact that each one of us embodies—with incidental particularities—a certain physical type, we are drawn far too urgently into a circle of likes and dislikes not to become quickly mesmerized, whether we like it or not, by our own outward appearance and that of others. Unfathomable mystery, against which a Cardan's or a Lavater's attempts at reduction seem fairly childish. A gathering of human faces, even select ones, always reminds me of a rather vulgar masquerade in which resemblances to animals are most in evidence, where doubles move enigmatically through the crowd, and that is only enlivened by the presence, here and there, of a few very beautiful black velvet masks. Inner life does not easily filter through this deceiving exterior: whenever we feel confident we can uncover it, whenever we fill a face with it to saturation point, it is, alas, because we already know it is there (as in the case of Pascal, Baudelaire, Rimbaud). And what disillusionment if we should put side by side—at the risk of being sacrilegious—the photograph of Nerval by Nadar and that of some movie star. There is no doubt that the human face is a cipher, like everything else, but the key to it is forever being recast and thus remains incandescent, more unreachable than any other.

25 April 1949

The Engineer

His steps as uncertain now as they seem to have been when he approached the year one thousand, man is getting ready to pass the mark of the second millennium of the era he chose for himself—the "Christian" era, to which he is now tied only by threads that are growing slacker every day. Once again he lives in the same dread of the end of the world while the bomb is being fused before his very eyes, no longer in the heart of religious faith, as it was at that time, but in the heart of the hope placed on scientific progress, which has gradually replaced that faith. Those who think they can deny the impending danger or who, at least as far as they are concerned, intend to keep on going as if nothing had changed, cannot prevent this torment from infecting them in ways against which they are defenseless. The truth is that today, to quote the anxious witness who speaks in the first person in one of Jean Ferry's finest short stories, "we are all in a terrifyingly unstable state of equilibrium that the slightest thing could upset." By virtue of a well-known law of ambivalence, this lurking prospect of a very possible and imminent rending of the space and time that are held real exacerbates the need to recover a "sacred" time and a "sacred" space, by definition out of reach, and gives free rein to these two yearnings—restrained, not to say repressed, in the West for centuries—that M. Mircea Eliade calls the "nostalgia for paradise" and the "nostalgia for eternity."[1] The conflict between these causes for despair and the rekindling of these

Introduction to the stories by Jean Ferry published in 1950 under the title *Le Mécanicien* [The engineer] under the aegis of the Cinéastes Bibliophiles.

obdurate yearnings results in this shuddering, which is peculiar to our times, the one that it is the function of art to register, since all we ask is for art to grasp at every moment *what is in the air*, so that it may isolate it on white-hot plates made of an elective metal.

I am not talking here with much less regard for the understanding of what I am saying than did Freud when he would pronounce the word "sublimation," which used to wring a sigh of contentment from us even though we would have found it difficult to know exactly what he meant and whether or not this word introduced a flaw into his system. Be that as it may, some individuals—escaped from God knows what jungles where everything seemed bound to turn out badly for them—have the ability, thanks to a mental "pull-up," so swift that it escapes the observer's notice and eludes their own powers of recollection, to reach a place where they are not only virtually immune to the madness and crime that would have embraced them but where they also act as lookouts, taking the pulse of the body of *events* and auscultating it with an infallible ear. Jean Ferry is one of them.

A position such as his own, that of the artist aware that he is expressing a new dimension of the world and, consequently, that he owes very little to his precursors, typifies in condensed form the pathos of present times.

I got into enough trouble with the English the time I took the liberty of stating that the gothic novel was the product of the revolutionary upheavals that, at the end of the eighteenth century, had shaken the feudal system and that its whole set of props—the thunder and lightning, the underground passages, the ghosts—had no other meaning than to give concrete expression to the great problem of the sensibility of the times: to account, on the one hand, for the elation caused by the setting up of the new order and, on the other hand, for the terror inspired by the abolition of the old one.[2] Yet I think that literary history should be entirely rewritten from that point of view, provided it is harmonized with this other viewpoint, so heretical these days, namely, that it is not so much "facts" that history as such disseminates but symbols of spiritual realities. Jean Ferry writes upon the stillness of the cloud that Hiroshima created in our consciousness.

As can be expected under these conditions, depressive themes prevail at first sight over others and we have only ourselves to blame, since the common reasons for dejection are innumerable. One of the other truly inspired authors of today and not of yesterday, Malcolm de Chazal, vigorously stresses one of them: "French thought is now at an impasse. After Descartes came along, two equally suitable pathways were open to it: reason and intuition. The French chose reason and developed it fully. Thereby, they paved the way for the present scientific world. Hence, they are the great precursors of the modern era, the shepherds of this flock whose fold is the deified atom, matter transubstantiated into the offsprings of physics. The atom bomb was first conceived in Descartes's brain."[3] At a time when the issue of the guilt of states and peoples has just been raised, as it was at the end of the war, with a greater or lesser degree of rigor and good faith, and when it has aroused passions that, even after they have abated, leave a lingering obsession in their wake (new resentments are presently smoldering under their embers, fanned by the constant reminders of the wrongs attributable to the United States according to some, to Russia according to others), it would indeed be desirable for intellectuals to try and go back in time to the real—and lasting—causes of perturbation. This would at least have the advantage of bringing the debate to a slightly higher level. Meanwhile, we must admit that the *scandal* is growing greater every day. Only yesterday, I thought I was in a fairly good position to verify this, as I have been staying at an inn in Brittany, where, curiously enough, I am finding out for the first time what an "inn" is (Rimbaud speaks of it in mysterious terms: "Never the green inn . . ."). In this house, very well located in the middle of a forest, where both bed and fare are good, recommended even by tourist agencies, and which has no difficulty in glittering from day to day with all its room keys and all its cutlery, it is a wonder to me to see that gypsies and vagrants of all kinds, sometimes even the least "presentable" ones, are greeted with the same discretion and the same consideration as the guests who arrive in cars. Under this roof overgrown with ivy and constantly hemmed with swallows, they are for a short while at home and sheltered from everything. Only last night I saw a wild and proud couple, the man—carrying a four-pound loaf of bread when he came out—a bit abstracted under his extraordinarily patched-up cap, the woman much shorter and with a somewhat comical corpulence, but with such dignity in her guileless eyes—the two of them so close and as if inured to poverty (I am told they were married a few days ago); they stopped for a few seconds in the doorway before setting off again, borne away by the ray of light that springs from *Jude the Obscure*.

When they came by, I was leafing through one of those illustrated periodicals that plague our times in ever-increasing numbers. Current events provided it with a pretext for introducing its readers into the private life of a M. F——, "the 135th successor, it said, of Saint Denis to the archbishopric of Paris." Actually, it was the second time that evening I read about that fascinating personage—someone who thought I was starving for weeklies had provided me with a liberal supply—and I already knew that, without overly distinguishing himself in the Resistance, he had been the best "shooter" on the football team at the seminary and that, during the Occupation, he had gone on to promote the ever so wholesome idea of the "worker priest" and to put it into practice. This particular magazine displayed various photographs: one of F—— quite obnoxious looking; one of his "arms" above the slimy motto: "I belong to my flock"; a picture of his hand—enlarged, let us hope—adorned with the amethyst; another of his miter and his crosier, the latter with its five sections unscrewed; another of his servants; finally, there was a photograph of his private chapel with its "secret door" (so secret that he saw fit to have his picture taken while opening it). Between the two categories of representations that met my eyes at that moment, I think it is hardly worth asking: Where is the sacred, where is the profane? Where is greatness, where is true wretchedness?

"This attractive young man" (who, in another picture, no doubt obligingly lent by himself, is shown "during his stag party") is now archbishop of Paris; not far from here, that homeless couple walks on while dogs are barking at them. The depredation in Indochina and the dismal exactions in Madagascar, among all the other crimes committed against humanity nowadays, the least forgivable of which is to corrupt, to systematically distort the meaning of words that inspire ideals (justice, democracy, peace, freedom), all this *plus* all the other curses that weigh on man and that are inherent in the misleading direction given to his thought a long time ago are just waiting to be written in the margin of this naive moralizing picture. Do you agree, Jean Ferry? I wanted to give *them* an immediate, concrete idea of what for us constitutes scandal.

Only by squarely and courageously facing the extent of present human misery, as depicted in this collection of stories, can we assess the importance of the remedies the author brings to it and extract some of the reasons for being that we can find for ourselves today in spite of everything.

The most consistent leitmotiv of these twenty stories or so is that of man being *lost*. One is all alone, the boat has sailed off again without warning, the passengers are scattered God knows where. The island is deserted, although one can surmise that there are people about at night. Here, it is no longer man who is moving, it is the earth. The perceptible world is made up of those innumerable traps that, until then, man would only encounter at distant intervals: "Have you ever stepped, in the dark, on the last stair, the one that does not exist? Do you remember that feeling of utter confusion you had for one brief moment?... Well, this country is always like that! The matter of which that absent stair is made here constitutes matter itself." Genghis Khan, in his feverish drive to possess and destroy, runs the risk of self-negation, on account of the roundness of the planet, by attacking his own forever scorched lands. Not only is it impossible to know from *where* one issues, but from *whom*: nothing in common, at any rate, with those who pass themselves off as the writers of your time—what time? Better to make up a genealogy for oneself after one's fancy and one's heart—but what if *they* do not want it? (We can see, on this occasion, the unbridled expression of one of the major denials and demands of the child: he is *someone other* than who he is said to be, he has been the victim of an abduction. Be as alarmed as you wish, this is the stage we have reached: it is the parents' turn not to be "acknowledged" by their children.) What matters here is that man is lost in the time that immediately precedes him—which only shows, as a mirror image, that he is lost in the time that follows him. You may sometimes happen, in conditions of extreme psychological deprivation, to pick up a message that appears exciting: although its manifest content does not directly concern you, it has the virtue of setting you back on your feet. Should something occur to bring you back for a few seconds to the external world, once you resume listening, you will be able to catch another fragment of the message but not to solder this fragment and the previous one back together, the nodal point of the story has been lost: lost forever the bobbin that was to enable you to make sense of it, where precisely the thread of the fictional narrative intertwined with that of your own life. The engineer driving the train does not stop at any station; it is specifically stated that one cannot get off the moving train and besides, there is no point hemming and hawing, it is much simpler, one does not get off: the alarm bell is strictly for show. From birth to death, the meaning of the journey is lost: "The Chinese astrologer wastes his years reckoning the time when he will die." The Robinson of this day and age, having left well behind his feats of ingenuity, only longs now to "sleep a dense sleep."

One of the major sources of humor in Jean Ferry is that the fatigue he so readily displays does not miss any opportunity to express itself and to this end expends boundless energy before our eyes.[4] This fatigue is for him an extraordinary springboard, which reminds me of the pantomime of those two entertainers—the "eccentrics," as they were known—who could be seen about thirty years ago at the Olympia, performing a variety act entitled *The Self-Deflating Man*. While acting the parts of masons building a house, of which in the end no stone was left standing, one of them constantly had to pick up the other one, who, when left to his own devices, with a vacant look in his eyes, would immediately start swiveling round slowly while he gradually subsided until he was completely flat on the ground with only the thickness of his clothing visible. I have not seen anything so irresistibly funny and unsettling since. I believe that in Jean Ferry these two characters are no less closely associated. They even have a common letterhead that reads: "Jean Ferry—All kinds of scenarios undertaken—Speedy and conscientious work—Specializing in psychological constructions—Wide selection of paradoxes, daring ideas, etc. Constant supply of compelling subjects of human interest—Poetic details: on request—Dashes of humor: by the ounce." Without entirely losing sight of Jean Ferry II, "even more tired than usual," Jean Ferry I managed for years to apply himself to a most difficult task, that of solving the riddle left by Raymond Roussel, and he is just as capable of presenting to us, with "Le Mécanicien" and other stories, a house duly decked with the traditional little flag.

The idea of the double—the intruder, the parasite one has to put up with— proves to be, from one story to the next, a rather obsessive one. This double is something very much alive: "And how he ate, the bastard! He ate as much as four real people, at a time when, more often than not, my breakfast consisted of coffee and a croissant." In his avatars, he goes so far as to beg with an empty can: "He had taken such pains to grow by feeding on our garbage ..." or else he turns into creepy-crawlies shut up in a box, the possessor of which knows they are hatching the worst designs against him, although he is condemned to feed them. The sole concern is to get rid of the box by any means possible (sending it off in a trunk, carrying it away on a shovel); at the very least, to protect oneself against an unexpected attack (to lock it away in the drawer under the marble top). Whatever opportunities for humor this theme may offer, one cannot doubt that fatigue is viewed as a tragedy. In this respect, one hears unmistakable accents here and there. "How dark it must be in the center of an air bubble trapped deep inside a thousand-pound wheel of Swiss cheese!" Sleep is resolutely cherished for its own sake, fanatically disconnected from the idea of rest, of recuperation, one usually associates with it. Pessimism reigns supreme; the only thing that mars sleep is dreaming, which Jean Ferry in any case confines to its superficial levels. The one he extols is the "unexploitable sleep, the one that cosmically puts man in his true place in the world." Nothing as grim, nothing as empty of starlight had been heard since Jacques Rigaud. "If the Church," he also says, "had rated abstinence from sleep as the highest renunciation, instead of ranking it slightly lower, the world would now be one vast chapel." Even if it means repeating myself on this point (it is worth doing so), I shall point out that Stakhanovite Stalinism, which certainly intends to benefit from this lesson, has undertaken a scientific offensive against sleep and has led people to expect any day now a discovery that would universally do away with "this useless luxury" (to quote *L'Humanité* when it announced that good news).

Nevertheless, the feeling that one is lost, however alarming it may be, is not—far from it—one of those feelings that leave man in the depths of despair, precisely because it instinctively begets the question of *how to find a way out*. Far more hopeless from the mind's viewpoint is the case of our innumerable contemporaries who come to terms with the present situation inflicted upon mankind and who convince themselves that it is all "business as usual," even if the power has been shut off. In spite of the reserve deliberately shown by the author, not only does his penchant for subversion keep him in a state of constant alertness but it is also clear that he has never ceased to take a very keen interest in everything that pertains to dreams, to the marvelous, and to love.

As for me, I revere—more than ever today because they are so rare—works that are electrified by this need for subversion that alone can give full scope to individual resistance against general domestication. On condition of course that the means made available to subversion are equal to it, otherwise they are liable to compromise it radically. In view of the present choking of "revolutionary" ideas by those very people who claim proprietary rights to them, of the subjection of those ideas to a rule that cannot be broken and that hinders their progress, of the historical chances that those ideas will be corrupted, and of the certainty of seeing them flaunted by people who in no way endorse them but who, in these strange times we are living in, derive substantial benefits from them, subversion, as it is practiced particularly in art, remains the great reservoir of new strength; it alone today can claim to represent the full extent of human protest against absurdity, cowardice, and iniquity in every form. A day will come when people will turn to works as completely unfettered as this one in order to seek the principle of a readjustment of the human condition to its fundamentals— a principle that, in this second quarter of the twentieth century, will not be found anywhere else. I believe, I have never ceased to believe, in this final disillusionment, I even think it is just around the corner: it will show conclusively where—as frontline snipers—the clear-sighted and the just stood, where the mercenaries and the traitors to the cause of mankind lurked.

Even if he intends to banish them from sleep, dreams are far from always being disparaged by Jean Ferry. Raymond Roussel, ushered into paradise by Jules Verne and Camille Flammarion, "realized that his thought now painlessly followed the difficult paths that had led him previously to write some of his books. . . . Henceforth, the external world corresponded to his own world." Jarry, even though he was as much a skeptic as Jean Ferry is, also expressed—in a letter to Rachilde written on the eve of his death—the idea, somewhat unexpected coming from him, "that the brain during decomposition keeps on working after death and that its dreams are what make up paradise." Hence dreaming is vested by both with exceptional powers extending in some direction beyond human life; here is the idea of a possible redemption of so-called active life by the dreaming process and consequently an invitation to cultivate dreaming so as to maximize its yield by all means available, including especially the most "difficult" ones. Besides, other than the ability to dream, what could possibly enable Jean Ferry to successively identify, to the extent of not leaving anything to improvisation, with so many diverse characters, or to show himself so perfectly sure of his bearings in places or circumstances of which he will never have any experience?

Whatever efforts may be made to deny it or to avoid taking it into account ("One must put up with it. But it requires a tremendous amount of work"), the only thing preventing the "marvelous" from flooding into ordinary life is a sluice that, as is plain to see, is rapidly deteriorating. The truth of the matter is that we are suffocating in a closed system barely adapted to the needs of practical existence, and even so, this system is falling apart at the seams. Is there any refuge? Although the attitude of "absolute doubt" with regard to all inculcated ideas and of "absolute deviation" from all prevailing opinions, expressly advocated by Charles Fourier, did not generally prevail, at least it was lent invaluable support and assistance by poets (Rimbaud, Cros, Nouveau, Lautréamont, Jarry, Roussel) following entirely different paths, and this has undeniably left its mark on modern sensibility. Between the idea that "true life is absent" and the idea that no element of art should be taken from the world surrounding us, a construction has sprung up: we can see that huge parts of it are still in darkness and that, as a result of having taken a wrong turn centuries ago, we have lost access to it, but, if we were to backtrack, we could find the door again, and at the same time what we see and what is hidden from us would stand revealed in the same dazzling light. In his last book,[5] Saint-Yves d'Alveydre imperturbably maintains that an association of some twenty million members—the Paradesa—keeps, deep underground, a record of everything that has been thought and of everything that has happened on the surface of the earth; that the insides of the planet have been methodically explored on the natural as well as on the supernatural level; that this association is in possession of the universal language: "The actual university archives of the Paradesa," he says, "stretch for thousands of miles. . . . The libraries of previous cycles can be found under the ocean that swallowed up the ancient austral continent, and even in the underground constructions of the antediluvian Americas. . . . The reader should imagine a colossal chessboard extending underground throughout most of the areas of the globe. . . . [There] everything speaks and everything has meaning, everything has its name visibly inscribed in its very form, the symbol of its nature—from the insect to the Sun, from the underground fire that devours all matter to the celestial fire that resorbs every essence within itself." This idea that the lost treasure (perhaps not lost for everyone) might be in the possession of a minority who have been entrusted with it and who must protect it at all cost from profanation, does not fail to cross the most skeptical minds. One may recall Jacques Vaché's statement: "My current dream is to be a member of a secret, purposeless Chinese society in Australia." *Purposeless*: out of some self-defense mechanism, Jean Ferry even goes one step farther: "Everyone has known for a long time that this purpose is to keep the secret." To this, it will be easy for the advocates of the esoteric tradition to reply that the actual secret in question could not possibly consist, as the common herd might think, in concealing the rites and the means of recognition, since "it pertains strictly to the inner man" and, as such, it can "never be betrayed in any way."[6] This last observation will certainly not detract from the significant reservations expressed by Jean Ferry in his reflections on Kafka with respect to the arbitrary recruiting of followers and to the risk, which any organization of this kind may incur, of lapsing into a bureaucratic morass. The fact remains that here, the marvelous has faced the temptation to reconnoiter its lands, that it is toward them that it turned to seek its credentials. The feeling that there is an occult presence about, if necessary in the guise of "this pallid little man with weary eyes" (everything needed to pass unnoticed) but who has the *knowledge* and the *will*, is the great lever of the most compelling story in this collection, a story that I unhesitatingly greeted as a masterpiece when it first appeared.[7]

It is this story also that probably best exemplifies the author's conception of love, a conception that I am not loath to characterize as sadistic since, I hasten to say, I attach no pejorative meaning to this epithet. Freud has shown that the sadistic temperament can beget, as well as vices, virtues of a very mundane nature, such as extreme punctiliousness, while in Jean Ferry it continually generates lyricism. Woman is regarded as one of the poles of the cosmic universe whose only meaning accessible to us is given by sexual attraction. Her eyes, serving as vehicles for this attraction, tend to transcend all dimensions ("immensely green eyes . . . never-ending eyes") and, in front of the great trapeze artist whom, among all others, he chooses as his mother (a doubly perilous motif), Jean Ferry is filled with the same enthusiasm as Cyprien in Huysmans's novel: "The sight of those sublime buttocks ascending toward the sky was deeply moving." To exalt this attraction and to liberate it from the taboos under which it is placed, no sacrifice is too great, not even that of a freedom that does not take it into account. The riddle left by the Marquis de Sade, on the borders of courtly love and of the most discourteous kind of love, is tackled here head-on and solved without ambiguity: "The Marquis de Sade, as he did not want to be disturbed, went and checked whether the door of his dungeon was properly shut. It was double-locked on the outside. He shot the inside bolt, with which the governor had obliged him, came back to his table, sat down, and resumed his writing."

Paimpont, August 1949

The Art of

the Insane,

the Door to Freedom

In the review dated October 1948, which is a real manifesto of Art Brut, our friend Jean Dubuffet stresses quite rightly our interest and special affinity for the works that "are created by individuals considered to be mentally ill and confined to psychiatric institutions." It goes without saying that I fully support his declarations: "The criteria by which a man is deemed unfit for social life are not ones we feel any need to uphold." I declare myself to be in no less perfect agreement with Lo Duca, the author of a remarkable article entitled "L'Art et les fous" [Art and the insane] that was passed on to me, unfortunately without its reference, and from which I will simply quote the following: "In a world crushed by megalomania and arrogance, by mythomania and dishonesty, the notion of madness is quite a vague one. In this regard, it has been observed that an inordinately small number of megalomaniacs are being treated by psychiatrists. Naturally, as soon as madness becomes collective—or expresses itself through the voice of the group—it becomes taboo. . . . In our eyes, the genuine madman is revealed through admirable expressions in which he is never constrained, or subdued, by 'reasonable' objectives. This absolute freedom invests the art of the mentally ill with a greatness that we are only sure to find also among Primitives. . . . My purpose here is to attempt to convince the public to *experience* before having *understood* a work of art. Someday the public will be made to question the value of their 'understanding': it will be enough to suggest to them that we are not even 'sure' of time and space. . . . The public know nothing of beauty, which they still confuse with what is pretty, charming, nice. They are not aware of the part played by intensity, rhythm, tempo. The art of the insane will instill doubt into them, that salutary doubt that will lead them toward a superior and serene comprehension." I have only quoted this text at such length to show that the idea of a resounding reparation is in the air. We will not rest until we are rid of that blind and intolerable prejudice that has for so long affected the works of art produced in asylums and until we have disentangled them from the pernicious atmosphere that has been created around them.

It should be noted that the question of how to deal with such works has caused increasing embarrassment over the last fifty years in psychiatric circles—that is to say in a sphere where those works were nonetheless essentially considered in terms of their "clinical" value. Already, in his book *L'Art chez les fous* [Art among the insane], published in 1905, Marcel Réja objected to their "pathological" character being used as an excuse to consider them as "off-center, completely outside the norm," and he was responsive to the beauty of some of those works. Hans Prinzhorn,[1] by bringing to public attention those he considered most remarkable (particularly works by August Neter, Hermann Beil, Joseph Sell, and Wölfli) and by providing them with a presentation for the first time worthy of them, called for a comparison between those and the other contemporary artworks—a comparison that, in many respects, would turn to the disadvantage of the latter. Jacques Lacan,[2] while making a masterly analysis of his patient Aimée, shows the highest and most justified esteem for her literary production. Gaston Ferdière, when he spoke quite recently at the Psychiatric Conference in Amsterdam, began his lecture with two epigraphs, the first by Edgar Poe: "Men called me mad, but science has not yet decided whether madness might not be the highest intelligence," the other by Chesterton: "Any sequence of ideas may lead to ecstasy; all paths lead to the fairy kingdom." As you can see, the salutary doubt Lo Duca was talking about may not have reached the public yet, but it does appear more and more among specialists of madness.

In order to overcome the public's lack of receptivity and their deep-rooted prejudice, we will have to tackle them at the source and show conclusively what causes them. I ascribe the blame for this to both Christianity and rationalism; the perpetuation to this day of this state of affairs can also be assigned to the inadequacy of art criticism, inimical as it is to anything outside the beaten track.

Everyone knows that primitive peoples honored or still honor the expression of mental abnormalities and that the highly civilized peoples of antiquity were not different from them in that respect, nor are the Arabs today. As Réja observes, "The ancients, who did not even suspect the existence of mental illnesses, attributed the origin of psychological disorders to a divine intervention, the same as for genius. . . . In the Middle Ages, delirium was no longer regarded as a sign of God's favor but as a retribution inflicted by Him. At least it still emanated from Him (through the Devil's agency)." This last notion, violently stirred up by the trials and exorcisms of "possessed" individuals, the memory of which remains quite vivid, proved enduringly alarming and is still today far from being revised.

Rationalism did the rest and it is not the first time that we see those two apparently contradictory ways of thinking unite, in fact, in order to sanction a blatant iniquity. "Common sense," which stands on very shaky ground but takes advantage unashamedly of the minor reassurances it provides within the sphere of practical life, tends to use violent means to brush aside and even to eliminate anything refusing to compromise with it. Common sense becomes all the more despotic as its authority rests on foundations that are increasingly more unstable and worm-eaten: at the smallest infraction, it is ready to inflict a ruthless punishment. It distrusts absolutely anything exceptional and sees to the proper maintenance, through its specially appointed journalists, of the famous corridor (A word to the wise. . .) that connects genius to madness and into which, so we are assured at every opportunity, artists can move quite far without needing too much of a push.

It should have been up to art criticism, faced with visual works of superior quality like those presented by Prinzhorn, to take stock of the situation, I mean to compare those works with the ones on which it usually focuses, to apply to them without bias its own set of criteria. But in order to do so, it should have retained some measure of genuine independence and its criteria should be less desperately inadequate. The suffocating smoke of incense with which it feels obligated to surround a few established artists and the bias toward extensive denigration that gives it status in its own eyes do not leave it much time to discover new values, and they make it all the less suited for explorations of a risky nature. It is far better for art criticism to enjoy peace and quiet as it fawns upon the celebrities of the moment, reiterates endlessly the same twaddle, and—just in case—belittles anything that deviates from the small line it has drawn. The public can rest easy: the padded door has been shut not only on those individuals who have not always been able to show their credentials but also on everything admirable that they sometimes do and that could remind it of their existence. You can well imagine that with such service records, art criticism as we know it today is not about to try and turn to advantage—its own as well as ours—those trophies of the true "spiritual chase" that leads through the great "distractions" of the human mind.

I am not afraid to put forward the idea, a paradoxical one only at first sight, that the art of those who are presently categorized as mentally ill represents a store of mental health. That is because it remains unaffected by everything that tends to distort the modes of expression with which we are concerned: external influences, self-interested motives, success or disappointments experienced on the social level, etc. In this instance, the mechanisms of artistic creation are freed from any constraint. Through a deeply moving dialectical effect, confinement and renunciation of all profits as well as of all vanities—despite what they mean in terms of individual tragedy—guarantee the total authenticity that is lacking everywhere else and that we crave more and more.

Pont-Neuf

For Jindrich Heisler

She feigns sleep and will not let us rest while her hair softly bubbles on the pillow of her banks. Her hand, the only part of her slightly awake on the edge of the bed, lit up a moment ago at all the feathers talking from the farthest horizons; once the birds flew off, it hid under her head, thereby accentuating the pose of voluptuous nonchalance. At once, all the fragrance of the flowers came to rest in the exposed armpit. Barely arisen from the night, almost unopened yet, they gather, shivering as if they could not survive outside the blond warmth of this basket. Her imperceptible breath can only be surmised from the slight quiver of her skin that it brings on at short intervals. This becomes more pronounced and almost slightly electric near the tenderest flesh of the belly, where one of the thighs forms a wider arc so as to cover part of the other one, creating the impression that the entwined legs, especially when the trees are covered with leaves and obscure the window, taper and ripple into an endless mermaid tail.

I am talking about a river to which I am bound by a spell, having been very early on confronted with her and with no other: I have not had time to grow indifferent to what is reflected, albeit so hazily, in her beige and gray eye. Other rivers are limpid and fascinating, others are turbulent and trout fly into their arms when they rise and rumble, other ones still roll nuggets or comb long red grass, but the Seine in Paris keeps a bittersweet surface that conceals a deep shiftiness. *Gone with History*, that is the title of a movie whose advertising posters I recently saw on walls. A clever title, I thought; indeed, in this respect history could teach the wind a thing or two. Of course "the old Paris no longer exists," but what do we care about the nostalgia for what it used to be and the melancholy periodically inspired by its spurious improvements, compared to the river that keeps on irrigating it, still propelled by the same force and no doubt barely altered in its essence? This water flows immutably here and there, neither more nor less muddy than when the newly built sumptuous mansions on the quai des Augustins sneered at the hovels of the Vallée de la Misère from above the île aux Treilles. Only this water can combine the cloudy green of the willow plantations, such as they existed on the Left Bank before the constructions ordered by Philip the Fair, with those gleams that, on the other bank, the stagnating runnels from the tanneries deposited on the clay.

Kleist is thought, at the beginning of the nineteenth century, to have projected his own moods on the physiognomy and temperament of certain rivers: the Main that curves round the slightest vineyard hill, the Elbe lingering with utter delight in its valley, the haughty Rhine pushing aside the rocks in its path. My own perception of the Seine is more static but entails no less effusion on my part.

The steps that, for no external reason, bring us year after year to the same spots in a city prove how increasingly sensitive we become to some of its parts, which appear in some obscure fashion to be either favorable or inimical. If one pays attention while walking along a single street that is moderately long and presents sufficient variety along the way (the rue de Richelieu, for instance), one will discover between two spots that could be pinpointed alternating zones of well-being and discomfort. A map that would probably be quite revealing should be drawn for *every individual*: the places he haunts could be shown in white, the ones he avoids in black, and the rest in various shades of gray according to the degree of attraction or repulsion. This classification should be ruled by a measure of objectivity, and there is no doubt that, in this as in other matters, the "privileged structures" prevail in the choices that are made. But, when it comes to a city as ancient as Paris and endowed with such a rich past, it seems to me impossible to think that those structures are strictly physical ones. What is interesting about them is that they arise to a large extent from *what happens* here or there and that, if we tried to elucidate the matter, they would make us more aware of what causes us to falter as well as of what helps us regain our balance. This entirely intuitive way of looking, this groping around through what brings us felicity or gives us umbrage, could be of great assistance to us in how we conduct our affairs.

In line with that effort to fathom what is incorrectly and so carelessly regarded as unfathomable, I can point out without much hesitation the spot from where the Seine in Paris would appear in the most favorable light to eyes that had never seen her before—which also happens to be the spot from which her general configuration can best be observed. In my opinion, that spot is located *somewhere* between the intersections with the embankments of the rue du Louvre and of the rue de l'Arbre-Sec. Referring to Edouard Fournier,[1] Fulcanelli points out that the rue de l'Arbre-Sec [Street of the Dry Tree] owes its name to an inn whose sign was still there in the seventeenth century and where pilgrims to the Holy Land must have stayed about 1300 (the dry tree being the hieroglyph used by the alchemists to represent "metal inertia"). At any rate, in the sixteenth century, according to the plans for building a new bridge "for the relief of the Notre-Dame and au-Change bridges," this one would be a continuation of the rue de l'Arbre-Sec. Judging from a distance and taking into account the roads available to human traffic at the time, this was indeed the most rational solution. The idea that prevailed, however, namely that of erecting the bridge some six hundred feet farther upstream so that it would stand on the western tip of the île de la Cité, seems to me to correspond to gratifications of an entirely different nature.

Whether he reaches the embankment by passing in front or in back of the church of Saint-Germain-l'Auxerrois, the observer stands there on the pivotal point of Paris. A short distance away, on his right, he can hear the dull creaking of the chain forged in the fourteenth century that, at the close of the day, used to link the tournelle du Louvre [small tower of the Louvre] with the tour de Nesle and marked one of the city limits. If for one second we picture the Seine like a woman letting the arm she held bent on her forehead slide down her side, the point I mentioned is invariably found between her fingers like the stem of a flower.

I should add that for me the immediate vicinity of Saint-Germain-l'Auxerrois is permeated with darkness and alarm. The contrast is all the more startling with the impression of a sudden unveiling given by the Seine when, from that spot, one looks at her upstream. It would be trivial to repeat that the heart of Paris is beating in the île de la Cité: for a whole country, everything really started here; moreover, however small it is in size, no one will deny that its destruction would be a mortal blow for this country and much more besides—maybe the only truly fatal blow. But this image of a heart yet conceals the suggestion of a shape that I am surprised did not become clearer long ago, at least to some people.

When I began, I tried to delimit that shape by what surrounds it: the quai de la Mégisserie and the quai de Gesvres, which until the war were deafened by birds and monkeys, and the flower market, where sheer freshness is reengendered night after night. If hideous buildings along the way force one to hurry on, it is fortunately not forbidden to blot them out using the Zen masters' method (closing one's eyes would still be too much) so as to restore the monuments that had soul and whose place they usurped, such as the fountain on top of which sat an astronomical clock with a set of bells and a mechanical ringer, the fountain from which sordid "department stores" stole even its name: "Samaritaine." Besides, whoever wants to peek through the successive layers of time can easily focus beyond on the tour Saint-Jacques or on the Hôtel de Ville, which, in the distance, look as if they could stand on a woman's palm, as in that beautiful popular image from the Chartres printing works that shows Saint Clotilda presenting a church tower. Those jewels from another age—jewels much less because of what they are than because of the circumstances out of which they arose or the events that unfolded therein—are standing in their smoked crystal through which faint lights are glowing, right next to the Seine as though she had just set them down after her ablutions or as if they had to stay at hand. Similarly laid out on her left, the schools like a half-read book waiting to be taken up again or thrown aside.

I say that the square de l'Archevêché on the one hand, the Pont-des-Arts as it stands nowadays, on the other, mark the limits within which the course of the Seine begets a being endowed with organic life whose essential organs, from the head to the junction of the lower limbs, are all enclosed within the île de la Cité—which in fact marked the boundaries of the early Lutetia—and that the configuration of that being, as well as the power of seduction that emanates from it, cannot bring to mind any other picture than that of a woman.

I do not think we need look elsewhere for the secret of her glamour. It lies entirely in the erotic appeal of that beautiful body, lascivious even when showing lassitude. There is nothing around her but sheets tossed aside, still permeated in fact with the smell of her. What comes to mind is Baudelaire's young giantess, and sometimes we also see that magnificent nudity, at once provocative and guarded, as well as everything that keeps on talking about her to the wind, with the eyes of Charles Cros when he opened them to capture the purest light of Paris in his wonderful poem "Matin" [Morning]. Whether we like it or not, Paris compels recognition in other countries because of its luxury goods industry, which is reflected in its culture as well, in what is most specific to it. This figure stretching on the water into an almond and a mistress is primarily, if not solely, concerned with seduction. Behind the elbow with which she pretends to conceal her face, her eyes blaze out in the great rose window of Notre-Dame whenever the fancy takes her. But what gives her away and clearly identifies her is elsewhere.

I once said that the place Dauphine "is really one of the most secluded places I know, one of the worst wastelands to be found in Paris. Each time I was there," I added, "I felt I was progressively losing any desire to go anywhere else, I had to argue with myself to break free of a very gentle embrace that was all too pleasantly insistent and, all in all, draining."[2] Only later did that impression become clear to me, but when it did, it nearly dazzled me. I find it unbelievable today that others before me, upon entering the place Dauphine from the Pont-Neuf, were not grabbed by the throat at the sight of its triangular conformation, a slightly curvilinear one at that, and of the slit that bisects it into two wooded areas. Unmistakably, what lies revealed in the shade of those groves is the sex of Paris. Its down is still lit, at various times of the year, by the execution of the Templars that was carried out on that spot on 13 March 1313 and was largely responsible, according to some, for the revolutionary destiny of the city. More often a wind of distraction blows there, inducing one to forget everything, leaving only *frenzy*. After nightfall, concealed Chinese lanterns illuminate, as in full daylight, the thousands of street performers who have been congregating there for centuries. Could it be that their twirling shadows contribute to how amazingly unsafe and at the same time how *detaining* the place seems? I believe, on the contrary, that this very configuration is what brought them to gather and settle for so long on that spot—not surprising, if that is indeed what I made it out to be. Needless to say, finally, the couples who stray onto that square on summer nights exacerbate their desires and become the playthings of a volcano.

To those who would tend to repress such a representation, even if it meant blotting out the square du Vert-Galant and refusing to recognize, mounted on his horse, the king who provided the design for refining the triangular shape of the place Dauphine,[3] I would also point out that the physical considerations supporting my theory could be coupled, if necessary, with arguments that apply on the "moral" level. In this respect, it seems to me positively significant that the base of the triangle, on the rue de Harlay, coincides with the back of the Palais de Justice [Law Courts], whose curved double staircase—so that everyone may know—is guarded by two stone lions. The proximity of the seat of punishment—framing as it does that infinitely precious machine of expiation that is the Sainte-Chapelle [Holy Chapel]—emphasizes even better the taboo associated with the place Dauphine and, for everything that has to do with Paris, marks it out as the *sacred* place.

From the time the city started taking shape, there has been a constant oscillation whenever it came to determining the elective location of the bridge that was to be thrown over the Seine between the Châtelet and the Louvre (in the ninth century, a wooden bridge continued the rue de Harlay toward the present quai de la Mégisserie: it is on the tower that dominated the Seine on this latter side that the Norsemen's attack broke up; moreover, let me remind you specifically that, in the reigns of Henry II and Henry

III, it was part of Spifame's plan that the projected bridge would link the Louvre with the old hôtel de Nesle, while the latter would be converted into a palace of the university). There was no chance that oscillation would come to an end before the natural magnetization point that needed to be reached could be found. I think it is clear by now that it could not have been located anywhere else.

The bold decision to trace the line between the two banks through that point, with the Pont-Neuf resting lightly and brazenly on that distracting angle of the delta, is what must have put that final accent of supreme immodesty on the city. The collective unconscious was so pleased with this masterpiece that the first equestrian statue of Henry IV, erected in 1635 and destroyed during the Revolution, was considered by the people to be badly oriented, on account of the fact that "instead of facing the entrance of the place Dauphine, it was at an angle to it." So, the functional value of the bridge did not eclipse the triangle of temptation that it brushed in passing.

I am reminded of that cry, ringing so true despite its enigmatic character, let out by one of the most engaging poets of the last century: "Paris, your obscene glory!..."[4] Never had the two ideas confronting each other in that cry combined more intimately in the course of time in a more exiguous space. From the rue de la Monnaie to the rue Dauphine, and straying inevitably toward the rue de Harlay, a wind of exhibitionism blows like nowhere else. The pilfering and debauchery that had concluded a treaty of alliance on that spot have been uprooted by the ruin and the replacement by a regular roadway of the old Pont-Neuf, but the place Dauphine, at dusk, is still endowed with an infinite magnetizing force and suggestiveness. The old Pont-Neuf remains there in the background, where Gaston d'Orléans and his retinue have come to rub elbows with the cutpurses. Under that streetlamp over there, the maréchal d'Ancre is not a pretty sight, hanging upside down like the figure on the twelfth arcanum of the tarot. That red blur that turns out to be a cardinal's cape, around which the roused mob mutters and yields, that is Gondi, a fine talker if ever there was one. That cheeky and bitter taunting of the river belts out all its refrains, punctuated by Cartouche's pistol. As night draws nigh, the high spectral cart still goes by, carrying the Friend of the people by torchlight,[5] with his head lolling on his shoulder and the dagger wounds showing on his bare chest. The "enchanted hand" conjured up by Gérard de Nerval beats time quietly. Two figures can be seen walking away cautiously arm in arm: both unusual as well as insipid in other respects, they could not be better suited to each other, Restif de la Bretonne and Bluet-d'Arbères, count of Permission.

February 1950

Open Letter

to

Paul Eluard

Paris, 13 June 1950

Fifteen years ago, at the invitation of our friends the Czech Surrealists, you and I went to Prague, where we gave lectures and interviews. More recently, I know you were much feted there but in a more conventional and official way. You must not have forgotten the welcome we were given in Prague.

Nothing came between us at that time: from the political point of view, we certainly did not pretend to toe the party line. Our only strength resided in the ideas that the small group of us had jointly developed. Our way of thinking was in our view strictly dependent on the poetic activity that had been our primary concern from the start. Along the way, we became involved in the movement for social change, a change that, for us, could not be dissociated from the ardent example of the Bolshevik Revolution, and we spared no effort to try and lessen, between various "cultural" views held by the Communist party and our own, the differences that remained. However, we always deemed it necessary to defend our positions when they were based on convictions within the purview of our own particular exploration. What was at stake was the authenticity of our testimony on both levels: the least compromise either way would have seemed to us liable to distort entirely that testimony and would have discredited us in our own eyes.

That was our frame of mind when we arrived in Prague, though we did feel some anxiety about how our message would be received. It is one thing to face a foreign audience when one is determined, whatever happens, to express one's own convictions and nothing but; it is quite different to come as the duly appointed spokesman of powerful organizations without having to express anything in one's own name. I will say it again: we were, you and I, nothing other than ourselves. In the slightly frantic bustle of those first few days, there is, if you recall, one man who comes by, who joins us as often as possible, who does his best to try and understand us, a man who is *open*. That man is not a poet, but he listens to us just as we listen to him: what we tell him does not seem to him inadmissible, and his occasional objections are instructive, convincing even. He is the one who, in Communist papers, provides the most penetrating analyses of our books and the most valid write-ups of our lectures. He will not rest until he has won us the favor of large audiences made up of intellectuals and workers alike.

On the level of human interaction, his help and generosity were invaluable to us at the time. The "Bulletin" that was published in Prague on 9 April 1935, in Czech and in French and signed by both of us, states this explicitly.

I think you remember the name of that man: he is—or was—Závis Kalandra. I dare not decide which tense to use since the papers have just announced that he was sentenced to death last Thursday by a Prague tribunal—after the usual "confession" in due form, naturally. You used to know, as I did, what such a confession was worth. Kalandra knew it as well in 1936, when he was expelled from the Communist party on account of his comments on the "trial of the 16" in Moscow. I am well aware that he then became one of the leaders of the International Communist party (in the Czech section of the Fourth International), but how could you blame him for doing so when you yourself, a few months before, signed a text entitled "At a Time When Surrealists Were Right" that declared our positive distrust of the Stalinist regime—a text that anyone can reread today?

Could it be because the war and the Occupation created such a division between men that Kalandra has obviously gone over to the wrong side? Could it be that he is guilty vis-à-vis the Resistance? Certainly not, since it is precisely the articles he wrote in 1939—in which, at the height of the Nazi Occupation, he was not afraid to deride Hitlerian propaganda—that earned him six years of incarceration in the camps (in Ravensbruck and Sachsenhausen, among others).

No way! No traitor has ever been cut out of such cloth. I have known you for a long time as someone who reveres and holds the human voice sacred, even in its very inflections: tell me, do you recognize Kalandra's voice under these castoffs of sordid propaganda: "My goal was to obtain a tightening of the discriminatory embargo laid on Czechoslovakia by the Western imperialist powers so as to hinder its economic prosperity and force it toward Marshallization"?

How can you tolerate, deep down, such degradation to be inflicted on a man who was a friend to you?[1]

The Donator

Around the age of twenty, one may find oneself irresistibly drawn
to a side of the human voice as one is drawn to a woman, and the die is
cast, there is no chance the attraction will fade. I am among those who loved
Eloges [*Eloges*] as one may love, at that age, in poetry and in art, everything
that enjoys the privilege of increasing the capacity for loving in the one who
loves. It was—how fortunate—a work that had not yet been consecrated:
its light was undimmed, it still burned brightly when it entered my bush.
That light will not fade; for the secret being abiding within the self, there
is no release from such a hold. I still remember, when we were in Nantes,
watching Jacques Vaché's face for his reaction to the thirteenth canto in
that collection, lest he should underestimate its "modernist" qualities (as
we used to call them). I am still captivated by its echo and fascinated as
well by the endless vistas that Saint-John Perse, from *Anabase* [*Anabasis*] to
Vents [*Winds*], has since been able to open up in the wake of that first book.
From the point of view of the "madly" daring contribution that anticipates
the specific need of an era—without anyone being aware yet that, from the
multicolored cartridges, flares will shoot up and illuminate the depths of a
whole world—no one has a greater right to say:

> *Others drank the new wine from fountains painted in red lead. And among
> those we were.*

But the enjoyment would be short-lived if we did not know where that
wine was coming from, on which hillsides are grown those choicest grapes

that only exceptional men with winged feet are able to reach and gaze at as they hold them against the sunlight:

O freshness, O freshness recaptured amongst the springs of language!...
New wine cannot be any truer nor new linen any fresher.

That place is, for that matter, plated with mirages, overcast with illusions, torn, just as is our present time, between the "established totality" (moral law included, could this totality have been different or not?) and the "conjectural" sphere (which for the past five years has been stricken, for the first time, in its very principle):

Ho! giant tree of language peopled with oracles, maxims and whispering whispers of one born blind in the grove of knowledge ...

The trails are all tangled up now. How are we to bring the Word back to that Beginning?

I salute Saint-John Perse, not only as a water-diviner in that domain but also as the man of my time who has tried the most unremittingly to reach all men, each according to his occupation. In the same way that Apollinaire's turn of mind is encapsulated in the phrase "There is"—the great leitmotiv in his poetry that enables him to bring together the simultaneous appearances, devoid of any noticeable common characteristic, that this world may take on while we are in it—Saint-John Perse's imagination is never any freer than when he uses the phrase "The one who." This expression opens the gate to the celebration of the most disparate activities alloted to men by the modern-day world, among which the least utilitarian, the most whimsical, are not necessarily the least well respected. Who would have conceived of such a magical census? Each individual being dignified by his particular assignment ... The poet hereby retains, or rather regains, the position from which everything today conspires to dislodge him—it is as if Saint George's spear suddenly gleamed:

And you who belong to the masses and the greater number, do not apply

your standards to the men of my breed. They have lived higher than you
in the depths of opprobrium.

They are the thorn in your flesh; the very point of the sword of the mind.
The bee of language is on their foreheads.

And on the heavy human sentence, kneaded out of so many idioms, they
alone sling the stones of scansion.

Which artist, among the most famous ones today, will dare vie with the
man who shows:

The governors in prune-violet with their russet-fleshed daughters smelling
of ferret.

The image—the star at the tip of the fingers—was never held any higher.
Here is the snow:

Dawn, silent in its plumage, like a great mythical owl possessed by the
breath of the spirit, swelled its body—a white dahlia.

Flying in the face of everything, here is desire:

And here again upon the New Year the virgins swarm, each concealing
under nylon the fresh almond of her sex.

As

in a

Wood

I would be in contradiction with myself and disavowing what defines me in my own eyes if I were to appear unduly upset, as is customary nowadays, over the disappointments caused by cinema as a means of expression that was once believed to be better suited than most for promoting "true life."

In this era of *inhumanism*, most writers feel honor-bound to "engage" in politics, which means that, with complete disregard for what might warrant their spiritual influence (providing a record of their times with complete freedom and an absolute respect for the meaning of words), they side with one of the two opposing camps, whose only intent is to exterminate the other. Artists who have always professed atheism now work with great fanfare on the decoration of religious buildings.[1] For a whole hour, on 28 September, the French Broadcasting Corporation, under the title "The French Variety Cup," was able to inflict upon its listeners a concert given by the "artists" from the Paris police headquarters that included an inspector's monologue, a great aria from *Pagliacci*, a piece for piano played by a handcuffed man, a poem by Prévert recited "with great feeling," and the choir of the "little singers of the pointed tower" (*sic*). In such times as these, I do not think that cinema is necessarily the medium most deserving of public abuse.

My dissatisfaction with the undeniable vulgarity of film production was never more than an altogether secondary, incidental concern. When I was of "cinema age" (it must be acknowledged that there is such a time in one's life—and that one outgrows it), I never began by reading the weekly program to try and guess which film might be the best one, nor did I inquire about the time when a particular movie would start. Jacques Vaché and I were particularly like-minded in that respect, and there was nothing we enjoyed so much as to choose a theater at random, barge in when the movie had already started, and leave at the first sign of boredom—of surfeit—to rush off to some other theater where we behaved in exactly the same way, and so on (of course, this would be too much of a luxury nowadays). I have never experienced anything quite as *magnetizing*: it goes without saying that more often than not we left our seats without even knowing the name of the movie, to which we were completely indifferent. Within a few hours on a Sunday, we had gone through all the movies that were being shown in Nantes: the important thing is that we came out of it "charged" for a few days; by tacit agreement, value judgments never came into play.

It did happen, however, that some "comic" films held our attention: as can be expected, those were Mack Sennett's, the first of Chaplin's, and a few in the *Picratt* series. I remember rating very highly around that time a certain *Diana la charmeuse* [Diana the charmer], in which a beautiful actress in the title role wandered bewitchingly among innumerable towers (no need to dwell on this: from this distance in time, all I remember seeing between those towers is a magnificent wasteland). We only kept up more or less assiduously with those serialized films that were already disparaged (*The Exploits of Elaine*, *Le Masque aux dents blanches* [The mask with white teeth], *Les Vampires* [The vampires]): "Starting on Saturday in this theater, XIX: *The Crawling Glove.*—You can count on us."

What we saw in movies, whichever they were, was only a lyrical substance that had to be mixed and stirred in bulk and haphazardly. I think what we prized most in them, to the point of being indifferent to anything else, was this capacity to transport the mind elsewhere.

This change in mental scenery takes place on several levels, by which I mean that it allows for various stages. The *marvel*, compared to which the merits of any given film are of little consequence, lies in the freedom granted to anyone to remove himself from his own life whenever he feels like it, at least in cities, as soon as he goes through one of those soundproof doors that opens onto darkness. Between the moment he sits down and the moment he enters the fictional world that unfolds before his very eyes, he goes through a critical point as captivating and as elusive as the hinge between waking and sleeping (the transition is incomparably slower with books or even with plays). That solitary spectator lost amidst faceless strangers, how is it that he can, along with the rest of the audience, become at once part of an adventure that is neither his nor theirs? Could we possibly plot on a graph the radiations, the vibrations, that account for such a unison? Think of everything that could be undertaken under such a constellation, while it lasts. . . . There is a way of going to a movie theater just as others go to church, and I think that, from a certain point of view, quite irrespective of what is showing on the screen, it is there that the only *absolutely modern* mystery is being celebrated.

There is little doubt that the main forces within this mystery are desire and love. "To a hundred and fifty million human beings, every week," writes René Clair, "the screen talks about love. . . . And one wonders whether these representations of love are not one of the essential appeals of movies, one of the secrets of the spell they cast on the masses. . . ."[2] It is surprising that he is not more certain of it. Among the means available to cinema, the most specific is quite obviously the capacity to give concrete expression to the forces of love that, in books, remain somewhat deficient by the very fact that writing is incapable of conveying a seductive or anguished look, or some of those priceless expressions of ecstasy—not to mention the total ineffectuality of visual arts in this respect (just think that not a single painter has been able to depict the radiance of a kiss). Only cinema has been able to annex that province, and that is more than enough to deserve consecration. In that regard, what incomparable, everlastingly scintillating trails such films as *Ah! Le Beau Voyage* [What a beautiful trip] or *Peter Ibbetson* have left in our memories! How they have lit up the supreme opportunities in life! Even if the tension is in other respects far less sustained, nothing can alter the fact that, on the edges of the least sacrificed as well as the most worthless lives, the shading on a beautiful arm will bring out an illuminated expanse.

So great is the temptation to prolong and extend to impossible limits this feeling of disorientation that it sometimes induced my friends and myself to adopt paradoxical attitudes along the way. Precisely because what was at stake was the will to *go beyond* the boundary of what is "allowed," a boundary that, nowhere as much as in a movie theater, seems to me to be an invitation to enter what is "forbidden." And what if we settled permanently in that arbitrary but changing world that—just as it is—is so much better than the other one, isn't it? To some extent, it is from this point of view that I once recounted how "with Jacques Vaché, in the orchestra of the old 'Folies-Dramatiques' theater, we would settle down to dinner, opening cans, slicing bread, uncorking bottles, and talking in loud voices as one does over a regular meal, which dumbfounded the rest of the audience, who did not dare to complain."[3]

(Just as I was quoting this sentence, I received a printed *Declaration* by Malcolm de Chazal, dated 25 September 1911, Curepipe, Mauritius, that concludes with the following: "What provides the Opening Key is the *Meaning of the Night* revealed. There is no other key, nor can there be. For the Secret of Success consists only in breaking up the contradictions. And only the Night has that power." Cinema is the first wide-open bridge connecting the "day" to that night.)

In my unwavering pursuit of increased disorientation, there was a time when I sought delectation in the most execrable film productions. I found it mostly in French films, as I mentioned elsewhere: "I have always felt a powerful attraction to the treasure trove of idiocy and coarse burlesque that, thanks to them, can be found sparkling on the screens of Parisian theaters. I for one set great store by French screenplays and French acting: with those at least, you can be sure of a good laugh (unless of course it is a 'comic' film, in which case human emotions, with their need for extreme externalizations, have a chance to reappear."[4] Here, an extreme form of disorientation is expected, not from the transfer of an everyday activity into a space dedicated to an *other* life, which it profanes, but from as great a discord as possible between the "message" intended by the film and the frame of mind of its recipient. I mentioned in *Nadja* a naked woman going about her business, as if she were at home, among the side rows of the "Electric-Palace" (well screened from sight of the center seats): her white figure would not have seemed as phosphorescent had she not caught my eye while I was watching an utterly absurd movie in which everything served as a pretext for exhibiting the "holy table." This was the work of a priest who dubbed himself Pierre l'Hermite, and I think its title was *Comment j'ai tué mon enfant* [How I killed my child].

It is plain to see that, in regard to motion pictures, I am content to remain in a neutral zone, which is by and large unaffected by the laudatory or derogatory comments aroused by any given film. Of course, this does not prevent me from stating whether I am "for" or "against" or from being passionate about it if need be. This is required by the necessary interplay of emotions and ideas that can only be sustained and kept alive by what is at hand. In this respect, the only thing to do is to make the best of a bad bargain. Once again social, ethical, and aesthetic criteria scramble for the spoils.

In this as in other regards, it is difficult not to feel somewhat nostalgic when one thinks of what cinema could have been and could have made possible if the sordidness of this era, combined with the requirements, worse than any other, of its "exploitation," had not clipped its wings before it could leave the nest. Only Charles Fourier had enough revolutionary vision to argue and to demonstrate that the whole cultural development of humanity did not follow the direction it did out of any internal necessity but as a result of various pressures that might have been different and might have been borne differently. This conviction in no way entails a detraction from human achievements on any level; it does emphasize, however, the fact that they are strictly contingent, and therefore embryonic. We can still distinguish today what the original means of motion pictures were and appreciate what parsimonious use has been made of them. Twenty-five years have elapsed since M. J. Goudal, in the *Revue Hebdomadaire*, pointed out how perfectly suited to the surrealist expression of life those means were, and *second by second* at that. Nowhere as in motion pictures have we been provided, in particular, with this Opening Key of which Chazal speaks, the one that triggers the mechanism of *correspondences* as far as the eye can see. But, of course, it was deemed preferable to stick to a theatrical type of action. One can judge the results in the light of this comment by a professional: "I must confess that I now seldom go to the movies. Most of them bore me and I find it very difficult to understand what is going on. People always have to explain the plot to me afterward."⁵

I once said: "Now we know that poetry must *lead somewhere*." Cinema had everything it needed to catch up with poetry, but as a whole—that is, as a controlled activity—the least that can be said is that it did not set out in that direction.

Foreword to the

Germain Nouveau

Exhibition

   "At last a work outside all literature, and probably superior to it all." This judgment, which Félix Fénéon passed with such lucidity on Rimbaud, could just as well be applied to Germain Nouveau and—with the exception of Lautréamont—to no one else. For that matter, they rode for a long while along the same path, their mounts rearing up with sparks flying from their back hooves as they came to the edges of the same chasms, before jumping synchronously between the two peaks of noxiousness and utmost salubrity. The inseparable black-and-white horsemen vie with each other in impetuosity. Only at the close of this unbridled race—when they are (at least apparently) at such a distance from each other—does lightning strike these two phoenixes, which, upon closer examination, are revealed as one. This phoenix is the *meaning* of life: in this search, they gave up all of what are called the "accommodations" of daily life. "Where do we come from? What are we? Where are we going?": obsessed with this one question, Rimbaud goes so far as to discard all that is most precious to him, and Nouveau deprives himself of the most basic necessities, going hungry and sleeping under bridges, a prey to vermin. At least, thanks to them and to the exorbitant price they had to pay, a new, unhoped-for, invaluable shoot has sprung up from the tree of human dignity, grown increasingly weak and stunted since Pascal and Rousseau.

   In his unmarked grave, sheltered from idle curiosity, Nouveau, who chose to endure all possible vicissitudes, who, more than anyone, flew

The exhibition was held in the Jacques Doucet Library in October 1951.

in the face of public opinion, certainly has nothing but disdain for the circumstances under which his writings have come down to us. It is a shame nevertheless that they should reach us in such a deplorable state. Since he did not authorize the publication of any collection, the volumes that came out under his name or his pseudonym—Humilis—present serious shortcomings: there is little justification for the actual ordering of the texts, and the accuracy of some of those is fairly doubtful. *Valentines*, for example, includes isolated instances of texts written in an entertaining vein ("Cas de divorce" [Divorce case]) that are in sharp contrast with the rest and appear quite out of place. The reconstitution from memory of the *Poésies d'Humilis* [Poems by Humilis] (first published under the title *Savoir aimer* [Knowing how to love]) is bound to be unreliable. The sequence within *Vers inédits* [Unpublished poems]—which, moreover, includes far less interesting prose fragments—follows no justifiable pattern. Finally, *Calepin du mendiant* [Beggar's notebook], were it not for the compelling introduction by Jules Mouquet, would hardly deserve a separate publication. We hope that this exhibition will prompt some researcher to devote his work to Germain Nouveau, bringing to his writings the clarification that is now very much needed and providing at least the preparatory work for a critical edition.

Here we have the opportunity to examine, outside of books, that which remains of one of the greatest adventures ever. No doubt some of these documents—the so-called ghost letter to Rimbaud dated 12 December 1893, the beautiful still lifes that are the very celebration of frugality, the cheap notebook in which the last lines of verse meander around faint sketches—will be seen and treasured as relics by others besides myself. Here we come close to some of the crests of the mind on the Heraclitean road, where "the way up and the way down are one and the same." On those lines crisscrossing in all directions, stretched between vertigo and ecstasy, I have seen the most wonderful verbal dewdrops hatch and sparkle like never before:

All snuggled up in a cheerful smell of laundering
—"Les Hôtesses" [The hostesses]

Poverty, so rich and golden

—"Cantique à la Reine" [Hymn to the queen]

When Athanasia was a merry queen
—"Toto"

A gray courtyard where the laced shoes of the older girls go round and
*   round*
—"Rêve claustral" [Claustral dream]

Yellow Sugar

Let the music start. Yes, good folk, it is I who command you to
burn, on a red-hot shovel, the vermouth-lipped duck of doubt with a
dash of yellow sugar . . .—Isidore Ducasse

I was dumbfounded to read in the last issue of *Cahiers du Sud*[1] an article by Albert Camus, the title of which, "Lautréamont et la banalité"
[Lautréamont and banality], might in its own right appear like a challenge.
In that article—very likely an excerpt from an essay entitled "La Révolte,"[2]
whose forthcoming publication is announced by the author of *Les Justes*
[*The Just*]—he takes for the first time a moral and intellectual stand that is
untenable.

"Moral": the very first lines are unsettling. Lautréamont "is, like Rimbaud, someone who suffers and who has rebelled; but, as he mysteriously
recoils from saying that he rebels against what is, he puts forward the dissident's time-honored alibi: the love of mankind." Besides the fact that
nothing could be more untrue (Lautréamont declares that his "purpose was
to attack man and the One who created him"), it is appalling that someone
who might have been considered noble-hearted should deny the dissident
the belief that he is acting not for his own good but for everyone's good.
Who is going to believe that Sade and Blanqui spent most of their lives
in jail because they rejected their own individual condition and not what
is the common lot? Such an insinuation is patently slanderous and utterly
intolerable. The word "alibi" is horrible: it belongs to the vocabulary of
repression. The man who utters those words has suddenly sided with the
worst conservatism, the worst "conformism."

"Intellectual": nothing as superficial, as trivial, has ever been written on Lautréamont. It almost seems as though the author of the article has only secondhand knowledge of his writings, that he has not himself read them. This work, the most inspired one in modern times, poses innumerable problems of "intention," unfolds simultaneously on several levels, overflows with interweaving meanings, plays on continual interferences of seriousness and humor, and systematically baffles rational interpretation. Now, it is reduced by Camus to an outline that would at most be appropriate to the type of synopsis found in serials: "Maldoror, despairing of divine justice, will side with evil. To inflict suffering and, thereby, to suffer himself, such is the program."

Yet, in his beautiful essay on Lautréamont[3]—to which Camus refers in a footnote, albeit perfunctorily—Maurice Blanchot had forestalled such oversimplifications. He was able to show that Lautréamont's heart "is also the heart of the universe" and that his struggle turns his torments into "the painful expression of the universal struggle." No one has better understood that Lautréamont enjoyed surprising the reader because "he himself is that reader and what he must surprise is the tormented center of his own self as it flees toward the unknown." Nor has anyone been better able to call attention to that deep pulsation within a work that is entirely focused on "desire" and whose movement is patterned after the erotic experience. However peremptory those warnings were, Camus paid them no heed. All he cares to see in Lautréamont is a "guilty" adolescent whom he—as the adult he is—must sermonize. He goes so far as to find in the second part of his works, *Poésies* [*Poems*], the punishment Lautréamont deserves.

According to Camus, *Poésies* is nothing more than a hodgepodge of "laborious platitudes," the expression of "absolute triteness," of an utterly "dreary conformism." Needless to say, this judgment would not stand up to the most cursory reading. There is no doubt that this little book propounds an enduring and singularly tiresome riddle; however, to use such a crude sleight of hand in order to make that riddle disappear is simply unacceptable. It is true that it is difficult to conjecture Lautréamont's reasons for doing a sudden about-face or (who knows what to expect with him) for pretending to do one. Maurice Blanchot, here as well, has stressed the ambiguity of the text. ("Many of the 'thoughts' may well celebrate virtue, but they do so with such contempt or, inversely, with such excessive extravagance that praise turns into denigration. . . . What is that power within him, even if it is turned toward the light, what is that creative overabundance in vain placed at the service of rules, but so great that it can only humiliate those rules and, beyond them, glorify immeasurable freedom?") Camus—who blames Hegel for most of the calamities in our times—would do well in this instance to avail himself of the resources of dialectics. The prevailing device used in *Poésies*, which consists in obstinately—and always with great subtlety—contradicting thoughts written by Pascal, La Rochefoucauld, and Vauvenargues, besides being unquestionably subversive, points to a process of generalized—dialectical—refutation that would invert the sign under which the whole book appears to be constructed. Camus, who, moreover, remains impervious to the unique tone of *Poésies*, does not seem to have been aware of this at all.

The shallowness of these views would not be of any great consequence if they did not aim at promoting the most questionable thesis there is, namely, that "absolute rebellion" can only engender a "predilection for intellectual enslavement." This is a totally gratuitous, ultradefeatist assertion that must be held in contempt, even more so than its erroneous demonstration.

It is scandalous that writers who find favor with the public should apply themselves to belittle what is a thousand times greater than they are. Not so long ago, someone was portraying Baudelaire as being entirely "lifeless or life-destroying," racked by an "aimless, sterile tension," killing himself in a deliberately "measly and protracted way," and whose character traits included "frigidity, impotence, sterility, lack of generosity, refusal to serve, sin." Carried away by his portrayal, that author even exclaims: "I would be willing to bet that he preferred to have his meat cooked in sauce rather than grilled and to eat canned vegetables rather than fresh ones." Your Lordships have an easy life: permit us to recall you from time to time to some sense of decency.

Alfred Jarry

as Precursor

and Initiator

"To paint is but to feign": this remark by Corneille Curce, the author of a book entitled *Les Clous du Seigneur* [The nails of the Lord] (1634), was taken up by Alfred Jarry in a well-documented article on the same topic that was published in the fourth issue of *L'Ymagier* in July 1895.[1] Jarry is undoubtedly at present the greatest victim of one of the worst curses of our times, which consists in oversimplifying, usually in a spirit of partisanship, the works of great authors. It is as if, out of all his writings, only *Ubu roi* [*Ubu Rex*] and later texts in the same vein were worthy of attention, as if his humor, more pervasive in those plays than anywhere else, had bitten like an acid deeply enough into the plate to obliterate all the other facets of a personality yet so rich and complex (but this complexity is precisely what is not wanted: it is easier to deal with only one aspect of such a thought, especially if by chance it has left an exceptional mark). And yet, just as we cannot reduce Sade to the perversion named after him, nor Baudelaire to the obsession with death, nor Lautréamont to the desire to glorify evil in *Maldoror*, then to glorify good (?) in *Poésies* [*Poems*], we can no longer accept that everything *else* Jarry wrote should be sacrificed to his predilection for puppet shows—to which he managed like no one else to bring recognition. The author of *Ubu roi*, of *Ubu enchaîné* [Ubu in chains], of *Les Almanachs* [The almanacs of Father Ubu], and of *La Passion considérée comme course de côte* [*The Passion Considered as an Uphill Bicycle Race*] is nonetheless also the one who wrote the first and last acts of *César-Antéchrist* [Emperor Antichrist], of *L'Autre Alceste* [The other Alceste], of *L'Amour absolu* [Absolute love]—all works that are quite different in the echoes they awaken, if not in their final intention. In fact, Jarry's curiosity was an encyclopedic one, if we understand the word not from the standpoint of the eighteenth century but from that of the transition from the nineteenth to the twentieth century. The doorway through which that transition occurred is still of great interest to us, so much so that we feel compelled to look back at it, since we only half know where it leads—and that in itself is not too reassuring. In the sphere of sensibility, Jarry's works are the hinges of that door, for no one has been able to look both as far ahead and as far back as he did. Not only did Jarry prophesy and stigmatize in *Ubu roi* and *Ubu enchaîné* the absurd and lethal propositions with which we were to be faced after his time, not only did his innovative genius inspire him with such lyrical flights as the "Course des dix mille milles" [Ten-thousand-mile race] in *Le Surmâle* [*The Supermale*] and as "La Bataille de Morsang" [The battle of Morsang] in *La Dragonne* [The persecuted], the "modernism" of which has never been surpassed or even equaled, but also it is as though, by some miracle, he could foretell what would be our own questions about the past, questions that he defined and answered in advance. It is high time to drop the plastered mask of a "Kobold" or of a "clown" with which Gide and some others who did not like him—and for good reason—covered Alfred Jarry's face. Whether or not he performed parody or burlesque in front of audiences of "men of letters" is of small importance: given the range of his vision, what is needed is to restore it to its true inner light.

There can be no better contribution to this task than to divest him of that theatrical role he played in daily life, for a dare as it were, and in order to do so we have to show which aspects of art, and of the art of his time in particular, were able to capture his attention. Was he the unrepentant iconoclast that his ostensible identification with Ubu would lead us to expect, or, if the opposite is true, what do the works that found favor with him reveal about his innermost sensibility? To settle this question, we only need to refer to the first books he was instrumental in publishing. The design of *Les Minutes de sable mémorial* [The records of the black crest] and that of *César-Antéchrist* show the keen interest he took in woodcuts, from the printmakers of old to Georgin, with a prolonged pause in front of Dürer. *L'Ymagier*, which he started in 1894 with Rémy de Gourmont, even suggests an elective predilection in this regard. The proponents of narrow-minded anticlericalism, upon seeing the "Calendrier du Père Ubu pour 1901" [Almanac of Father Ubu for 1901], are quick to enlist Jarry in their enterprise, yet we may observe that almost all the prints chosen and commented on by him are of religious inspiration and that, quite evidently, no trace of sarcasm is implied: "Vincent de Beauvais, Jacques de Voragine, the brocade of the Virgin of Lyon, the serge of Our Lady of Brittany, the animals in the restored Eden by Dürer (the Virgin with Rabbits, the Virgin with the Owl, the Virgin with the Monkey) and those in Epinal prints, the Marriage and the Demise of the Blessed Virgin—the image makers carve images and gild legends for the sake of the little Child sitting on his mother's lap who would make the blind see the light." None of the capital letters are missing and the tone is undeniably one of tenderness. Thanks to the magic of popular art and of Dürer's talent, not only did Jarry manage to warm to the spirit permeating the works in question but he also grew so keen on them that he then devoted himself exclusively to publicizing them. This is so true that, when his contribution to *L'Ymagier* came to an end with the fourth issue (for reasons quite unrelated to the orientation of the journal), he wasted no time starting, this time on his own, another journal called *Perhinderion*, entirely devoted to the celebration of engravings by Dürer and Georgin.

We can thereby appreciate the extent of his almost fanatical fascination with art forms in which the traditional Christian iconography figures most prominently but that also make room next to them for representations of mythical figures or animals from Cochin China or the Sandwich Islands. That is because Jarry was inclined to venerate all "monsters" indiscriminately and wanted to be a prey to them all, but, he adds, "it is customary to apply the word MONSTER to the unusual combination of dissonant elements; the Centaur, the Chimera are so described by those who do not understand. I call monster any original inexhaustible beauty."

Any original inexhaustible beauty ... It is clear that the nihilism much too quickly ascribed to the author of the Ubu plays is far from being absolute since it does not extend to "Beauty," which is even regarded as an object of worship. But Jarry's attitude in the presence of beauty is as far as can be from dumb admiration, it is a fervid inquiry into the ways and means by which beauty was achieved, a desire of total possession through the reconstitution, beyond the manifest content, of the *latent* content. Nothing shows this better than the commentary on the *Martyrdom of Saint Catherine*, the most significant passage of which is herein quoted under the partially masked reproduction of the engraving.[2] Jarry's posture as he scrutinizes Dürer's engraving prefigures that of an Oscar Pfister discovering in Leonardo's *Saint Ann*, in the Louvre, the contours of the obsessional vulture whose psychoanalytical meaning was to be brought out by Freud.[3] It points the way to the "paranoiac-critical method" outlined by Max Ernst and systematized by Dalí. Jarry was probably the first to start from the conviction that "indefinite dissection always uncovers something new in works of art."[4] Moreover, there is no doubt that this idea of the "inexhaustible," deep-rooted in Jarry, led him to focus his attention on the loftiest (which are also the most difficult) immemorial constructions of the mind. The opening act of *César-Antéchrist*, as well as *L'Amour absolu*, clearly indicate that he was particularly familiar with John's book of Revelation and with Gnostic writings[5] (on the one hand, the third issue of *L'Ymagier* includes three representations of the Antichrist that are replicas, drawn by Jarry himself, of fifteenth-century prints; on the other hand, "Emmanuel's Confession" in *L'Amour absolu*, from which I shall quote the following excerpt: "I am God, I do not die on the Cross . . . the New Adam, who was born an adult, I was born at the age of twelve, I shall vanish *but it is not I who will die*, at the age of thirty, tomorrow"—the emphasis is Jarry's own—almost certainly refers to Basilide, for whom "Jesus took on a body that was only apparent and suffered only apparent torments"). Everything remains to be done to provide an exegesis of Jarry's works along these lines, which may be the only key to a proper understanding. Here, I am merely pointing out a second basic determining factor of Jarry's sensibility: the first one, as we have seen earlier, kindled in him a passion for popular images from the printing works in Chartres, Orléans, Rennes, or Epinal, while this one impelled him to inquire deeply into the meaning of the pictures through which the esoteric tradition was handed down.

It may be especially interesting, under these conditions, to know what

Jarry's reactions were toward the art of his time since his curiosity was exceptionally wide ranging and since, moreover, he was in contact with all the coteries and constantly remained, until his death in 1907, in the forefront of intellectual life. During the previous twenty years, so rich in theoretical discussions about art, did he take an active part in the debate or did he at least indicate where his sympathies lay? No sooner is this question asked than it seems susceptible of a most brightly illuminating answer.

First of all, Jarry has, in this respect, a superior right to our gratitude: it is thanks to him that we know Henri Rousseau. "The Douanier," Apollinaire wrote, "had been discovered by Alfred Jarry, whose father he knew well. But, if the truth be known, I think Jarry had been initially won over much more by the simplicity of the fellow than by his qualities as a painter.[6] Later, however, the author of *Ubu roi* became quite appreciative of the art of his friend, whom he called the fabulous Rousseau. Rousseau painted his portrait, including in the picture a parrot and the famous chameleon that was Alfred Jarry's companion for a while. That portrait got partly burnt; when I saw it, in 1906, only the head was still intact: it was very expressive." It is most unfortunate that no one until now has been able to elucidate the circumstances of their meeting: we do not even know if it took place in Laval, their native town, nor what circumstances (according to Trohel) led Henri Rousseau to lodge Alfred Jarry in his residence at number 14, avenue du Maine. Thanks to Apollinaire, we also know that Rousseau was introduced by Jarry to Rémy de Gourmont, who was sufficiently won over to publish in *L'Ymagier* his lithography entitled *Les Horreurs de la guerre* [*War*] (Apollinaire recounted that "Rémy de Gourmont had been told by Jarry that the Douanier painted with the purity, the grace, and the ingenuousness of a Primitive"). We are told, it is true, that Gauguin had noticed Rousseau from the time he first exhibited in the 1886 Salon des Indépendants, but we have no information on what had aroused his interest. On the other hand, it is easy to understand that, on account of his extensive knowledge of art, Jarry was in a far better position than anyone to recognize and to bring attention to the Douanier's genius. He remains for me the man who established Rousseau's reputation—and the only one who could do so— *with full knowledge of the facts*. He did it with all the understanding and emotion that were required and most certainly not with the intention of playing a hoax, something he was credited with by those whose lack of sensibility is betrayed by their perpetual fear of being taken in.

Here, we are approaching a zone of pure affinities that, to some extent, eludes rational analysis. Even so, it is still remarkable that Gauguin "noticed" Rousseau, considering the attraction they both felt for a certain tropical light that also floods the islands where the "ace" in *Doctor Faustroll* landed. Let us not forget, moreover, the elective love that Jarry as well as Gauguin felt for Brittany (the last painting done by Gauguin, in the Marquesas Islands, is *Breton Village in the Snow*): it is to be expected that, on the emotional level, their conjunction did not stop there. At the end of 1893, Jarry devoted three poems to the celebration of paintings by Gauguin (*Ia Orana Maria, Man with an Axe*, and *Manao Tupapau*) exhibited in the Durand-Ruel gallery: it is the only tribute of this kind he will pay to a contemporary artist. (I should say that, this once, I have no objection to or complaint with the commentary given on these poems in a recent collection.[7])

In *Gestes et opinions du docteur Faustroll* [*Exploits and Opinions of Doctor Faustroll, Pataphysician*], chapter 32, entitled "How One Obtained Canvas" and dedicated to Pierre Bonnard,[8] is particularly interesting in that it tells us what Jarry's other predilections were in terms of modern painting and how he graded them. Bosse-de-Nage, the monkey, is asked by Faustroll to go to the National Department Store, called Au Luxe Bourgeois [Bourgeois Luxury], and there to buy several ells of a canvas: "You will convey my compliments to the department managers Bouguereau, Bonnat, Detaille, Henner, J.-P. Laurens, and Whatshisname, and to their horde of assistants and other sales clerks." Then he told him, "So as to wash the shoptalk out of your prognathous jaws, go into a small room arranged for this purpose. There the icons of the saints shine forth. Bare your head before the *Pauvre pêcheur* [Poor fisherman], bow before the Monets, genuflect before the Degas and the Whistlers, grovel in the presence of Cézanne, prostrate yourself at the feet of Renoir, and lick the sawdust in the spittoons under the frame of *Olympia*!" Faustroll adds that, above all others, the true "artisan of the Great Work," the one who created pure gold, is Vincent Van Gogh. Jarry goes on to say that "after aiming the salutary hose of the painting machine at the center of those quadrilaterals dishonored by irregular colors, he entrusted the operation of the mechanical monster to M. Henri Rousseau, a set artist, known as the Douanier."

Cézanne, Renoir, Manet, Gauguin, Van Gogh, Rousseau: it is amazing to see how this judgment was confirmed by posterity. Not a single professional critic of the time—even chosen among those with greater insight—came up with this set of names presented *in this order*, which still seems to me the most exciting one and the one that is coming closer every day to a general endorsement.

This is why I think I should publicly try and rescue from oblivion the name of a painter particularly dear to Jarry and no doubt to Gauguin as well, since he lived with him for a long time and would mention him with great interest in his letters. The artist in question is Filiger, and we know, thanks to a letter from the engraver Paul-Emile Colin to M. Charles Chassé,[9] that he joined Gauguin in Le Pouldu in 1890: "All four of us were there: Gauguin, Filiger, de Haan, and I. We had settled by the seaside, in the Hôtel de la Plage, where we were the only guests of Marie, a good soul whose sole income came from the little money we paid for our board. It was only with great reluctance that Filiger, driven away from Paris for lack of funds, had gone to Brittany: he was never to leave it. . . . I can still see the common room in that small secluded inn surrounded with sand. The ceiling had been decorated by Gauguin with geese serving as a motif. The doors as well were decorated with paintings. A large picture in blue hues represented Marie the Breton and her son. Finally, one day, to complete the decoration of the room, Filiger painted the Blessed Virgin on a panel after a charming little gouache, like all those he was so good at painting. . . . I do not think you would get anything from Filiger if you were to find him, wherever he may be: he was a very nice fellow, but so far away from our whole culture—so far above it, I should say." This would already be most engaging, but there is something else. M. Charles Chassé[10]—with whom, needless to say, I am in marked disagreement over Jarry and Rousseau, but to whom I am nevertheless very grateful for having gotten on Filiger's track, which had been lost until he came along—describes him as "one of the most enigmatic characters that ever were." However much of a mystic he was supposed to be, M. Chassé is inclined to see in him a great deal of deadpan humor: it would be difficult indeed otherwise to reconcile his refusal to enter the Café des Voyageurs in Concarneau on the pretext that it is not "a place worthy of a painter," with the recollection of Louis Le Ray, according to whom the aperitif he extolled was a mix of bitter Picon and of the Carmelites' melissa cordial, which he called a "symbolic drink." We should also note that, during the years before his death (in 1930, at Plougastel-Daoulas), Filiger had switched from that pseudo-Christian mysticism to a "total paganism."

There is something else, I said: if you open volume 6 of Alfred Jarry's *Oeuvres complètes* [Complete works] and look at the "Art Criticism" section,[11] you will realize that the only important text—out of the two that are included—is entirely devoted to Filiger's glorification, a fact that, together with the quality of the emotion showing through, entitles M. Chassé, at least to a certain extent, to consider Filiger as the "favorite painter" of the author of . . . *Ubu roi.* I must limit myself to quoting—but it already speaks volumes—part of Jarry's peroration: "Of the two eternals who cannot exist one without the other, Filiger has not chosen the worst one. But since the love of what is pure and pious does not cast that other purity, evil, off like a rag into material existence, Maldoror incarnates a God that is also beautiful under the sonorous cardboard hide of the rhinoceros. And perhaps a holier one . . . The demons that do penance between the long slopes, like beasts caught in nets, climb to heaven with their four claws—the only march along the steep paths . . . that is why Filiger's art surpasses him with the innocence of his chaste heads in the expiatory style of Giotto. It is quite absurd that I seem to be doing this sort of write-up or description of his paintings since (1) if they were not beautiful, I would take no pleasure in citing them, therefore I would not cite them; (2) if I could clearly explain point by point why they are very beautiful, they would no longer be paintings but literature (discounting the distinction between genres) and they would no longer be beautiful at all. . . ."[12]

The very small number of works by Filiger that were presented to the public, due no doubt to the fact that most of the other ones were buried in the collection of the count Antoine de La Rochefoucault (who helped the artist financially for years), the scarcity of photographic reproductions that might somewhat fill in this gap, and the lack of any chronology applicable to what is shown at rare intervals seem to justify my including a personal note.

According to Julien Leclerc, "looking at Cimabue's painting in the Louvre, Filiger would go into raptures over the fact that the angels' faces are similar to that of the Virgin." I remember ascribing to the same cause my own wonderment when I first saw that painting. Two years ago I was able to acquire in Pont-Aven a gouache by Filiger that is reproduced as plate 8 in this book.[13] The eight arches on top, as well as the sky around the constructions, are royal blue; the horses are painted a moss green that is slightly thinner than the horizontal stripe against which light dots form a wavy line with trifoliate patterns. Cherry red is used for the bottom spikes, which, two by two, flank a chicory-colored flower, the entire design being as if filigreed with a crown suspended over a butterfly. . . . The symmetry is only upset by the small branch that uncoils from left to right, from one green lateral tower to the other, and from which, between two light-colored hearts, an unknown fruit similar in color to the red spikes is hanging. Even though I am aware that a description of this kind is futile, my love for this work has impelled me to write it: my excuse is that nothing has put me under such an enduring spell nor has proved to be less vulnerable to the vagaries of my mood. In 1888 Gauguin painted a small board for Paul Sérusier: it went down in history under the name of *Le Talisman* [*The Talisman*]. If this title had not already been used, I would give it to this unnamed and hardly larger painting by Filiger.

According to Emile Bernard, Filiger owed his inspiration solely "to the Byzantines and to the popular images of Brittany": I would not know. Be that as it may, as I was leafing through a recent issue of *Sciences et Voyages* that listed the only flowers that, in our lands, made up *all* the ornamental vegetation in the Middle Ages (snowdrops, primroses, daisies, narcissi, violets, lilies of the valley, columbines, foxgloves, centauries, bellflowers, and wild roses), Filiger was the only one I could think of who brought back Griseldis.

If only out of consideration for Alfred Jarry's judgment, which has proved to be nearly infallible in this domain, let us hope that a gallery—if not a national museum—will undertake, whatever the difficulties, to put on a comprehensive exhibition of Filiger's works, so that, even at this late date, he may receive due recognition.

October 1951

Why Is Contemporary

Russian Painting Kept

Hidden from Us?

"Form is my property, it represents my individuality. *The style is the man*. I should say so! The law permits me to write, but only provided I write in a style other than *my own*! I have the right to show the shape of my mind, but I must first confine it *to the prescribed mold*! Any man of honor would be ashamed of such a claim. . . ." One can imagine the vituperations with which such a declaration would be greeted in Russia nowadays. I would not bet on the life of a "formalist" who would dare speak that way. Here is someone who would be in for it, a blabbermouth who would be gagged in no time! And he dares keep on about it: "You admire the inexhaustible richness of nature. You do not ask for the rose to have the fragrance of the violet, but what is richer than anything else—the mind—should only be able to exist in *a single* fashion?" Enough is enough! Unfortunately, the one protesting here is Marx, and these remarks, which sound seditious to millions of men under the dictatorship of Moscow, are found in his *Oeuvres philosophiques* [Philosophical works].[1] He is the one who underlined the words italicized above.

These truths have been established for so long that it is astonishing to see them being challenged in the middle of the twentieth century. But it is even more appalling to realize that what neither religious persecutions nor the imposition of "absolute power" were able to do, namely, to stifle forever the voice of those who kept thinking more or less outside the dogma or who strove to undermine that power, has been successfully enforced by a regime backed up by police terror upon all those under its sway. If the Church or the monarchy had had such means at its disposal, neither

Eckhart nor Pascal nor Rousseau would have been heard of. In that distant past, obscurantism still had its limits. The greatest tragedy is that today, thanks to fanaticism and other factors, it does not remain confined within Russian borders, but, not content with having already managed to take over several countries, it keeps reaching out farther and farther with its tentacles. Admittedly, the working masses, outside of the areas under the direct control of the alleged "communist" party, are not very interested in the problem of "enlightenment." They can easily be convinced that, like everything else in Russia, arts and letters are in full bloom and developing freely. That is what they are being told by some "intellectuals" who can misrepresent the truth with all the more impunity as they hardly need fear a concrete refutation: the few Russian books being translated are confined to apologetics, and we can only glean some idea of Russian painting and sculpture from reproductions that are even fewer and buried in confidential publications.

Fortunately, the "USSR" is less stingy when it comes to reporting the "artistic discussions" that, so it seems, rivet everybody's attention over there. It is to one of those discussions, a quite recent one, that we owe the publication, in *Les Lettres Françaises* of 27 December and 3 January, of an article from *Art Soviétique* that says a great deal about the actual situation. According to *Les Lettres Françaises* itself, it is a response to the question asked by many French readers: "What do we know, in general, about the architecture of that country where so much building is going on? As for painting, we know even less about it. . . ." That article, so we are told, "has been given great importance by the artistic circles in the USSR." Finally, it addresses the following basic question: "What does the Soviet public today expect from painting? . . . Is socialist realism satisfied with having won the fight over the subject? What are the ambitions to which Soviet painters must aspire in order to fulfill the expectations of the people? And what must be the role of criticism?"

It is unfortunate that the editorial staff of *Les Lettres Françaises* has preferred to illustrate the article in question with a self-portrait of Henri Matisse smoking his pipe, rather than with some of the works that brought about the debate. In fact, the drawing by Matisse and the accompanying sentence by Picasso ("Never has any painter tickled painting to such bursts of laughter as Matisse has. Vallauris, 22-12-51") are ruthlessly negated and condemned by the very context in which they are inserted. Who would believe that in Russia such a drawing (already inadmissible given the "frivolity" of the subject) would not be regarded moreover as something that is "neither done nor to be done" and that Picasso's pleasantly piquant sentence, summing up after its own fashion Matisse's aspirations, would be tolerated for one moment? Just think of what happened to the great poets and artists whose creative vigor coursed for a short while through the Russian revolution: Majakovsky, Yesenin, Pilniak, Lissitzky, Malevitch, Rodchenko, Tatlin (fortunately, Chagall and Kandinsky were able to clear out in time).

I must confess to a bitter gratification even now when I happen to read a piece such as the one we owe to *Art Soviétique*. When, some twenty-five years ago, along with Aragon and Eluard—a bit later with Tzara, Sadoul, Marcenac, and many others—we would note with a feeling of dread the symptoms of regression in the USSR, not only on the artistic level but on the level of the most general intellectual expression, we still harbored the illusion that this could be a passing illness and that a recovery, as well as a straightening up, was not impossible. I assume that, for those I have named, it is now out of the question. Under these conditions, it would be a matter of basic honesty for those who turn a blind eye to the situation to acknowledge the fact that, in their view, other interests take precedence over the interests of art and, beyond art itself, are worth the sacrifice of free human expression.

A bitter delectation: through a continuous process, on the artistic level, error raised to the status of a system and constantly soliciting the help of incompetence has, in the final analysis, no other resource than to take an increasingly aggressive turn. The alleged need for restoring the *subject* in painting to prominence, totally at odds with the historical factors by which painting has been conditioned for a century, has led to the pathetic confusion of that subject with the dullest, or the flashiest (when it is not the most sordid) kind of *anecdote*. From the list of the twenty "subjects" prescribed to painters by the minister of culture of Hungary, let us merely note the following ones:

> *The heroes of labor sit in their box at the theater;*
> *The first tractor arrives in the village;*
> *A policewoman helps a child cross the street;*
> *A view of the courtroom during the Rajk trial;*
> *The preparations for Stalin's birthday;*
> *The police arrest a foreign agent at the border.*

On this side of the "iron curtain" we would like to see, even among supporters of the "USSR," how many painters would be ready to accept such instructions. The titles of the paintings mentioned in the *Art Soviétique* article hardly fare any better. To wit:

> *Dimitrov Accuses;*
> *The Stakhanovites Are Keeping Watch;*
> *The Innovators of the Kolkhozian Fields;*
> *V. I. Lenin and J. V. Stalin in Razliv;*
> *J. V. Stalin at V. I. Lenin's Tomb;*
> *Children Offering J. V. Stalin Their Best Wishes*
>   *on His Seventieth Birthday.*

The critique of these last works and of other ones in the same vein, which forms the subject of the article, impresses one with its technical incompetence and its inquisitorial style. "After having successfully defeated the corrupting influence of formalism and kept securely to the track of socialist realism set by the great Stalin ... Soviet painters become more and more demanding of themselves." P. Kotov, who painted the study *The Stakhanovites Are Keeping Watch*, is guilty of having drawn the following comment from visitors of the 1950 exhibition: "The Stakhanovites are keeping watch but they are not doing anything." ("Indeed, in the foreground Kotov placed an idle young girl who, for no discernible reason, has a triumphant look in her eyes.") The sun is rather frowned upon: how could

F. Bogorodski, who until now glorified military heroism in his paintings, commit "such trivial, such incidental works as *Flowers in the Sun*"? A. Plastov, who painted a picture representing pioneers on a truck, "got carried away by patches of sunlight." The painting by M. Antonian, *J. V. Stalin at V. I. Lenin's Tomb*, is full of "inadmissible errors that play havoc with the basic rules of perspective and with correct proportions." Stupidity, coupled with the hysterical need to suspect and denounce, reaches its peak in the charges made by a "baffled female student" against E. Katzman concerning his painting *I Want Peace*: "Why is the dove of peace in his picture so big that it no longer looks like a dove? Why are the trees in the background of an unknown species? In which direction is the dove flying? If it is coming toward us, who sent it? If it is flying away from us, why isn't that made clear to the viewers? Why is it difficult to read the little girl's feelings in her face? Is she waiting for the dove, is she the one who released it, does she admire it when the bird flies by her? Why is there a penholder in the book instead of a bookmark? Is it to show that the little girl can write? In school, we are taught to take care of books and not to put penholders inside them. None of that is clear."

As far as general views on art are concerned, what we have here is beneath the remarks exchanged by people out for a Sunday stroll through the "daub fair" and, as for moral and human decency, we are here exactly halfway between the local gossip center and the police station. Needless to say, the "confused female student" who demonstrates such a remarkable vocation as an informer is, in *Art Soviétique*, warmly congratulated.

All this bespeaks madness, all this exudes terror. The publicity given both in the "USSR" and outside it to recurrent debates on art has long stopped fooling anybody. The decision taken more or less recently to fight "naturalism" as well as "formalism" is not one that is likely to rekindle any interest. There is not a single artist, both competent and free from constraint, who is not fed up with the perpetuation of the debate that sets "content" against "form" with no hope for a solution and that can only generate tautology and truisms. The truth, carefully concealed, is that contemporary

Russian painting, within the pathetically narrow limits where this mode of expression is permitted, has been incapable of producing anything that might go beyond the old calendar picture from department stores or the village chromo. At least this is what the numerous documents that I was able to consult to date and that have to be obtained from specialized agencies are leading me to infer until I see evidence to the contrary, if *Les Lettres Françaises*, for instance, is able to produce it. It will be very careful not to do so because the mere juxtaposition of such daubs with works by Picasso, Matisse, as well as by Giotto or Grünewald, to which that journal has the good taste to give pride of place, could not help emphasizing an intolerable hiatus. Anyone who, on this side of the world, is not completely blind would judge the theory on its applications, based on the evident absence of composition, the total incapacity to portray any kind of expression, the meticulous attention to pointless detail, in short the mural-size enlargement of the worst sort of postcard. Needless to say, the color reproductions are even more dreadful: there is no attempt at harmony or balance of colors, and besides, we are back to the "dull" dominant of the official salons from before Impressionism. Considering the evolution in taste in Western Europe over the past hundred years, I do not know what will *horrify* true art-lovers more: the bombastic asininity of the themes—which would be enough to make us regret Detaille and J.-P. Laurens—or the total impersonality of style that reminds us of the "art" that is for sale in cheap department stores.

On 24 May 1949, Zamouchekine, director of the Tretyakov Gallery in Moscow (the Russian equivalent to the Jeu de Paume Museum), while opening the Budapest Salon, declared that:

> *Cézanne must be proscribed,*
> *Matisse does not know how to draw,*
> *Picasso will make your brains rot.*
> *Any artist who does not follow the example of Soviet art is an enemy of socialism.*[2]

Such views actually corroborate the opinion expressed in *Pravda* in connection with the 1947 Fall Salon: *the green women exhibited by André Marchand are the expression of the mental and physical decay of French women.*

Kroum Kiouliavkov, rector of the Arts Academy of Sofia, published in the December 1950 issue of *Chronique Culturelle Bulgare* an article that states:

"The lack of frames of reference made it possible for formalist movements to infiltrate all branches of art, to dictate and to establish 'art' (*sic*), that hallucination created by unbalanced painters.... The Soviet peoples, guided by the sound thinking of the Central Committee of the Communist party, turned their backs on the sacrilege that is modernism and, thanks to the healthy application of Marxist-Leninist criticism, they dealt it a decisive blow.... Soviet art is as necessary to Bulgarian artists as the sun is to every flower."

It would be tedious to extend those quotations to Romania, to Czechoslovakia: I will come back to them if need be. Enough has been said to establish the fact that we are dealing with a scheme of systematic destruction, of eradication by all means of what through the centuries we have learned to consider as art worthy of that name and most particularly of what can correspond to the concept of a *living art*, in the sense of a passionate quest for a new vital link between man and things, in which that man and those things find their common and loftiest expression. All those who have some notion of what this art is about understand that what is at stake is a spiritual adventure that simply cannot be interrupted at any price. They know that it is along that royal road that are inscribed in modern times the names of Blake, Delacroix, Géricault, Füssli, Courbet, Manet, Cézanne, Gauguin, Van Gogh, Seurat and that it extends magnificently all the way to us. Those individuals were *free* and complete *masters of their worlds*. It is all too obvious that not a single artist of their stature could nowadays find favor with the improvised critical tribunals that sit in Russia, their sole code consisting of a few rudimentary academic notions while they are equipped with an ever-increasing list of prohibitions (the *nude* is banned, the *still life* less and less tolerated, and so on).

The whole question is whether, in countries where art is not put in chains, we can tolerate the idea that that royal road is to remain closed—its monuments obliterated even in memory—until it is opened to the crowd of drudges and mercenaries.

The policy adopted by Stalinism in this country toward great artists of international repute, such as Matisse and Picasso, comes as no surprise. It is no different from the one carried out with regard to some statesmen in countries that had not yet been occupied, from whom Stalinism could expect, while they were still in power, a more or less conciliatory attitude or even a minimum of cooperation. Once on the inside, it made it clear enough that they had become expendable. In order for Picasso, Matisse, and those who followed their lead to side with the wolf or to flirt with it, they would need to be naive to a degree that is unbelievable to me. They cannot possibly close their eyes to the fact that the *travesty of art* (just as one says a travesty of justice) that alone has the approval of Moscow is the peremptory and inflexible negation not only of their own art but of any art as they are able to understand it. It is impossible for their ears not to be burning with the wild praises heaped upon them over here by those who pillory them over there. Whether or not they feel that this situation will last as long as they do, they nevertheless assume the heaviest kind of responsibility when they lend their names to a scheme demanding that a mortal blow be dealt to artistic conscience and freedom, which have been the whole justification of their lives.

Tower

    of

        Light

It is in the black mirror of anarchism that surrealism, long before it achieved self-definition, first recognized its own reflection. This was shortly after World War I and we were still nothing more than a free association of individuals united by our spontaneous rejection of all the social and moral constraints of our times. Among the shrines on which we converged and that could not fail to bring us together there was this conclusion of *Ballade Solness* by Laurent Tailhade:

> *Stab our tattered hearts*
> *Anarchy! Bearer of flaming torches!*
> *Dispel the night! Stamp out the vermin!*
> *And build, sky-high, with our tombstones even,*
> *The Tower of Light that dominates the sea!*

At this point, surrealism rejects everything: no political movement could harness its energies. All the institutions on which the modern world is resting and that have led to the First World War we deem aberrant and scandalous. Above all we challenge the whole apparatus society uses to defend itself: the army, the police, "justice," religion, psychiatric and forensic medicine, education. Our collective declarations as well as the individual texts written by Aragon and Eluard (as we knew them at the time), Artaud, Crevel, Desnos, Ernst, Leiris, Masson, Péret, Queneau, or myself manifest the same common intention to reveal their true nature as corruptions that must be recognized as such and fought against. But in order to fight them with some measure of success, one has to undermine the framework supporting them, which in the final analysis is based on *logic* and *moral sense*, both fraudulent labels for, on the one hand, a morality that has been falsified by Christianity so as to deter all resistance against the exploitation of mankind and, on the other hand, for a so-called reason that serves as a poor disguise for the exhausted notion of "common sense."

A great fire was smoldering then—we were young—and I should emphasize that it has been continually rekindled by what radiates from the works and lives of poets:

Anarchy! Bearer of flaming torches!

Aside from Tailhade, those poets are Baudelaire, Rimbaud, Jarry, and all our young libertarian comrades should know them just as they should know Sade, Lautréamont, and Schwob when he wrote "Paroles de Monelle" [Monelle's words].

How is it that the organic fusion of the surrealist and (strictly speaking) anarchist elements did not occur at that time? I still ask myself this very same question now, twenty-five years later. It was undoubtedly hindered by the idea of efficiency, which served as the prevailing mirage for that whole period. A whole new change in perspective was brought about by what was believed to be the triumph of the Russian Revolution and the advent of a workers' State. The only blotch marring this perfect picture—it was to develop into an indelible stain—was the brutal suppression of the Cronstadt uprising of 18 March 1921. The surrealists were never able to forget it entirely. Nevertheless, around 1925, only the Third International seemed to have the requisite means of transforming the world. One could assume that the symptoms of degeneracy and regression already distinctly visible in the East could still be remedied. The surrealists' behavior at that time rested on the conviction that social revolution, as it spread to all nations, could only promote a *libertarian* world (some say a surrealist world, but they are one and the same). All of us thought so at first, including those, such as Aragon, Eluard, and so on, who have forsaken their original ideal to the point of carving out a career for themselves within Stalinism, and a fairly good career at that—for businessmen, of course. But human desire and human hope will never be at the mercy of those who betray them:

Dispel the night! Stamp out the vermin!

Everyone knows how ruthlessly those illusions were destroyed during the second quarter of this century. Through some dreadful irony, the libertarian world we had imagined has given way to a world where the most servile obedience is expected, where the most basic human rights are denied, where all social life revolves around the policeman and the executioner. As in all cases where a human ideal reaches such depths of corruption, the only cure is to immerse oneself anew in the great current of sensibility where this ideal originated, to *go back to the principles* from which it had sprung. Those who complete the journey, one that today it is more than ever imperative to undertake, will discover that anarchism alone is the only remaining solution. Let us dismiss the caricature, the scarecrow we are expected to see: anarchism was best described by our comrade Fontenis "as the very essence of socialism, that is the modern demand for the dignity of man (his freedom as much as his well-being); socialism conceived not simply as a solution to an economic or political problem but as the expression of the exploited masses hankering after a society that will be classless and Stateless, where all human values and aspirations may be realized."

This idea that revolt and generosity cannot be dissociated and that they *both* remain *equally* boundless (whether Albert Camus agrees or not), we surrealists have now adopted as our very own. As it emerges from the deathly mists shrouding our times, we are convinced it is the only idea capable of bringing back within the range of vision of an ever-increasing number of people

The Tower of Light that dominates the sea!

Letter to a

Young Girl Living

in America

Dear Sir,

I am a twelve-year-old French girl residing, for the time being, in Washington DC. At home we subscribe to *Arts* and I follow your life of Picasso, which I cut out and paste into my "scrapbook."[1]

In my school we all give reports and for the next one, I have chosen Matisse. In museums children can often be seen copying modern paintings and Dad told me that doing so is probably a mistake because they are not old enough yet to understand.

I would like to have your opinion on this matter since I know you have a daughter who is older than I am and who has lived in New York: has she gone to school there? Do you think Americans are right to give so much freedom to children or is it better, as in France, to subject them to strict discipline? Your answer would help me a lot with my "report." Do you recommend artists such as Matisse or Picasso to children? You may find me rather audacious for writing to you this way . . . demanding like a little French girl, ill-mannered like an American one.

Let me end this letter the way it is done here,

Very sincerely yours,
Maguelonne Car
6023 5th St. NW
Washington DC

Paris, 9 February 1952

Dear Maguelonne,

Only someone as young as you are could ask such difficult questions and, given your determination, I can see that you will not let me off easily. Do not think that I just have to open a drawer to find the answers you are expecting, ready-made and (in a flash) fitted to your size. It isn't that the drawer is missing, the small secretary to which it belongs is in fairly good condition, but the problem is this: I don't know what happens but every time I open that drawer to examine the precepts I tucked away there I find them all topsy-turvy. It must be another of Queen Mab's tricks (have you heard about that charming creature?). This has mostly taken on curious proportions over the past while.

Well, if you had been able to question me earlier, you would have found me much more self-confident. In particular, my choice would have been quickly made between the methods of art teaching that are currently used in the United States and in France. It is so much nicer to think of a child drawing and painting according to his or her fancy than forced as they are here to concentrate on reproducing a saucepan or a grimy plaster cast! In perfect contrast to those exercises, which have left me with such bad memories, I think that you are very fortunate to have been introduced already to Matisse's beautiful harmonies. At any rate, the report you are preparing suits you like a bouquet of flowers.

Almost two hundred years ago, a very great mind addressed the problem that you have raised; you must have heard about him already and I am almost sure that you will grow fond of him. It is true that he was not writing for children, he was writing for those who take care of them, but what is so endearing about him is first and foremost that he took the children's side as no one, or almost no one, has been able to since. Nor had anyone before him taken such an interest in children or tried with such perseverance and passion to find what might best suit their needs, both in relation to what they *are* and to what they will *become*. Don't you find it touching that, in order to increase his chances of communing with the little girl, and later on the young girl whom he wanted to educate *in the ways of happiness*, he should have felt the need to go and dream about her "in a deep and delightful solitude, amidst woods and streams, surrounded by a chorus of birds of all species, steeped in the fragrance of orange blossoms"? Here was a master with nothing forbidding about him: his name was Jean-Jacques Rousseau.

I really could not find a better refuge from your questions sprinkling down in arrows. Let us begin, if you like, with what he says:

"Since children are great imitators, they all try to draw: I would like my own child to cultivate this art, not really for art's sake but to develop a discerning eye and a supple hand; and generally it does not really matter whether he is familiar with any particular exercise as long as he acquires the keen sense and trained dexterity that are the benefits of that practice. Hence, the last thing I would do would be to hire a drawing master, who would only give him imitations to imitate . . . I want him to have no other master than nature, no other model than objects. I want him to look at the actual thing, not the paper that represents it; I want him to sketch a house after a house, a man after a man, so that he may get used to observing objects and appearances carefully, and not to mistaking false and conventional imitations for genuine imitations . . . I do not intend him so much to be able to imitate objects as to know them; I would rather he showed me an acanthus plant and that he drew with less skill the leaf-work on a capital."

Here, I think, is the basic truth, to which we must refer time and again. Provided we do not lose sight of it, I have no objection, on the contrary, to it being supplemented by other ways of seeing and knowing.

Better than anyone, our friend Jean-Jacques understood that childhood reproduces, in its successive stages, the evolution of mankind. It is therefore very important to make the child aware of that evolution, and this could not be achieved in a more accurate and tangible fashion than by showing him the artistic accomplishments that have succeeded one another, starting with the most primitive. However, you should understand that the work of art to which the child is being introduced must never belong to a stage in the evolution of mankind that comes later than the one that corresponds to the stage in the development of the child's mind (your dad will explain). To illustrate what I mean, suppose you tell me that, when you were younger, you just loved Lewis Carroll but that now you feel a greater inclination toward *Atala*: I will say that you seem to me to be on the right track toward knowledge, whereas if you assured me that you were reading Rimbaud, I would object. Rimbaud did speak about childhood in wonderful terms, but to appreciate what he said, you will see some day that one must have left one's whole childhood behind. As eager *to know* as I can see you are, it cannot be helped if this annoys you.

Having said this, since the school system tries hard (without much discernment, to my mind) to bring within grasp of the students in the various grades "selected passages" of literature with the attendant indispensable "text commentary" exercises, I think it would be a good idea to do the same for art. Here as well, however, one should select items that are suitable to the hearts and minds of each age group and bring them to life by showing the original to the students, or at least a cast or a color slide, and by providing commentaries that are at the same time *informed* and *appealing*.

This way, one would avoid "putting the cart before the horse," which is, from what I could observe, what happens too often in America. Do you begin to see what I mean? When we are very young, everything we see is only either pleasant or unpleasant. Associations of color and structure only come afterward and even later the notion of generality, which leads by degrees to the *abstract* (I am sure this word will not scare you: I have no doubt it is widely misused in Washington). You will discover yourself, a few years from now, that there are artists called, particularly in America, "abstract" who have been able to keep their connection with nature and that those who have lost this connection, whether in "representational" or "nonrepresentational" art, have lost *everything*. The fact remains that a teaching method that would begin with abstract art or get to it too hastily would warp all young minds because it would impede their normal development.

To go even farther, I don't think that intentional "distortions," which, for many modern artists, are the product of what adults call with a fancy word "intellectual speculation" (by definition, something beyond the reach of children), can be held up as a model for children. But it is true that some modern artists have done everything to get back in touch with the world of childhood: I am thinking particularly of Klee and Miró, whose works should have pride of place in all schools.

Thanks to my daughter, who still lived there when she was your age, I was able to get an idea of the methods that are used in the United States to awaken the artistic sensibilities of the child. It started with the elementary school in New York where, when she was about seven, she was asked to use her imagination to do a drawing inspired by a fairy tale. Then, in a Connecticut school, similar assignments would center on a holiday, such as Christmas, Easter, or Thanksgiving, and the students would vote to select the best drawing, which would then be enlarged and hung on a wall. Finally, in a progressive school in Vermont, whose walls, as it happened, were decorated with reproductions of Miró's paintings, the student was expected to fill in—it was made clear it had to be in a nonrepresentational way—a "background" that he or she had to prepare beforehand, guided only by his or her personal taste and sensibility. Apart from the objections I raised earlier in respect to this last matter, I have no complaint with that as far as freedom is concerned. Unfortunately, the quality of the fruit is what a method of cultivation is judged by (it is true that the nature of the soil also has to be taken into account). Now, having spent quite a bit of time in art galleries, it seems to me that the fruits that have come to maturity over there do not come close to the flavor of those over here. So what? you'll say. Well! I definitely do not have the makings of an educationalist. Would you believe that, with your letter in my hand, I ended up consulting my daughter: at least her opinion has an invaluable advantage in that it still partakes of childhood. She thinks that we could adopt a solution that, for my part, I find fairly clumsy. (What about you?) This would be to alternate quite regularly, on the one hand, exercises that aim at representing real objects and at recording the relationships between them (these exercises would be done in the very relaxed atmosphere that Rousseau recommends) and, on the other hand, exercises that rely entirely on the imagination.

As you will come to realize only much later, this solution will always be opposed by all the people who think that life, as soon as childhood is over, can be nothing but effort and adversity, against which it is better to have been hardened over time. This is enough for them to justify imposing all the constraints possible on youth. I don't need to tell you that I am not on their side, even though they might be partly right.

You see how full of nuances all this is: with your nice acidulous voice that I can hear from here, I find you fully qualified to speak about Matisse. You have a key that opens his house, and that, in a very young girl, is an innate sense of adornment. If it were a matter of Picasso, however, I would firmly advise you to let several years go by.

With kind regards.

Of "Socialist Realism"

as a Means of

Mental Extermination

A few months ago, I asked that we be brought up to date on the output of present-day Russian art: a greater willingness to do so might disabuse us of the idea that it was not a degenerate but an *irreparably degraded* art, due to the very conditions imposed on its production.

As a result, we have been treated since then to some lengthy articles by Aragon in *Les Lettres françaises*, and, for our greater enjoyment, that series is being continued.[1] The least we could say about those articles is that they do not show any great impatience to come to the point. Aragon has long been considered a master of this sort of evasiveness. (Let us recall his rejoinder, during one of his lectures, to a member of the audience who, exasperated by his digressions, had interrupted him to bring him back to his title: pointing to the buttonhole on his jacket, the author of *Traité du style* [*Treatise on Style*], no less peremptory than he used to be at that time: "My titles, Sir, I wear them on my lapel.")

The fact remains that those articles, whose "syrupy consistency" is made hardly more palatable by nugatory remarks of a coquettish or impertinent kind, present at least the great advantage of including illustrations that are quite representative since they are photographic reproductions of works that have received the "Stalin Prize."

So now we get to look at what Russian contemporary sculpture and painting can offer that is best in keeping with the line laid down for them. So now we can evaluate the contribution of so-called socialist realism by its works rather than its pomps (Zhdanov and others). Although Aragon, unwilling to overtax our strength, was careful not to throw them at us one right after the other, the two most striking examples he offers for our contemplation (*We Demand Peace*, *Les Lettres françaises*, 31 January 1952, and *A Meeting of the Presidium of the Academy of Sciences*, *Les Lettres françaises*, 10 April 1952) surpass in horrification all that could be apprehended. It is obvious that no one had ever gone so far in the most absurd "cemetery art" nor in that sort of triteness that aspires to pomposity. The sample we are shown from another work that won the same prize (the series of drawings illustrating Mayakovsky's book *Of America*), namely, "the head of Liberty at Long Island, whose eyes are made with two policemen's ugly mugs" (I am quoting Aragon), emphasizes the distinctive characteristic of this production, which is none other than hostility, not to speak of aggressiveness. Need I add that one must be Aragon to have the *front* to maintain "that, no, Prorokov (the one who made those drawings) cannot be said to be a surrealist, but that the diversity of design among the Stalin prizewinners this year attests a great fact: the freedom *of means* within socialist realism"? Who will doubt that this modicum of liberty on the formal level is granted exclusively to those who apply themselves to spreading hatred—in this case, of America? And what would Mayakovsky have thought of this recent illustration of his book, Mayakovsky, who—Aragon is very well aware of this since he is the one who told me about it—committed suicide when he was refused the passport that would have allowed him to follow out of Russia the woman he loved?

Enough tomfoolery! It is not surprising that even people close to Aragon expressed serious worries—something he could not avoid mentioning as his articles kept coming out. Could he actually love what he was defending? Could he believe, even to the smallest extent, in what he was defending? Was he not, once again, yielding to his tendency to go overboard, as he did at the time of "Le Scandale pour le scandale" [Scandal for scandal's sake] and of *Moscou-la-gâteuse* [Moscow-the-dodderer]? What concern, under those conditions, could he still have for artistic pursuits, for instance, for painting, to which certain individuals, by far the majority, have been drawn *before* they defined themselves politically and to which an irrepressible need drove them to dedicate their lives? There cannot be the least ambiguity about this. We know where Aragon really stands on this point. He expressed his position in *La Peinture au défi* [Painting challenged] (1930), a title that, by itself, is a whole program: "Painting has not always existed, an origin can be ascribed to it, and we have been told so often about its development, about its peak periods that we may assume not only that it goes through temporary declines but also that it will come to an end just like any other concept. Absolutely nothing would be changed in the world if there were no longer any painters. . . ; we can safely suggest that painting, with all the superstitions it involves, from subject to material, from the spirit of decoration to that of illustration, from composition to taste, etc., will certainly be regarded in the near future as a harmless diversion for young girls and old provincials, as with versifying today and novel writing tomorrow. There is reason to prophesy this. . . ." *To crush art forever*: this intention with which, in *Arts*, I credited the Stalinist leaders, I hope I have shown convincingly that it can only suit Aragon's purpose.

There are plenty of us throughout the world who think that "socialist realism" is but one more imposture to lay at the door of a regime that alienates human freedom, systematically corrupts all the words that could predispose men to universal brotherhood, and eliminates in an ignominious way those individuals who did not bow their heads soon enough. That regime, for the very reason that it is a totalitarian one, must be judged as a whole.

On the occasion of the meeting held on 23 and 24 April of this year by the "plastic artists, members of the French Communist party," the Paris newspapers—it may never happen again—have shown some ingenuousness. Considering that this meeting was convened to repress the stormy reactions that Aragon's interminable homily had triggered around him, with his compulsive and customary excessive shows of zeal, they seemed to expect spectacular exclusions or resignations. Nothing, of course, was less likely to happen. I am among those who hold the solution that was reached as extremely satisfactory, insofar as it accentuates in depth the difference of opinion and brings to a peak the internal contradiction. For one thing, such an absolute critical abdication had never yet been required, in France, of the intellectuals within the party: in their address to Maurice Thorez, they agree to endorse the accusation of bacteriological warfare brought against the

Americans, and they also confirm the statement made by the party secretary that states that "all cultural values have gone over to the proletariat" (an allegation easily refuted by the simple remark that such a meeting gathers, all in all, some two hundred artists and critics, that is, less than 1 percent of those who could be found living in Paris). They thank Thorez for his advice, which "has already enabled them to win great victories over themselves" and which opens up for them "prospects of the total self-actualization" of their art.

To listen to them, with one accord they would pit against art for art's sake, against pessimism, existentialism, and formalism, "an art that would draw its inspiration from socialist realism and would be understood by the working class," that is to say, exactly the same one the models of which Aragon produced for us. This would be terribly disappointing if the "letter to Maurice Thorez" were not offset by another letter assuring Pablo Picasso, whose work has been for the past fifteen years the passionate negation of such an "art," of their "confident affection" and of their "respect." It is clear enough that this letter allows all those who have signed the previous one to avail themselves of all the resources of *mental reservation*. In 1937 or 1938 Picasso told me that what disposed him favorably toward the Stalinist leaders was that they reminded him of the Spanish Jesuits, whom he had held in high esteem when he was young. The motion of 24 April, which took the form of a double letter to Thorez and to himself, is certainly meant to strengthen the sentiment to which he was referring. A motion with a double meaning such as this one betrays nonetheless, among the intellectual cadres of the Stalinist party, increasing antagonisms that will inevitably prove irreducible and, before long, will overtly take the shape of a *conflict*.

Notes

Nonnational Boundaries of Surrealism

1.   Karl Marx and Friedrich Engels, *Etudes philosophiques* [Philosophical studies] (Paris: Editions Sociales Internationales, 1935), pp. 150–53.

2.   See "Crise de l'objet" [Crisis of the object], *Cahiers d'Art* (1936).

3.   See *Nadja* (Paris: NRF, 1928) [*Nadja*, trans. Richard Howard (New York: Grove Press, 1960)]; *Les Vases communicants* (Paris: Editions des Cahiers Libres, 1932) [*Communicating Vessels*, trans. Mary Ann Caws and Geoffrey T. Harris (Lincoln: University of Nebraska Press, 1990)]; *L'Amour fou* (Paris: NRF, 1937) [*Mad Love*, trans. Mary Ann Caws (Lincoln: University of Nebraska Press, 1987)].

4.   "Il y aura une fois" [There will be once] in *Le Revolver à cheveux blancs* [The white-haired revolver] (Paris: Denoël et Steele, 1932).

5.   Marcel Lecomte's book *Les Minutes insolites* [Strange minutes] (Bruxelles: A l'Enseigne du Paradis Perdu, 1936) is of exceptional value in this regard.

Memory of Mexico

1.   See *Minotaure* 12–13 (1939).

2.   It is so difficult to depict such places with words. I have just reached this point in my description when a letter from a friend is handed to me. Although it is about something else entirely, I see this letter as something of an occult assistance, coming just at the right moment to fill the gaps in my memory and make up the deficiencies in my writing ability. The sense I get of the obscure necessity of such interferences prompts me to quote this letter in its entirety rather than reduce it to its more particularly interesting postscript.

Marseilles, 21 March 1939

In a book stall in Marseilles, I chanced upon and bought (for one franc!) the *Ombres de poésies* [Shades of poetry], by Xavier Forneret. That copy, which must have belonged to the "famous" critic from Pontmartin, contained handwritten verse by the aforesaid in an ironic style! It also included this "critical" review that I am sending you.

I am waiting for what you will have to say about Mexico. Has there been any new issue of *Clé*? Has the publication of *Minotaure* ceased? I am working right now on one of your favorite topics: Saint Theresa was only a saint.

François Secret

Do you know the Tower of the Madman between Lourmarin and the castle of La Coste (Sade)? In the middle of the Lubéron region, a tower built like a lighthouse, flanked by a house with iron bars, protected by fortifications in Vauban style. This castle has no high walls, but it does have a covered way that leads to a hunting lodge with loopholes. There are cloister arches standing in the middle of the garden planted with boxwood. One inscription: 1880.

Manifesto for an Independent Revolutionary Art

1. Although Diego Rivera is one of the signers of this manifesto, it was actually written by Leon Trotsky and André Breton. For tactical reasons, Trotsky asked that Diego Rivera's signature be substituted for his own.

Visit with Leon Trotsky

1. A Stalinist network of public reading rooms. (Trans.)

Golden Silence

1. Edmond and Jules de Goncourt, *Journal des Goncourt: mémoires de la vie littéraire*, vol. 2 (Paris: G. Charpentier, E. Fasquelle, 1888–96) [*The Goncourt Journals, 1851–1870* (Garden City NY: Doubleday, Doran and Co., 1937)].

2. Cocteau. (Trans.)

3. "Le Message automatique" [The automatic message], in *Point du jour* [Daybreak] (Paris: Gallimard, 1934).

4. Taine, *Essais de critique et d'histoire* [Critical and historical essays] (Paris: L. Hachette et Cie, 1858).

5. Italics mine.

6. Isidore Ducasse (le Comte de Lautréamont), *Poésies* (Paris: Au Sans Pareil, 1920) [one translation of these "poems" can be found in Comte de Lautréamont, *Maldoror and Poems*, trans. Paul Knight (Harmondsworth: Penguin, 1978)].

7. "Le Message automatique," in *Point du jour*.

A Tribute to Antonin Artaud

1. After he came out of the Rodez hospital, Artaud still had a fairly extravagant recollection of the events that, according to him, had taken place in Le Havre in October 1937 just before he was institutionalized. He was convinced that I had died while coming to his rescue (in spite of the fact that he was writing to ask me to meet him). He had not seen me since that time when he wrote on 31 May 1946: "Don't tell me it wasn't you who came and got *killed* (I do say *killed*) in Le Havre in October 1937, shot by police machine guns in front of Le Havre General Hospital, where I was kept in a straitjacket with my feet strapped to a bed. There you left more than your consciousness and you did keep your body, but barely, for, after dying, one does not come back intact." The next day, as we sat together at the terrace of a café, he insisted that I should publicly corroborate this incredible account so as to put an end to the protests and objections with which it was met. I had no alternative but to refute his story as tactfully as I could. As soon as I did, his eyes filled with tears. The whole time we stayed together that day, he would not give up the idea that I was concealing the truth from him, either because I had the same motivations as the others—something he could not willingly resign himself to accept—or because, much more probably, thanks to God knows what devious operation, my true recollections had been stolen from me and replaced with false ones. However, he later went back on his position, partially at least, when he wrote on 3 May: "I believe, since you told me so, that in October 1937 you were indeed not in Le Havre but in the Gradiva Gallery in Paris. I maintain that I was never raving, that I never lost the sense of reality, and that my recollections—or what is left of them after fifty comas—are real. For three days in Le Havre I heard the police machine guns in front of Le Havre General Hospital, I also heard the tocsin being rung in all the churches during a whole morning. I have never heard anything like it *since*. One could spend a long time discussing the interpretation of these facts. I had been told by various people that André Breton wanted to rescue me by forceful means. You have told me that you did not: I believe you." (*Author's note*, March 1952)

Before the Curtain

1. Let us merely quote a few titles: "The Surrealist Fun Fair," "The Clowns' School," "A Gallery of Grotesques," "The Geriatric Rebels," "When Dada Becomes Gaga," "The Complicated Perverts," etc., in contrast with the obituary clichés "Surrealism Dead, Exhibition to Follow," "The Surrealist Funeral," "Surrealism Not Dead Yet," "Surrealism at Death's Door," "Collapse of Surrealism," etc., that for the last twenty years seem to have brought jubilation over their brainwaves to the most wretched gossip columnists.

2. *Gringoire, Candide, Le Temps Présent, Je Suis Partout*, to mention only the more rabid among them.

3. As evidential examples for the benefit of skeptics, and to show that this kind of prediction can range from the particular to the general and from a trivial occurrence to a historical event of the first order, I will quote the following: "La Ménagère department store could catch fire . . ." (A. B. and Philippe Soupault, "S'il vous plaît" [If you please], in *Littérature*, September 1920): that store burnt down the following year and the site on which it stood in Paris, on the boulevard Bonne-Nouvelle, has oddly remained vacant ever since; the sentence in my "Lettre aux voyantes" [A letter to seers] (*La Révolution Surréaliste*, October 1925) forecasting the war for 1939; this explicit confirmation of the aforementioned date: "What does 1940 have in store for us? 1939 has been disastrous. . . . Should we miss chivalrous trench warfare or favor the inglorious immobile exterminations of today?" Louis Aragon and A. B.: "Le Trésor des jésuites" [The treasure of the Jesuits], in *Variétés*, June 1929; "La Nuit du tournesol" [The night of the sunflower] (*L'Amour fou* [*Mad Love*]); the sentence in my Yale lecture predicting "a spectacular discovery in physics" (December 1942). See also Pierre Mabille: "L'Oeil du peintre" [The painter's eye] (*Minotaure* 12–13 [1939]).

4. Is there any need to stress that the aforementioned attitude is diametrically opposed to the one recently adopted by some of those members of the former surrealist group in Brussels who rallied around Magritte? Because they realized, as we did, that events had often confirmed beyond all expectations some of our most venturesome declarations, they took it into their heads to foster in their works only that which was "charm, pleasure, sunshine, objects of desire" and exclude anything that might be "sadness, boredom, threatening objects"! Even though this might be on their part a desperate attempt to straighten out their position with respect to the resolution of the Leningrad Writers Committee (1946) prescribing an unconditional optimism, it is difficult not to liken that gesture with that of a (backward) child who, in order to make sure he will have a pleasant day, would dream up the idea of blocking the pointer of the barometer at the "fair weather" mark.

5. William Blake, quoted by Jean Wahl (foreword to the W. Blake exhibition, Paris, 1947). [The first line of this secondhand quote in French includes a curious mistranslation: what Blake wrote, of course (in *Milton*), is "faith in the saviour," which was translated as "la foi dans le savoir." Breton would certainly have avoided quoting that particular line had he known! (Trans.)]

6. "Suspiria de profundis," trans. [into French] Alexis Pernau (*L'Age d'Or*, December 1946).

7. "If surrealism," as suggested by M. Jean Maguet, "leaves behind Eluard and his derivatives, abandons automatism and the Freudian unconscious, magic, and primitivism—and a certain Marxism as well, too quickly absorbed—in a word, gives

up everything, it will still retain what it was in addition to all that, and what it should have been in essence: an action brought against itself, an experiment conducted under heat, an incitement to its own ruin; in short, organizing and internalizing rebellion" (*Troisième Convoi*, October 1945).

8. Let us note, for our own information, that "Heidegger, in one of his opuscules, has tried to construct a kind of mythical rather than mystical philosophy, enjoining us to commune with the earth and the world and claiming, to that end, to draw on the thought of Hölderlin" (Jean Wahl, *Petite histoire de l'existentialisme* [Paris: Ed. Club Maintenant, 1947] [*A Short History of Existentialism*, trans. F. Williams and S. Maron (Westport, Conn.: Greenwood Press, 1971)]).

Surrealist Comet

1. The first phrase, "Là-bas fuir," is from Mallarmé's poem *Brise marine* [Sea breeze]; the second is an allusion to Rimbaud, characterized by Verlaine as "l'homme aux semelles de vent." (Trans.)

2. *Le Surréalisme et la peinture* [*Surrealism and Painting*] (Paris: Gallimard, 1928).

3. Address to the Eleventh International Congress of Pen Clubs.

Second Ark

1. Where the International Exhibition of Surrealism, to which this text served as introduction, opened at the end of 1947.

2. Jean Paulhan, "De la paille et du grain" [Chaff and grain] (*Les Cahiers de la Pléiade*, April 1947).

3. Nakladatel Joza Jicha.

The Lamp in the Clock

1. Quoted by Georges Blin, *Le Sadisme de Baudelaire* [Baudelaire's sadism] (Paris: José Corti, 1948), p. 53.

2. In particular the so-called revolutionary surrealists who cannot even see that the combination of the two titles with which they crown themselves is nothing but a gross pleonasm.

3. See Fulcanelli, *Les Demeures philosophales* [Philosophal dwellings] (Paris: Schemit, 1930), p. 22.

4. In a letter of 20 July 1870 addressed to Engels, quoted by Charles Thomann, *Le Mouvement anarchiste dans les montagnes neuchâteloises et le Jura bernois* [The anarchist

movement in the mountains around Neuchâtel and Bern] (La Chaux-de-Fonds: Impr. des Coopératives Réunies, 1947).

5. For more information, contact Front Humain, 46, rue Lepic, Paris (XVIIIᵉ).

6. From an article quoted by Maurice Nadeau, "Politique et culture," *Combat*, 22–23 February 1948. Two weeks earlier, in the same paper, Péret and myself were called "eunuchs" by the same Kanapa, whose name is obviously predestined if one should adopt for one moment his loutish idiom: Kikana? Kikanapa? (Article quoted by Armand Robin in *Le Libertaire*, 29 January 1948.) ["Kanapa" can be read as a colloquial version of "Qui n'en a pas" (He who hasn't got any); hence the play on words: Who's got some? Who's got none? (Trans.)]

7. Fulcanelli, *Les Demeures philosophales*, pp. 184–293.

8. For bibliographical references, see *Critique* 20, p. 3.

9. Particularly the pervasive occultist influence and, from a religious standpoint, the fundamental heterodoxy.

10. See *Le Figaro Littéraire*, 21 February 1948.

11. An allusion to Raymond Roussel's play *L'Etoile au front* [The star on the forehead]. (Trans.)

12. See "Raymond Roussel," in *Anthologie de l'humour noir* [Anthology of black humor] (Paris: Sagittaire, 1940).

13. *Du sang, de la volupté et de la mort* [Of blood, pleasure and death], first published in 1894. (Trans.)

14. Pages 520–22 in the original edition.

15. *Le Magasin des enfants* is a collection of "moral tales" written by that prolific author of books for children, Marie Leprince de Beaumont. *La Chute d'un ange* is the opening fragment of an uncompleted epic by Lamartine intended to depict the gradual purification of the human soul. (Trans.)

16. A "treatise on journalism" by Marcel Schwob (Paris: Société du Mercure de France, 1903). (Trans.)

Thirty Years Later

1. Jacques Vaché, *Les Lettres de guerre* (Paris: K., édit., 1949).

Caught in the Act

1. The original French text is actually a misquotation from Apollinaire's poem in *Calligrammes* [Calligrams]: this line should read "you will never know" ("tu ne connaîtras") and not "you will never recognize" ("tu ne reconnaîtras"). (Trans.)

2. *Carrefour*, 1 June 1949.

3. See Pierre Macaigne, "L'Affaire Rimbaud" [The Rimbaud affair], *Le Figaro*, 28–29 May 1949.

4. The latest news is fortunately that it decided against it (see the appended documents: "The Rimbaud Affair Comes to a Close," *Le Figaro Littéraire*, 2 July 1949).

5. See the appended documents, "A Note to André Breton," *Combat*, 26 May 1949.

6. "André Breton poète" [André Breton, poet], *Combat*, 12 March 1948.

7. André Breton, "Un nouveau précieux" [A new *précieux*], *Combat*, 10 February 1949.

8. Kandinsky, *Regard sur le passé* [Looking back], trans. Gabrielle Buffet-Picabia (Paris: Galerie René Drouin, 1946).

9. *Combat*, 26 May 1949.

10. *Combat*, 10 December 1947.

11. Daniel Anselme, "Rimbaud mort fait une chasse spirituelle à trois critiques" [While dead, Rimbaud spiritually hunts three critics], *Action*, 26 May 1949.

12. *Le Figaro*, 25 May 1949.

13. *Le Figaro*, 28–29 May 1949.

14. *Combat*, 9 June 1949.

15. Pierre Macaigne, "La 'bataille' de Rimbaud" [The "battle" around Rimbaud], *Le Figaro*, 23 May 1949.

16. "Pour ou contre la Chasse spirituelle" [For or against The Spiritual Chase], *Carrefour*.

17. Those two letters as well as "The Dispute over 'Poison perdu'" by P. Petitfils are included in the appended documents.

18. Pierre Petitfils, *L'Oeuvre et le visage d'Arthur Rimbaud* [The works and the face of Arthur Rimbaud] (Paris: Nizet, 1949).

19. "Seuls les naïfs vont à 'la chasse spirituelle'" [Only fools go on a "spiritual chase"], 26 May 1949.

20. It is easy to see that "Rêve" exerts a decisive influence on several poems that appeared in my first collection, *Mont de piété* [Pawnshop] (Paris: Au Sans Pareil, 1919), such as "Forêt-Noire" [Black Forest], "Pour Lafcadio" [For Lafcadio], "Monsieur V." [Mister V.], "Le Corset mystère" [The mystery corset]. See also "Paratonnerre" [Lightning conductor], in *Anthologie de l'humour noir* (Paris: Sagittaire, 1940).

21. André Rousseaux, "Une autre affaire Rimbaud" [Another Rimbaud affair], *Le Figaro*, 11 June 1949.

22. By the same author: a critical edition of *Poésies* [Poems] (Paris: Mercure de France, 1939); a critical edition of *Une saison en enfer* [A Season in Hell] (Paris: Mercure de France, 1941); a new edition of Arthur Rimbaud's *Oeuvres* [Works] (Paris: Hazan,

1946); a critical edition of the *Les Illuminations* [*Illuminations*] (Paris: Mercure de France, 1949).

23.   See Jules Monnerot, *La Poésie moderne et le sacré* [Modern poetry and the sacred] (Paris: Gallimard, 1945).

24.   For the fun of it, M. Ernest Raynaud had already published in *La Muse Française* (10 March 1923, p. 129) a poem of his own composition that he signed with Rimbaud's name. No one took him seriously and nothing ever came of it.

Oceania

1.   Guillaume Apollinaire, "Zone," in *Alcools* (Paris: Mercure de France, 1913) [*Alcools*, trans. Anne Hyde Greet (Berkeley: University of California Press, 1965)].

2.   Georges Buraud, *Les Masques* [The masks] (Paris: Editions du Seuil, 1948).

3.   Michel Tapié, *Au pays d'Henri Michaux* [In Henri Michaux's country] (Paris: R. Drouin, 1948).

Fronton-Virage

1.   Etiemble, "Le Requin et la mouette" [The shark and the seagull], *Les Temps Modernes* (December 1947).

2.   Roussel went further than I in that direction: having gone on a cruise to the South Seas, when he reached the Tahiti harbor he refrained from going ashore.

3.   Raymond Roussel, *Comment j'ai écrit certains de mes livres* (Paris: Lemerre, 1935) [*How I Wrote Certain of My Books*, trans. Trevor Winkfield (New York: SUN, 1977)].

4.   See Jean Ferry, "Le Tigre mondain" [The sophisticated tiger], in *Le Mécanicien* (Paris: Les Cinéastes Bibliophiles, 1950).

5.   See *Second Manifeste du Surréalisme* (Paris: Kra, 1930) ["Second Manifesto of Surrealism," in *Manifestoes of Surrealism*, trans. R. Seaver and H. R. Lane (Ann Arbor: University of Michigan Press, 1969)].

6.   A popular collection of magic recipes attributed to Albertus Magnus. (Trans.)

7.   During the first performance of the play, a member of the audience accused the surrealists of being there as a claque (*claque* in French also means a slap), to which Desnos rejoined: "We are the claque and you are the cheek." Roussel later autographed his books for Desnos in appreciation of his support. (Trans.)

8.   This is a prime and oft-quoted example of a "holorhyme distich": all the sounds in the second line repeat those in the first but using different words. (Trans.)

9.   Marcel Duchamp, with his "wordplays," is situated precisely at this junction. From him grew Desnos (*Rose Sélavy*). A collateral branch was supplied at the same time by Leiris (*Glossaire: j'y serre mes gloses* [Glossary: Therein I keep my glosses]).

10. "Au lion d'or" (at the golden lion) = "au lit on dort" (in bed one sleeps). (Trans.)

11. "Sa grossesse" (her pregnancy) = "sa grosse **S**" (her large **S**). (Trans.)

12. Fulcanelli, *Les Demeures philosophales* [Philosophal dwellings] (Paris: Schemit, 1930), pp. 34–35.

13. "Bon appartement chaud" (nice warm apartment) = "Bonaparte manchot" (one-armed Bonaparte). [Trans.]

14. "Règles de lard" (rules of lard) = "règles de l'art" (rules of art, rule book); "taies d'eau rayées" (striped water specks on the eye) = "taies d'oreiller" (pillowcases). (Trans.)

15. The poetic resources of that language are invaluable (see, for instance, Valentin Andréae, *Les Noces chimiques de Simon Rosenkreuz* [Paris: Impr. Jouve & Cie, 1928]). [One recent translation from the German original is *The Chemical Wedding of Christian Rosenkreutz*, trans. Joscelyn Godwin (Grand Rapids, Mich.: Phanes Press, 1991).]

16. Ferry defines this as "a chain of nonexistent events that leads to the case of precious stones." The links are actually clues that must be deciphered in the course of the "treasure hunt" on which the play is centered. (Trans.)

17. It being understood that, to my mind, this particular childhood myth—one of the most powerful—and the kind of revelation that would deliberately follow the same pattern can only, in the final analysis, corroborate each other in the strongest way.

18. Fulcanelli, *Les Demeures philosophales*, p. 127, n. 2.

19. The original French phrases have been provided for easier reference to Ferry's book. Ambrosi is an Italian Renaissance poet—"Renaissance" understood here as "re-birth." (Trans.)

20. This refers to a sepia drawing (a sepia being also a cuttlefish) representing a huge local fossil, the "pterodactyl's stone." (Trans.)

21. The three principal phases of the Work: blackening, whitening, reddening. (Trans.)

22. Fulcanelli, *Les Demeures philosophales*, p. 136.

23. A *martinet* in French can denote the bird as well as a cat-o'-nine-tails. (Trans.)

24. One of the swallow's feathers conceals a piece of paper bearing a quote from *L'Astrée* [Astrea] by the seventeenth-century author Honoré d'Urfé. The characters in the play discover letters by d'Urfé, and in one of those letters, two words—"shepherdess" and "albino"—have been underscored. (Trans.)

25. Fulcanelli, *Les Demeures philosophales*, p. 229.

26. Fulcanelli, *Les Demeures philosophales*, p. 282.

27. Fulcanelli, *Les Demeures philosophales*, p. 87.

28. Fulcanelli, *Les Demeures philosophales*, p. 188.

29. The cross erected to the memory of the anonymous hero was paid for by donations (the "subscription"); 5 francs was the minimum allowed; anything else had to correspond to a power of five. (Trans.)

30. See Gérard van Rinjberk, *Le Tarot* [The tarot] (Lyon: P. Derain, 1947), p. 115.

31. Lotus de Paini, *Les Trois Totémisations* [The three totemizations] (Paris: Chacornac Frères, 1924).

32. Fulcanelli, *Les Demeures philosophales*, p. 208.

33. Fulcanelli, *Les Demeures philosophales*, pp. 84–85.

The Night of the Rose-Hotel

1. "Poetry must aim at practical truth," etc.

2. Marcel Granet, *La Pensée chinoise* [Chinese thought] (Paris: Renaissance du Livre, 1934).

3. See "La Lampe dans l'horloge" [The lamp in the clock].

4. The latter are the protagonists in Achim von Arnim's tale "Die Majoratsherren." (Trans.)

5. René Micha, "Une nouvelle explication de l'oeuvre de Kafka," *Le Figaro Littéraire*, 3 February 1949.

6. René Guénon, *Aperçus sur l'initiation* [Some insights into initiation] (Paris: Editions Traditionnelles, 1953).

7. Granet, *La Pensée chinoise*.

8. Which still implies: the Quest for the Grail is not far.

The Engineer

1. Mircea Eliade, *Traité d'histoire des religions* (Paris: Payot, 1949) [*Patterns in Comparative Religion*, trans. Rosemary Sheed (New York: Sheed and Ward, 1958)].

2. See "Limites non-frontières du surréalisme" [Nonnational boundaries of surrealism].

3. Malcolm de Chazal, *Message aux Français* [Message to the French people].

4. See "Le Voyageur avec bagages" [The traveler with luggage], "Mon aquarium" [My aquarium], and "La Grève des boueurs" [The garbage collectors' strike].

5. Saint-Yves d'Alveydre, *Mission de l'Inde en Europe* [The mission of India in Europe] (Paris: Dorbon, 1910).

6. René Guénon, *Aperçus sur l'initiation* [Some insights into initiation] (Paris: Editions Traditionnelles, 1953).

7. "Le Tigre mondain" [The sophisticated tiger].

The Art of the Insane, the Door to Freedom

1. Hans Prinzhorn, *Bildnerei des Geistenkranken* (Berlin: J. Springer, 1922).

2. Jacques Lacan, *De la psychose paranoïaque dans ses rapports avec la personnalité* [Paranoiac psychosis and its relationship to personality] (Paris: Le François, 1932).

Pont-Neuf

1. Edouard Fournier, *Enigmes des rues de Paris* [Enigmas of Paris streets] (Paris: E. Dentnu, 1860).
2. *Nadja* (Paris: Gallimard, 1928) [*Nadja*, trans. Richard Howard (New York: Grove Press, 1960)].
3. Henri IV, known because of his amorous temperament as the "Vert-Galant." (Trans.)
4. Michel Féline, *L'Adolescent confidentiel* [The confidential adolescent].
5. Marat. (Trans.)

Open Letter to Paul Eluard

1. This letter elicited no other response from Paul Eluard than what he said in *Action*: "I have too much to do for the innocent people who proclaim their innocence to care for the guilty who proclaim their guilt." Závis Kalandra was to be executed shortly afterward. See Louis Pauwels, "Des 'salauds' parmi les poètes" [Bastards among poets], *Combat*, 21 June 1950.

As in a Wood

1. What could be more scandalous than someone like Matisse declaring—or letting others say—that the decoration of the chapel in Vence is the "work of his life"? Is there anything more disgusting, in the same vein, than the contortions of that two-bit strong man who, not content with his success as the master of superficiality, inexpressiveness, and bestiality—after a spectacular evolution from Pétainism to Stalinism, not to forget Gaullism in between—finds a way to "girdle" the walls of a new church with stained glass while at the same time, in the "House of French Thought," under the title *The Builders*, he hangs up a few workers' caps crowning a total lack of ideas and of life? And that is not all, but I will come back to it . . .
2. René Clair, *Réflexion faite* (Paris: Gallimard, 1951) [*Reflections on the Cinema*, trans. Vera Traill (London: W. Kimber, 1953)].
3. *Nadja* (Paris: Gallimard, 1928) [*Nadja*, trans. Richard Howard (New York: Grove Press, 1960)].
4. *Les Vases communicants* (Paris: Editions des Cahiers Libres, 1932) [*Communicating*

Vessels, trans. Mary Ann Caws and Geoffrey T. Harris (Lincoln: University of Nebraska Press, 1990)].

5. Clair, *Réflexion faite*.

Yellow Sugar

1. First semester 1951.

2. Shortly afterward, that essay was to appear under the title "L'Homme révolté" [The rebel].

3. Maurice Blanchot, *Lautréamont et Sade* (Paris: Les Editions de Minuit, 1949).

Alfred Jarry as Precursor and Initiator

1. The object of this exercise was to demonstrate that, notwithstanding the iconography, from the ancients to the moderns, which is much debatable, there could only have been four nails used for the crucifixion.

2. The two plates mentioned in this chapter (Dürer's engraving with Jarry's commentary and later on, Filiger's *Gouache*) are not reproduced here.

3. Sigmund Freud, *Un souvenir d'enfance de Léonard de Vinci* (Paris: Gallimard, 1927) [*Leonardo Da Vinci: A Psychosexual Study of an Infantile Reminiscence*, trans. A. A. Brill (London: K. Paul, Trench, Trubner, 1932)].

4. Foreword to *Les Minutes de sable mémorial* (Paris: Mercure de France, 1894).

5. See Eugène de Faye, *Gnostiques et gnosticisme* [Gnostics and Gnosticism] (Paris: Librairie Orientaliste, Paul Geuthner, 1925); H. Leisegang, *La Gnose* [Gnosis] (Paris: Payot, 1951).

6. An unverifiable assertion.

7. Alfred Jarry, "La Revanche de la nuit" [The revenge of the night] (Paris: Mercure de France, 1949).

8. He was the perfect illustrator for Jarry's *Almanach illustré du père Ubu* [Illustrated almanac of Father Ubu] (Paris: A. Vollard, 1901).

9. Charles Chassé, *Gauguin et le groupe de Pont-Aven* [Gauguin and the Pont-Aven group] (Paris: H. Floury, 1921).

10. Charles Chassé, *Le Mouvement symboliste dans l'art du XIXe siècle* [The symbolist movement in nineteenth-century art] (Paris: Librairie Floury, 1947).

11. *Oeuvres complètes* (Monte-Carlo: Editions du Livre, 1948).

12. Alfred Jarry, "Filiger," (*Le Mercure de France*, September 1894).

13. One comes across works by Filiger so rarely that it is proper to cite the names of those collectors or friends of the painter who have his paintings in their possession in

Brittany. Such is the case of M. Le Corronc, of Lorient, who had kindly brought this one to my attention.

Why Is Contemporary Russian Painting Kept Hidden from Us?

1. Karl Marx, *Oeuvres philosophiques*, trans. J. Molitor (Paris: A. Costes, 1937–48, 1:124–27.
2. See *Les Meilleurs Peintres soviétiques* [The best Soviet painters] (Budapest: Maison de la Culture, 1949), and *Literaturnaya Gazeta*, October 1949.

Letter to a Young Girl Living in America

1. "Scrapbook," "report," and "Very sincerely yours" were in English in the original letter. (Trans.)

Of "Socialist Realism" as a Means of Mental Extermination

1. As soon as this text came out in *Arts*, that series of articles, which was *to be continued*, stopped appearing as if by magic.

In the French Modernist Library series

Louis Aragon, *The Adventures of Telemachus*
Translated by Renée Riese Hubert and Judd D. Hubert

Louis Aragon, *Treatise on Style*
Translated by Alyson Waters

Marcel Bénabou, *Why I Have Not Written Any of My Books*
Translated by David Kornacker

Maurice Blanchot, *The Most High*
Translated by Allan Stoekl

André Breton, *Communicating Vessels*
Translated by Mary Ann Caws and Geoffrey T. Harris

André Breton, *Free Rein*
Translated by Michel Parmentier and Jacqueline d'Amboise

André Breton, *Mad Love*
Translated by Mary Ann Caws

Blaise Cendrars, *Modernities and Other Writings*
Translated by Esther Allen and Monique Chefdor

The Cubist Poets in Paris: An Anthology Edited by L. C. Breunig

René Daumal, *You've Always Been Wrong*
Translated by Thomas Vosteen

Max Jacob, *Hesitant Fire: Selected Prose of Max Jacob*
Translated and edited by Moishe Black and Maria Green

Jean Paulhan, *Progress in Love
on the Slow Side*
Translated by Christine Moneera
Laennec and Michael Syrotinski

Benjamin Péret, *Death to
the Pigs, and Other Writings*
Translated by Rachel Stella
and Others

Boris Vian, *Blues for a Black
Cat and Other Stories*
Edited and translated
by Julia Older